ALL IN THE
FAMILY

ALL IN THE
FAMILY

THE TRUMPS
and how WE GOT THIS WAY

FRED C. TRUMP III

G

GALLERY BOOKS

New York   London   Toronto   Sydney   New Delhi

G

Gallery Books
An Imprint of Simon & Schuster, LLC
1230 Avenue of the Americas
New York, NY 10020

First Gallery Books hardcover edition July 2024

GALLERY BOOKS and colophon are registered trademarks of Simon & Schuster, LLC

Simon & Schuster: Celebrating 100 Years of Publishing in 2024

For information about special discounts for bulk purchases, please contact Simon & Schuster Special Sales at 1-866-506-1949 or business@simonandschuster.com.

The Simon & Schuster Speakers Bureau can bring authors to your live event. For more information or to book an event, contact the Simon & Schuster Speakers Bureau at 1-866-248-3049 or visit our website at www.simonspeakers.com.

Interior design by Jaime Putorti

Manufactured in the United States of America

10 9 8 7 6 5 4 3 2 1

Library of Congress Cataloging-in-Publication Data has been applied for.

ISBN 978-1-6680-7217-2
ISBN 978-1-6680-7219-6 (ebook)

To my wife, Lisa, to whom I am most grateful,
with love and appreciation.

To my children, Andrea, Cristopher, and William,
who have changed my life for good. I am humbled and honored
to be your father.

To Mom and Dad: Thank you for giving us hope and a better path
for the next generation of all of us. Dad, you would be so proud
of your grandchildren.

And to the families who are advocates for individuals with
intellectual and developmental disabilities.

"It's not personal, Sonny. It's strictly business."
—Michael Corleone, *The Godfather* (film)

"It's all personal, every bit of business."
—Michael Corleone, *The Godfather* (novel)

CONTENTS

PART III:
PUTTING US BACK TOGETHER

ALL IN THE
FAMILY

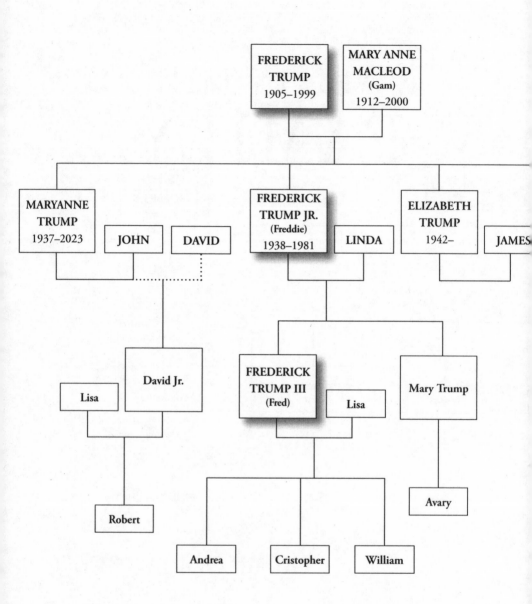

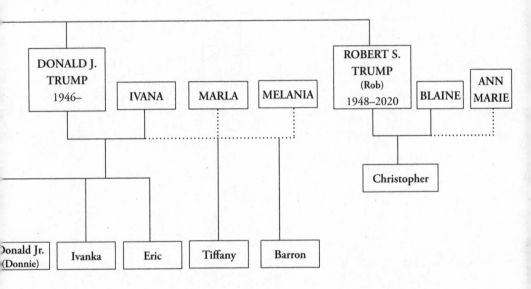

DONALD J. TRUMP 1946–ㅤㅤIVANAㅤㅤMARLAㅤㅤMELANIAㅤㅤROBERT S. TRUMP (Rob) 1948–2020ㅤㅤBLAINEㅤㅤANN MARIE

Christopher

Donald Jr. (Donnie)ㅤㅤIvankaㅤㅤEricㅤㅤTiffanyㅤㅤBarron

TRUMP FAMILY TREE

INTRODUCTION

DEARLY DEPARTED

I had no idea what we were in for.

June 29, 1999. On the day we buried my grandfather Fred Trump, whose name I carry and whose legacy I still bear, my son William Trump was just about to burst into the world. And I didn't have a clue what a long, dark shadow that first family milestone was going to cast on the second one . . . or which of my relatives had been secretly plotting to leave one branch of the family out in the cold.

Mine.

My father's father was the Trump who first defined what it meant to be a Trump, long before Uncle Donald marched the family name into Manhattan and gave it that shiny 1980s glow. It was sad for Grandpa to leave us, of course. But he was ninety-three and had been struggling with dementia for years. Six years earlier, when he was best man at Donald's wedding to Marla Maples, my grandfather had almost gotten lost on his way to the altar and had to be reminded what he was doing there.

"There wasn't a wet eye in the place," writer Julie Baumgold blurted to a *New York Times* reporter that awkward evening at the Plaza Hotel, after the "I do's." Just the kind of media snark we'd all been forced to get used to.

My grandfather had lived what could only be called a long and prosperous life. Having worked since he was a skinny ten-year-old, he'd risen to the very pinnacle of the New York real-estate world, ending up with a stunning portfolio that included scores of high-rise apartment buildings in Brooklyn and Queens. He had political juice from City Hall to Albany and was known everywhere he went, which is to say the outer boroughs of New York City, Grossinger's in the Catskills, and the Fontainebleau Hotel in Miami Beach. But he'd had a terrible relationship with my father, who blamed him for ruining his life. It was one of those can't-live-together, can't-live-apart situations. But it was my father, his namesake, who died just shy of his forty-third birthday with an ex-wife and two teenage children. So, you tell me: Who paid the ultimate price?

My grandfather wasn't the easiest man to get along with. After all the tense holiday dinners I'd sat through at my grandparents' twenty-three-room Colonial mansion in Queens, believe me, I knew. That was as plain as the three-piece suits, slicked-back hair, and Walter Cronkite mustache that became my grandfather's fashion signatures. He was an old-style patriarch, presiding over a large, rambunctious family, whose members he managed to dominate and sometimes pit against each other. But business was his passion—that's how he always defined himself, as a hard-driving businessman. In the office and at home, he had an emotional range that went all the way from stoic to judgmental to really pissed off. Not a lot of cuddling on the couch, and his later-in-life confusion didn't add much humility to the mix. In his prime, he'd been an undeniably commanding figure and a very present grandfather. There was no doubt he'd amassed a stunning list of accomplishments in those nine-plus decades of his, along with a fortune worth at least a couple of hundred million dollars. And you can't explain the personalities of any of his five children without knowing what he did for—and *to*—each of them.

Maryanne, the whip-smart but often cruel eldest child, whose public achievements as an attorney and federal judge were equally matched by her constant carping within the family.

My father, Fred Trump Jr., the charming black-sheep first son, whose free-spirited rejection of the family business was taken as a character flaw almost as severe as his self-destructive impulses and his alcoholism.

Elizabeth, the quiet middle child, who did everything she could to avoid the blinding glare of the Trump-family spotlight and almost succeeded.

Hard-charging Donald, the one most like their father, whose ferocious ambition and drive had to compensate for a lack of compassion, subtlety, and book smarts.

And finally, Robert, the chameleon little brother, who landed on one side or another of each fresh family drama, depending on who appeared to be ascendant that week.

No one can deny their many accomplishments. Grandpa built all those buildings and housed thousands of people, but he never achieved the intellectual stature that his daughter Maryanne did. He never became world-famous like his son Donald. He never sought that out. He certainly never hosted his own hit TV show or got himself elected president. But his towering presence launched all that and so much more, some of it worth being deeply proud of, some of it much better ignored. And that is the story of one generation of our family, all wrapped up in one paragraph.

I never planned to write a book. Up until now, I have stayed stubbornly quiet, even as those around me took their potshots. But silence is golden only when there is nothing that needs to be said. We are *all* in this family together, even when the "together" part isn't close to where it ought to be. Well, it's time for me to open up now, let some light shine

in, and reflect on how we got this way so we can move past all that *stuff*.
I have a name—Trump—that is extraordinarily polarizing, and keeps
getting more so. But there is more to my name than all that friction,
and I am ready to use it for something good. A cause near and dear to
my heart: advocating for individuals with developmental disabilities.
But we'll get to that in a bit.

This nation and this family are inextricably intertwined. As go the
Trumps, so goes America. For the sake of my generation and the generations to come, as well as the great nation we love, it's time to advocate
for policy over politics.

I realize the chapters ahead may ruffle some feathers. Things could
be tense on the golf course the next time Uncle Donald rolls up in his
cart. And I am certainly a flawed messenger. I have my faults—many
of them. Who *doesn't* in this family . . . or any other? The difference
between me and my relatives is that none of them will admit that, and
I just did. Thanks to some circumstances unique to my own life, I am
a different kind of Trump.

So where did the cruelty come from? I've wrestled with that question for years. Who planted the seeds of narcissism? When did winning
become everything? How did Trump loyalty become such a one-way
street? Were all the outsized achievements *in spite* of these complicated
relationships . . . or *because* of them? And what does all this mean for my
generation of Trumps—David Desmond (Maryanne's son from her first
marriage), Donald Jr., Ivanka, Eric, Tiffany, Barron, my sister, Mary,
and myself—and for our children and the generations that follow?

Excellent questions, and I will try to address all of them.

The cruelty, I can now see, didn't come from any one of those distinct Trump personalities. As I will explain, it came from the unique
way these strong-willed family members collided with each other and
anyone who ever stood in their way. And a lot of it started with my
grandfather.

Which brings me back to his send-off. He certainly deserved a proper one.

Six hundred and fifty people packed the pews at the Marble Collegiate Church on Fifth Avenue, a pulpit made famous by *The Power of Positive Thinking* author Norman Vincent Peale. Various Trumps had attended services there since the 1960s. It was quite a turnout that broiling June day. Relatives. Employees. Business associates. A who's who of machers from the worlds of New York politics, media, construction, and real estate. The only thing missing . . . friends. Old and single-minded as he was, Grandpa didn't have too many friends at the end.

My wife, Lisa, and I arrived at the church two minutes late. *"What the fuck . . . ,"* my aunt Maryanne snapped at us as we slipped in the back and headed up to the family pew. I didn't bother to answer. I just motioned toward Lisa's belly. She was nine months pregnant, already *out to here,* but not wanting to miss such an important family gathering. My superwoman of a wife had *willed* herself there.

I'd been asked to deliver one of the eulogies, along with my grandfather's four living children. Maybe I was a stand-in for my missing father.

Naturally, Donald spoke mostly about Donald. "I was having the greatest year of my business career," he began, a heavily edited portrayal of his ever-changing fortunes. "I was sitting having breakfast thinking about how well things were going for me," when he got the news that his father had died.

When it was my turn to speak, I got up there and looked out at all those people. It was the largest crowd I had ever addressed. I took a different path from the other eulogists. I didn't even want to mention my grandfather's wealth.

I accentuated the positive, saluting his potent influence on his family and his city. But I also wanted to touch on the hard history between my grandfather and his oldest son, which still hung so heavily over the family almost eighteen years after my father's demise. "One of them was completely driven," I said. "The other was a total free spirit. After all their clashes, maybe the two of them can find peace and comfort together in the afterlife."

We could hope, right?

I caught Ivana's eye just as I was saying that. After marrying twenty-two years earlier in this very same church, she and Donald had been divorced for eight and a half years by then. But she had been close to her father-in-law. Just as I got to "peace and comfort," Ivana began to sob. Then, I spoke directly to my grandmother. I'd always had a special connection with her and she with me. Like my father and like me, she'd sometimes felt like an outsider in her own family. I wanted to bring some kind of encouragement to her.

"Gam," I said, "don't worry. Your fellows are going to be okay."

I don't know where I got that. I'm not even sure I fully believed it. But in a family not always known for its small kindnesses, it felt like the right thing to say.

On that sad day, I had every reason for optimism, though I didn't choose to brag about it like some people had. My own real-estate career was hitting its stride—and not inside the protective womb (or the snake pit) of the Trump Organization, where Donald was now president, CEO, and twenty-four-hour-a-day publicity machine. I was beating a professional path all my own. Lisa and I had two happy, healthy children—five-year-old Andrea and three-year-old Cristopher—and a house we loved in Connecticut. We were delighted to know that our family would soon be welcoming another baby boy, the third child we had both been hoping for.

My precious son William was born the next morning. And without the tiniest heads-up, our whole world would suddenly be turned upside down.

PART I

MAKING US

CHAPTER 1

FRED ZERO

It's tempting to start the story of the Trumps with my grandfather, the man everyone called Fred Trump Sr.

Tempting but wrong.

The real story of the Trumps doesn't begin with him. It doesn't even begin with *Trump*. The original family name in the Pfalz region of southwest Germany was Drumpf, though the two spellings don't sound all that different if you mumble them in a strong enough German accent.

Various genealogists, amateur and professional, have tried to trace our family tree. They differ on key details, but they all seem to mention a man named Johannes Philipp Drumpf, who was born in 1667 and married a woman named Juliana Maria Rodenroth. They had a son named Johannes (1699), who had a son named Johann (1727). That Johann had a son or maybe it was a grandson named—guess what? Johannes, the German version of John, was clearly the Fred of its day. That Johannes was born in 1789 in Bobenheim am Berg before settling in the quaint Bavarian village of Kallstadt, which was also where he died. It went on like that for a while longer. It's impossible to say exactly when Drumpf morphed into Trump or why. But it wasn't until March 14, 1869, when my great-grandfather was born, that things started to get interesting. He was Friedrich Heinrich Trump, the original Fred Trump.

If my grandfather was Fred Sr., what does that make my *great*-grandfather?

Fred Zero?

As the youngest son, he did not get off to an especially promising start. But the details of his life are a remarkably prescient foreshadowing of Trump adventures generations into the future.

People haven't paid nearly enough attention to this part of our family history. It really shows the road map of things to come.

For centuries, the people of Kallstadt grew plump grapes and made crisp, delicious wines. I've never been there. I was hoping to visit during my college study-abroad program. I went skiing in Innsbruck instead. Sorry, Kallstadt. But from the pictures I've seen, it's a beautiful place of old stone buildings, rolling hills, and sturdy glassware in every living room. In the 1880s, there weren't many opportunities in Kallstadt for a young man who wanted to make a name for himself but didn't have much going for him. Friedrich, or Fred Zero, was a sickly child, considered too weak to work in the family vineyards with his five brothers and sisters. So, at age fourteen, he apprenticed with an experienced barber in nearby Frankenthal. But after returning to Kallstadt, he discovered that there wasn't enough business in his village of a thousand people to make a decent living shaving whiskers and snipping hair. And there was one other issue staring him in the face: He was approaching the age for the military draft, which started as early as seventeen. Having absolutely no interest in joining the army, he decided he would follow his mother's advice and emigrate to America.

(Making a quick note here: My uncle Donald wasn't the first Trump to sidestep military service.)

On October 7, 1885, my sixteen-year-old future great-grandfather boarded the newly built, iron-screw steamship SS *Eider* in the German maritime city of Bremen, carrying a single, bulging suitcase and a fistful of dreams. Traveling alone, he arrived ten days later at the Castle Garden Emigrant Depot in New York City.

Welcome to America, young man!

And this is where the Trumps' American adventure begins in earnest.

The sixteen-year-old had no money. He didn't have much English or so much as a high school diploma from back home. He could read and write . . . in German. Beyond that, he was lost. He did have an older sister, Katherina, who'd come to America a few years earlier to join her fiancé, Fred Schuster (another Fred). By the time Friedrich arrived, the couple had gotten married, had a baby girl, and were living in a tiny cold-water apartment in a ragged brick tenement building on Forsyth Street on Manhattan's Lower East Side. This sister and her husband were the full extent of the connections Friedrich had, the only people with any chance of smoothing his arrival in America.

And still, he was only two generations away from a president of the United States. What Friedrich Trump had going for him was drive.

Putting his childhood frailties behind him, young Friedrich discovered an extraordinary bravado inside himself and vowed to embrace every last opportunity this New World might deliver to him. The original Fred Trump was more than ready to ride the American Dream as far as he could.

His sister and her husband made room for him in that small apartment on the Lower East Side, a teeming neighborhood of newcomers that included quite a few immigrants from their part of Germany. That afternoon, Friedrich met a German-speaking barber who had an empty chair to fill. The ambitious young immigrant went to work the next day.

Barbering helped to get him settled in America, and he stuck with it for the next six years. But my great-grandfather wasn't about to spend his entire life with a leather strop at the ready and a straight razor in his hand. He had bigger plans and a real fearlessness about fulfilling them. He would soon become the first Trump in history to try his hand in the overlapping businesses of real estate and hospitality, showing promise in both those fields.

(Yes, there were Trump-owned hotels even all those generations ago . . .)

In November 1891, when he was twenty-two years old, he moved across the country to Seattle, where he bought a piece of property on the outskirts, then opened a restaurant on Washington Street in the city's raucous Pioneer Square, a lively district of saloons, gambling parlors, and brothels. He called his new business the Dairy Restaurant and offered food, booze, and very likely the same "Private Rooms for Ladies" its predecessor, an establishment called the Poodle Dog, advertised. The "gentlemen" were invited upstairs for what I have to assume was something more than conversation and chamomile tea.

It was in Seattle the following October that Friedrich Trump became a United States citizen (it was that easy back then), just in time to officially Americanize the spelling of his first name. Friedrich became Frederick. He registered to vote and cast his first ballot in the 1892 presidential race. I can't say which candidate he voted for. There is no record of that. But I do know the race was a hard-fought rematch between Benjamin Harrison, the Republican incumbent, and Grover Cleveland, the former Democratic president who was beaten by Harrison four years earlier. Cleveland's victory was historic, making him the first-ever president, and the only one to date, to serve nonconsecutive terms in the White House.

Sound familiar? History does have a way of repeating itself. I'm not saying this is some kind of omen, from 1892 to 2024. But for what it's worth, the challenger won the rematch that time, beating the incumbent 46 to 43 percent, with a third-party candidate collecting 8 percent of the vote.

My great-grandfather did well out West, especially during the Klondike Gold Rush of the late 1890s. He never actually mined any gold. Not personally. But he sold his Dairy Restaurant in Seattle and opened a successful saloon, restaurant, and boardinghouse in the mining boomtown of Monte Cristo and even got himself elected justice of the peace. And when the Monte Cristo boom went bust, he moved further north to open, with a partner, the New Arctic Restaurant and Hotel in Bennett, British Columbia, and then the Arctic Restaurant in White Horse, Yukon Territory. Again, instead of mining gold, he "mined the miners," to quote Gwenda Blair, whose impeccably researched 2000 book, *The Trumps,* is still the deepest dive anyone has done into this long-ago era of our family history.

And what were these establishments like? Well, the reviewer for the *Yukon Sun* praised the Arctic's "excellent accommodations" for "single men," but added a note of caution: "I would not advise respectable women to go there to sleep as they are liable to hear that which would be repugnant to their feelings and uttered, too, by the depraved of their own sex."

A lot of moaning, I guess. Putting the "wild" in the Wild West.

The businesses were undeniably profitable, as the flesh trade often is. His sisters back in Kallstadt didn't ask too many questions, but they greatly appreciated the gold nuggets their brother kept sending in the mail. When my great-grandfather returned for a visit in 1901, he arrived a wealthy man, at least by the standards of his modest village. It was on that visit that he met and married a local girl named Elisabeth Christ. It wasn't long after that he moved with her to New York City, where their first child, a daughter they named Elizabeth, was born in 1904. But the family didn't stay in New York for long. The new Mrs. Trump was terribly homesick. She claimed she could not tolerate the climate in New York. And she hated the idea of raising children so far from her own family. With Fred's agreement, they returned to Kallstadt later that year, with hopes of remaining in the Old Country for good.

But a piece of lingering business put an end to that.

In February 1905, Frederick Trump was ordered by royal decree to leave the kingdom of Bavaria within eight weeks for failing to perform his mandatory military service all those years before. My great-grandfather, conscientious objector or draft dodger . . . and not the last in the family.

There would be no repatriation for him. The decree didn't mince words. It ordered "American citizen and pensioner Friedrich Trump" (still spelled the German way) to leave "at the very latest on 1 May . . . or else expect to be deported."

Royal decrees were serious business.

My great-grandfather tried to plead his case. He wrote a fawning letter to Prince Regent Luitpold, addressing the prince as "the much-loved, noble, wise and righteous sovereign and sublime ruler." The suck-up letter did no good. On July 1, 1905, the Trumps left on the Hapag steamship *Pennsylvania,* bound again for New York City, this time to stay.

One other development worth noting: Six months before they boarded the boat, Frederick and Elisabeth Trump conceived a second child. The baby wasn't born until three months after they landed in America. That baby was my future grandfather Frederick Christ Trump.

It's the classic immigrant story. From Germany to America. From rags to riches. From pinched horizons to unimaginable opportunity. It has back-and-forths and fits and starts and a few seamy stops along the way. Under the laws of today, my great-grandfather's original arrival could certainly be considered illegal. He would have been classified as an "unaccompanied minor" unless his sister Katherina, who'd preceded him here, had taken official steps to be his legal guardian, in which case the whole family could promptly be denounced for abusing the practice of "chain migration."

None of that happened to my great-grandfather. America had greeted him with open arms and opportunity, as long as he did his part. For him, Germany was fully in the past.

He and his family, soon joined by a third child, John, settled into an apartment on East 177th Street in the Bronx, where the children spent their early years, before they all moved to a more suburban block in Woodhaven, Queens. Ever the industrious businessman, my great-grandfather got busy building a whole new New York career for himself. No more brothels this time for the father of three.

He was a multitasker before anyone knew the term. He opened a barbershop on Wall Street. He bought property on Jamaica Avenue in Queens. He managed the small Medallion Hotel on Sixth Avenue at 23rd Street in Manhattan. Things got a little dicey for him after Congress declared war on Germany in April of 1917 and the U.S. entered what was then called the Great War (we know it now as World War I). Eager to avoid the growing anti-German sentiment taking hold across America, my grandfather relied instinctively on his salesman's charm to downplay his German ancestry. No more *danke schöns* and *bitte schöns* on the New York sidewalk. With his skill and drive, even the rising prejudice couldn't slow him down. A landlord, a business owner, a hotel operator—he had every reason to think that the future was bright for him, that he could keep marching ever forward on this immigrant journey of his. America, he kept discovering, really was a land of endless possibility for him and his young family.

And so it was until May 29, 1918.

On that bright morning, he was walking with his twelve-year-old son, Fred, when he suddenly felt unsteady on his feet. He wasn't sure what the problem was, but he went home to bed. My great-grandfather never even made it to the hospital. By the next morning, he was dead at forty-nine. What was first diagnosed as pneumonia turned out to have been an early case of the so-called Spanish flu.

The Spanish flu didn't actually come from Spain. That was one of its many misconceptions. The outbreak almost certainly originated in America, perhaps at Fort Riley in Kansas, where the first case of the virus was recorded. It was said that overcrowded and unsanitary conditions created a fertile breeding ground.

An estimated twenty-one to fifty million people died around the world from that earlier pandemic, nearly 700,000 of them in America, many times larger than the death toll of World War I. And it left my great-grandmother an unexpected widow with three young children alone in New York, a city she'd never wanted to be in and now couldn't leave.

And there it was, another neat foreshadow for the Trump family: The Great Influenza of 1918–1919 was the COVID of its time, another sweeping pandemic that came out of nowhere and suddenly seemed to change just about everything.

It's strange, but through most of my life, I barely heard a word about my great-grandfather. It was as if the Trump family wasn't hatched until my grandfather came along. Not a single story about the original Fred Trump. His dramatic immigration journey, his outsized personality, his wild adventures out West, his striking successes in what would become the thoroughly Trumpy trades of hospitality and real estate— his extraordinary life would set a standard for generations to come, especially for my grandfather and my uncle Donald.

And yet . . . silence.

There were no colorful tales about his many adventures in Germany and America, no ancestral portrait in the hall. It was like Fred Zero got chopped right off the family tree. When his name came up at all, he was only described as "gone," as if he'd abandoned the family and moved off somewhere. As a kid, that was the impression I had, which could not have been any further from the truth. Not only did my great-grandfather die in a worldwide pandemic, he left his wife and children with a tidy estate. And he clearly set a compelling example for his older son. But you wouldn't have known any of that from the Trump family lore. I met my great-grandmother a few times when I was little. I didn't know to ask about her late husband. And I don't remember my grandfather ever once mentioning him.

When I finally saw a photo of him, I was struck by how much he looked like all the other Trump males. The prominent nose, the pinched mouth, the big, bushy eyebrows—they were every bit as notable a legacy as any property my great-grandfather left behind. In the late 1990s, when Gwenda Blair was researching her Trump-family history book, Donald called and asked me to speak with her. I told him I'd prefer not to.

"Okay, pal," he said. "I understand."

I was driven at that point to keep a level of privacy for my family.

CHAPTER 2

GO-GETTER

As if she hadn't had enough to worry about already . . .

With the nation still at war and a deadly pandemic rampaging across the land, now my widowed great-grandmother had to manage her grief and face her uncertain future as a single mother.

Elisabeth Trump wasn't exactly destitute. Her entrepreneurial husband had left her with a two-story, seven-room home in Queens, five vacant lots, $4,000 in savings and life insurance, $3,600 in stocks, and fourteen mortgages, according to Trump biographer Gwenda Blair. His net worth at death was $31,359 . . . in *1918* dollars, which would be in excess of $675,000 today. That part was fortunate. But was it really enough for his widow to make a comfortable life for herself and her three young children? How would she care for them in fast-paced (and high-priced) New York City? How would she feed, clothe, and educate them until she could send them off on their own? She was a thirty-eight-year-old woman with no obvious job prospects and no family to turn to in her time of sudden need.

At least she didn't think so. That's when her go-getter of an older son stepped up.

Twelve-year-old Fred hadn't yet started at Richmond Hill High School when his father passed away. But he had always been an industrious and resilient child. The family lore is filled with tales of my future grandfather's prodigious work ethic from an absurdly early age, even before his father died. At ten, he'd strapped a large wire basket on the front of his bicycle and taken a job as a delivery boy for a busy neighborhood butcher. He never stopped working after that. Though he wasn't old enough to shave yet, he was the man of the family now.

He stayed in school for the next few years, but he was never without two or three part-time jobs. Curb painter. Paper and grocery boy. Caddie at the Forest Park Golf Course on Woodhaven Boulevard, the first-known Trump-family connection to the potentially lucrative world of golf. Six decades later, when I needed a lift to that very same public course, my grandfather drove me there in his brand-new, dark blue Cadillac—he bought a new one every three years—and proudly pointed out the precise location of the old caddie shack.

"It was right over there," he said. "But some of the players were stingy tippers."

He could still remember which ones.

And he hung around long enough to hit a few balls. "That's how it's done," he deadpanned. "Do you need a ride home?"

Throughout his early teens, he worked for pay before and after his classes, not to mention every weekend, and diligently brought his modest earnings home. Which his widowed mother no doubt appreciated. At age fifteen, the fatherless boy had what certainly seems in hindsight like a life-changing revelation. Instead of working for other people, couldn't he earn more money by starting a business of his own? His timing could not have been better. The Great War was over. The veterans who'd made it through the conflict were establishing new lives back home. The docks and factories and retail establishments of New York City were buzzing with fresh activity. Immigrants were pouring in again. The nightclubs were filled with skinny flappers in bobbed hairdos and short skirts. Prohibition? What Prohibition? Fun-loving couples would soon be doing the Charleston. The New York economy hadn't hummed like this since—well, it had never hummed like this before. The Roaring Twenties were really beginning to roar. The subway was still the lifeblood of the working city. But families in far-flung sections of Brooklyn and Queens were also buying newfangled automobiles.

Young Fred saw all this happening around him, and he took it all in. While other boys his age were building tree houses in their backyards, he decided to start his own construction company. His mother would be his business partner. He would oversee the projects. Since he wasn't of age yet, she would write the checks. That was the division of labor at E. Trump & Son, the earliest iteration of the family-owned conglomerate that would eventually slap its five-letter name, T-R-U-M-P, all in caps, on skyscrapers, hotels, golf resorts, casinos, steaks, cologne, bottled water, dress shirts, neckties, vodka, mattresses, eyeglasses, chandeliers, coffee, pillows, a modeling agency, a get-rich-quick business school, and shiny-gold high-top sneakers with matching American flags for $399 a pair.

But that was way off in the future.

For now, the firm's first area of specialty: building garages for all those newly arriving automobiles. Garages were easier to build than houses. People had the money to pay for them. And as middle-class New York came into its own in the 1920s, the demand was certainly there. The Queens teenager's irresistible pitch: *Doesn't your shiny Model T also deserve a home?*

So how do we know so much about my grandfather's youthful work ethic and his rapid rise from preteen mogul to budding real-estate man?

No one was running a video camera as he made these early inroads. Was he really *that* diligent as a teenager? Was he that prescient about the automobile? Are all those stories true? Well, maybe not *all* of them. Most of what we know about my grandfather's early triumphs, we know firsthand . . . from him.

He always loved telling stories that featured his early hard work and unyielding ambition. After years at the family dinner table, I can vouch for that much. Some of these stories could certainly have gotten exaggerated over the years as they were repeated in countless newspaper articles and banquet talks. But I'm convinced there's enough truth in my grandfather's up-from-the-bootstraps origin story that it really does help explain him, and the diligent-boy-makes-good framing is revealing in its own way. From a very young age, my grandfather understood the importance of selling. And as any good salesman will tell you, you are always selling yourself.

After my grandfather finished high school in January 1923 (I'm still not sure he actually *graduated*), he took on another job delivering lumber to construction sites, and there was, literally, no stopping him. He signed up for night classes in engineering at Brooklyn's Pratt Institute and learned to read blueprints. He subscribed to correspondence courses in masonry, plumbing, and residential wiring. His mother incorporated E. Trump & Son, but young Fred did the heavy lifting. He was soon selling spec houses in Hollis, Queens, some of them before they were even finished to finance the next ones. Year by year, he built more and larger houses and expanded his footprint, one small step at a time, across the growing neighborhoods of Brooklyn and Queens.

As he moved from single-family houses to multistory apartment buildings, he hired more employees and settled into a suite of offices a two-minute drive from the Coney Island Boardwalk at 600 Avenue Z. The walls were soon covered in smiling publicity photographs: Fred with Mayor Fiorello La Guardia. Fred with a contingent of ministers or rabbis. Fred and a shovel, breaking ground at a new apartment complex. He teamed up with other builders and kept expanding the kinds of projects he was prepared to take on. It was basic math: Why buy a piece of land and put a single house on it when he could accommodate twenty families side by side and one above the other?

In the mid-1930s, he opened Trump Market in Woodhaven, one of the city's first modern supermarkets. "Serve Yourself and Save," his newspaper ads said. Six months later, he sold the store to Long Island's King Kullen chain. The following year, he and a partner bought a mortgage-servicing company out of bankruptcy. That gave him a chance to foreclose on deadbeat properties, which could be flipped at a tidy profit.

My grandfather had earned enough by then to send his younger brother, John, to private college and then to private graduate school—at Brooklyn Polytechnic Institute, Columbia, and MIT, an advanced education that the brother would eventually parlay into a tenured professorship in electrical engineering at MIT. However my grandfather felt about the value of higher education, he never considered it an option for himself. In his mind, he had a stronger obligation: He had to support the family. And everyone in the family seemed to agree: Let brother John pursue what he loved; Fred knew how to shake the money tree.

All these stories weren't just a case of self-aggrandizement—though don't rule that out entirely. It was more strategic than that. From a very early age, my grandfather had a keen appreciation for the value of hype. On sweltering summer Sundays at Coney Island, New Yorkers weren't greeted only by sideshow freaks, Nathan's hot dogs, and the rides at Steeplechase Park. Anchored in the water, measuring bow-to-stern at sixty-five feet, was the Trump Show Boat, a massive yacht adorned with giant TRUMP signs. Every time the loudspeaker played "The

Star-Spangled Banner," sandy men and women would stand up at their beach towels and salute, according to *The New York Times,* putting the Trump company firmly on the side of American patriotism. And every now and then, crewmen on the boat would release brightly colored balloons, redeemable for $25 or $250 toward a new Trump Home. The mayhem in the water was like a shark sighting, only the sunburned people were running *into* the surf to grab one of those prized balloons.

Success begets success, my grandfather understood—and so does the *appearance* of success. If people think you are successful, that will help you become so. Later on, he would hire a Madison Avenue public-relations firm to get this bold version of his rise published in New York newspapers. One typewritten press release boasted that the impressive young builder had a success story that "parallels the fictional Horatio Alger saga about the boy who parlayed a shoestring into a business empire."

Horatio Trump. The papers ate that stuff up.

So, no, Donald wasn't the first Trump with a talent for name promotion. His father and grandfather launched that rocket. Donald just rode it to the stars.

Still, there was no denying my grandfather's many business achievements and his expanding real-estate portfolio. If he'd exaggerated at the beginning, he caught up with his own boy-makes-good storyline—and easily surpassed it. In his case, the hype really was self-fulfilling. He amassed thousands and thousands of apartments over the years. Some he built. Some he bought. Almost all of them, he figured out how to leverage financially. Many of his buildings still stand. There's no denying this part. It really did take a clarity of vision, a tireless work ethic, and some superhuman drive.

Even the Great Depression didn't slow him down for long. By the mid-1930s, he was eagerly partnering with Washington, specifically the subsidized mortgage program of the Federal Housing Administration. That helped him close a lot of deals. By 1938, when my grandfather was thirty-three, he had more than three hundred workers on the company payroll. That year, *The Brooklyn Eagle* called him "the Henry Ford of the home building industry." Thanks, Madison Avenue PR. Things really took off for him in the lead-up to World War II. By Pearl Harbor, he'd built two thousand homes in Brooklyn alone, many in partnership with the FHA.

It was in this period between the two world wars that my grandfather felt a need to finesse one aspect of his background that he feared could become troublesome for him. His middle name: Christ. It had been his mother's family name, and he'd never given all that much thought to it. But with his rising prominence in New York real estate, he was doing business with a lot of Jewish people—landowners, developers, real-estate brokers, even workers in the construction trades, not to mention tenants from the large Jewish communities of Brooklyn and Queens. Would they have an issue dealing with someone named Christ? He thought about that. He'd always used the German pronunciation, as his mother's family had—"krist," like "mist." But still. His name was spelled the Jesus way, C-H-R-I-S-T, and he certainly wasn't looking for trouble with the Jews. He'd always made an effort to support Jewish charities and would soon donate a plot of land for the Beach Haven Jewish Center, where he called the rabbi, Israel Wagner, "my rabbi."

Though my grandfather rarely used his full middle name in business, he was widely known as Fred C. Trump. The newspapers often called him that. He often used the middle initial in his signature. So, what should he do?

My grandfather's solution? Drop the "h."

Which is why, in those years, he began writing the name C-R-I-S-T. He didn't change the pronunciation. He didn't need to. But from that point forward, if he had some reason for formality, he was Frederick Crist Trump.

As America shifted onto a wartime footing, so did my grandfather.

He built apartment complexes in the Navy city of Norfolk, Virginia. It was a great deal for him. He owned the buildings, and the federal government paid the apartment rents. By 1944, he'd constructed 1,360 of these wartime apartments, making him one of Norfolk's largest landlords, and he didn't stop there. He then built barracks near the shipyards in nearby Newport News.

When a whole new generation of veterans began returning home from World War II, my grandfather was there to house them and their families—and that is how his empire really found its scale. He built the Shore Haven Apartments in Bensonhurst, Brooklyn, thirty-six-story buildings and a shopping center. Next, it was the twenty-three-building Beach Haven Apartments in Coney Island. And he just kept on going. By that point, he was being called one of the major landlords in New York. No one could deny it now: Fred Trump had lived up to his hype. If his father had brought a gold-rush sense of adventure into the immigrant Trump family, my grandfather was the one who imagined the born-in-America version and nursed it to life.

And why him? He wasn't an intellectual. He wasn't especially erudite or well-read. He had no patience for windy discussions of culture, religion, or the arts. He was a practical businessman from the start. Focused. Driven. Always pushing for more. No fancy financial footwork, the kind his middle son would eventually get in trouble for, and no high-flying construction techniques. He had a few simple business principles, and he stuck with them.

Find a need and meet it.

Build something once. Rent it over and over again.

Buy distressed properties on the cheap from other owners who are struggling.

Push yourself hard. Push others hard too. Don't get sentimental. Ever.

Stick to white neighborhoods.

That last one wouldn't last forever in a changing city like New York. But all the others turned out to be sound business principles, even if they didn't always make him the easiest man to live with. When he set his mind on something, my grandfather did not give up.

It is easy in the Trump family to focus so much on the men and their many exploits that the women get left out of the story entirely or get consigned to a minor, helpmate role. In fact, my grandmother had just as dramatic an origin story as my grandfather Fred did . . . actually, more so. It's just that her influence on the family would turn out to be far quieter than her husband's was.

Mary Anne MacLeod had an excellent reason to leave her native Scotland and move to the United States. Things were bleak at home for her, and she dreamed of better opportunities, the same reason hopeful immigrants have always come to America. She was born in 1912, the tenth of ten children, in the village of Tong (say "tongue") on the outskirts of Stornoway in an isolated corner of the western Scottish isles. This was the Isle of Lewis in the Outer Hebrides. There may be a gloomier, more austere place on the planet, but you'd need a savvy anthropologist to find it and a crackerjack travel agent to get you there. My grandmother's father was a fisherman, a subsistence farmer, and the truancy officer at Mary's school. The family lived in a gray pebble-dashed croft house on a pockmarked road and worshipped under the stern strictures of the Scottish Presbyterian Church. Gaelic was spoken in the home. The children learned English as a second language in school. "Hardscrabble" is the word people often use for this kind of upbringing, and that's exactly what it was. When my grandmother was a child, bad things kept happening around her. The Western Isles had more men killed in World War I than anywhere else in the British Empire. Of the six thousand who served from the Isle of Lewis, more

than a thousand returned in body bags. Then, another two hundred
drowned when the ship that was carrying them home careened into a
massive rock just off the shore.

When Mary Anne's older sister Catherine had a baby even though
she wasn't married, that caused an immediate uproar on the isle. Catherine chose to distance herself from the sting of scandal by emigrating
to New York, where she quickly found work as a "domestic," cleaning
rich people's houses and looking after their children. One sister followed and then another before Mary Anne decided to make it four.
Given northwest Scotland's paucity of job prospects and eligible men,
she kept asking herself: Even in the midst of a Great Depression, how
bad could America be? It had to beat sitting at a loom in the Harris
Tweed plant or curing herring as a fish girl.

Mary Anne boarded the SS *Transylvania* in Glasgow on May 2,
1930 (some reports say November 29, 1929). Either way, the teenager arrived in New York Harbor nine days later with the intention of
staying. She moved in with her sister Catherine on Long Island, using
that as a base to find work in the same field her three sisters had. Scottish girls were good around the house, well-off New Yorkers seemed
to agree. In fact, Mary Anne worked as a maid at the Upper East Side
mansion of one of Scotland's most famous sons, industrialist turned
philanthropist Andrew Carnegie, according to Nina Burleigh's book
The Trump Women. Though he'd been dead for twelve years before Mary
Anne appeared at the doorstep, his widow, Louise, still lived in the
four-story, sixty-four-room Georgian Revival estate.

One night in 1935, Mary and Catherine reportedly went to a house
party in Queens, where they met a couple of American guys. Mary hit
it off with the one who said he owned a construction company and
built things in the New York area. They made a nice-looking pair. He
was tall and lean with slicked-back hair, six years her senior. She was
twenty-three, tall with wavy brown hair and porcelain skin.

They married the following January at Manhattan's Madison Avenue Presbyterian Church with a British-born minister named George Arthur Buttrick officiating. Rolls right off the tongue, huh? "Tong Girl Weds Abroad," said the short write-up in her hometown paper, the *Stornoway Gazette*, which also noted that the bride wore a "princess gown of white satin and a tulle cap and veil." The couple had a small reception at the Carlyle Hotel and honeymooned for a night on the boardwalk in Atlantic City, New Jersey. They would have stayed longer, but the groom said he needed to get back to work.

An assertion he would make over and over again, almost until the day he died.

An early glimpse of the life they would have together, she would soon find out. But she wasn't one to argue. So return to Queens they did.

The new life she had fallen into could hardly be any more different than the one she had left behind. Though she'd traveled 3,112 miles from her windswept corner of Scotland, it might as well have been a million and a half. Now it was on to the future for Mary Trump.

At first, the newlyweds lived with his mother, but they soon found a house of their own on Devonshire Road, as my grandfather continued to build his real-estate empire. Their first child, a daughter they named Maryanne—one word this time—was born in April 1937. A son, Frederick Crist Trump Jr.—again without the "h"—arrived eighteen months after that. Mary Anne was sworn in as a U.S. citizen in 1942, completing her immigrant journey, the same year her third child, a daughter named Elizabeth, was born. By then, they'd moved into a larger house on Wareham Place in Jamaica and hired a nanny to help with the children and the house, a position my grandmother had held not so many years before.

Let me repeat that: The family had its own nanny. What a distance my grandmother had already come.

There was still some tension between my grandfather's family and the woman he had chosen as his wife. To put it bluntly: My grandfather's German-born mother and some of the others didn't think she measured up to their social class. All these immigrant Scottish sisters. A baby out of wedlock. The bride's own parents didn't even make it to the wedding, leaving that to the sisters who were already here. Was this really the kind of woman who should be Mrs. Fred Trump? And that was just the start of it. For years, people on my grandfather's side of the family would bury the true story of my grandmother's arrival in America, trying to make her sound like something more than a poor immigrant who'd disembarked in the new country with little more than a battered suitcase and her dreams. The way they chose to tell the story, Scottish lass Mary Anne was in New York "on holiday" from her happy life across the ocean when she met her Prince Charming, conveniently skipping the part where she fled grinding poverty and the five years she had worked as a maid in Queens and on Long Island in other people's homes.

It was, in fact, an amazing journey that brought my grandmother to America, and her in-laws wanted to skip the most inspiring parts.

Thank goodness, none of the grumbles seemed to have much impact on her Fred. To his credit, if he even heard the whispers, my grandfather was headstrong enough not to care. He and his wife wanted a big family, and they got busy adding to the fold. Son Donald was born June 14, 1946, at Jamaica Hospital, followed two years later by another boy, Robert, bringing the Trump family child count to five.

My grandmother had a tough birth with Robert. She hemorrhaged severely, which required an emergency hysterectomy. That led to a serious abdominal infection, which led to more surgeries. At one point, there was genuine concern she might die. Her husband shared that rattling news with eleven-year-old Maryanne in a very Fred Trump way.

"Go on to school as usual," he told her. "We will update you if anything changes."

No, my grandfather could never be accused of being overly sentimental. Clearly, he was a bright and capable man in many respects, but emotional intelligence might not have been one of them.

My grandmother survived, but she was never pregnant again. So five kids it was—more than enough to carry them boldly into the future.

CHAPTER 3

FAMILY PLAN

Like water, every marriage finds its own level, and that was certainly true of the Trumps'.

My grandfather and grandmother, Fred and Mary Anne Trump, had a division of labor that seemed to suit both of them perfectly. He took care of his busy real-estate company, while she gave him all the room he could possibly need to do that and looked after almost everything else in their lives.

Only rarely did either of them step outside their lanes.

My grandmother would ride around to Trump apartment buildings and collect coins from the laundry machines. And when it suited him, my grandfather would step in as the big-gun disciplinarian, usually after my grandmother had been forced to utter those six immortal words: "Wait until your father gets home."

Grandpa had two kinds of workdays: long and longer. If he didn't have an evening meeting to attend, he was typically home by dinnertime. And everyone could hear him coming. That was the point of his distinctive six-note whistle as he bounded up the front steps from the garage.

C-A-F-F-C-A#, a note for those who read music.

It was the Fred Trump equivalent of "Hey, everybody, I'm home."

And once he came in, he could clean up any disciplinary issues that lingered from the day. Often, all that took was a glare. He could put the fear of Fred into most of his five children without even saying a word. And if he had to deliver a corrective lecture, the best way of making it stop was a two-word answer:

"Yes, sir."

Especially with the boys, my grandfather's disciplinary approach was simply to say, "Don't do that again"—period. He said it so sternly and directly, it usually ended the need for any further updates.

No one was guaranteed Fred Trump's approval, including his wife and children. It had to be earned . . . and earned, and earned. If my grandmother felt oppressed by any of that, she never let on. Given the bleak corner of northwest Scotland she'd left behind and her five years as a maid and nanny in New York, she must have figured that even her worst day as Mrs. Fred Trump was a nice step up. He was the star. She reflected his light. The brighter he shone, the stronger she glowed . . . and even more so in her theatrically blond-tinted hair.

She had her own proud role outside the home as an active volunteer with the Salvation Army, the Boy Scouts, the Lighthouse for the Blind, Booth Memorial Hospital, and Jamaica Hospital, where she would eventually rise to president of the Women's Auxiliary. But her true realm was as wife and mother and queen of the home, where she was the undisputed boss of everything—until the moment her husband came through the door.

"Hello, dear, can I get you a coffee or a Coke," she would call out from the kitchen in that wonderful voice of hers, a thoroughly original amalgam of Scotland, Long Island, and Queens. There was no mention of alcohol, ever. The only exceptions I ever heard about were the ancient parties my grandfather supposedly hosted in the basement for the local Queens and Brooklyn politicos. Those characters definitely did not come over for coffee, tea, or soft drinks.

It wasn't that my grandfather refused to engage with the family. It's just that he was the undeniable center of gravity whenever he was around, even when his mind was halfway someplace else. Among the phrases heard most often in the Trump family when the children were young: "Don't disturb your father, he's working" and "Can you boys please pipe down?" And when he *was* there, he wasn't the kind of dad to roll around on the floor with the kiddos or toss a ball out in the yard. Six-foot-one and barrel-chested with no noticeable slouch and a slicked-back, receding hairline, he had a general demeanor that was far too stiff for that. If he'd ever been young, you wouldn't know it by looking at him. Often, he didn't even take his tie off until he was ready for bed. But with his relentless work ethic and his ever-expanding real-estate empire, he set a powerful example for his children, whether they wanted to follow it or not. (Which would become a defining question later on.) For now, there was a right way and a wrong way to do everything, and not much was left to choice.

Fred and Mary Anne and their children—my grandparents, dad, and aunts and uncles—got rolling in a pleasant butter-colored house at 85-15 Wareham Place with five bedrooms, a sunroom, and a beamed Tudor-style roof. It was a perfectly comfortable family home with a flagstone walkway and red-brick front steps, but not quite a showplace that declared, "Successful builder lives here." When Uncle Robert was barely out of diapers and Aunt Maryanne was preparing her advance to upper school, their father bought a twenty-three-room mansion at 85-14 Midland Parkway on the opposite side of the same block. The house, which was built around 1930, looked like it could have come off a Southern plantation. Four white columns. A colonnaded portico. A two-car garage below the sprawling dining room. Lush landscaping out front and winding steps to the porch. Formal rooms on the main floor, bedrooms above that, and then rustic attic quarters for the household staff. During the war years, my grandfather had spent time working in Virginia. He must have gained an appreciation for the region's antebellum architectural style while there.

Now *that* was a house. And it would be my grandparents' forever home.

Anything seemed possible in the leafy Jamaica Estates section of Queens, where mature oak trees lined the streets and the spacious houses were thoughtfully set off by gently sloping, well-manicured lawns. No more Woodhaven. No more Richmond Hill. Jamaica Estates—even the name sounded swank—was a tight, protected enclave of doctors, lawyers, and other well-off professionals, hemmed in by one of the most diverse patches of real estate on planet earth. The old stone gatehouse still stood at Hillside Avenue, where the rest of the borough began. And four-lane Midland Parkway, with its wide, planted median, was the neighborhood's grandest boulevard, the Park Avenue of this heavenly patch of Queens. These were blocks that quietly stated, "Life is special here and we'd very much prefer to keep it that way." It's where my father, his two brothers and two sisters all came of age, in a house I would later come to think of as my second home, a place I would ride my bike to, endlessly.

As the oldest, Maryanne was smart and tough and athletic, an overachiever in the classroom and on the basketball court at her private Kew-Forest School. She was the first of many Trumps, including me, to attend the small, coed academy, where personal attention was a hallmark and many of the classmates stayed together for twelve years. Maryanne was tall and blond but never flashy, not a girly girl, and not one to shrink from anything. She made it on brainpower. High achievement, not family wealth, was her brand, to put it in Trumpian terms. As she would say later: "The first time I realized my father was successful was when I was fifteen and a friend said to me, 'Your father is rich.'"

Maryanne wasn't a goody-goody. She knew all the four-letter words and didn't hesitate to use them. She was already smoking by the time she started high school. And if she had an opinion, which she often did, biting her tongue was almost never her course of action. Put it like this: By the time she was fitted for a training bra, she was either a "mean girl" or a "truth teller," depending on whether she was talking about you or somebody else. And her unvarnished opinionizing extended even to the people she loved.

Maryanne liked to tell a story about having a guy over to visit. As they sat together on the couch watching TV, her father's voice suddenly came over the mansion intercom.

"Maryanne."

Let's just say she didn't hear from him again.

The firstborn son, my father, got the charm in the family.

He was Frederick Crist Trump Jr., which marked him as special right there, though everyone just called him Freddie. Tall, lean, handsome, easy to be with and quick with a funny comment, Freddie was the Trump who had personal skills and an effortless kind of charisma.

He didn't follow his sister to the Kew-Forest School. He started out in public school. Then, his father decided Freddie might be better off at St. Paul's, an all-boys Episcopal school in Garden City, Long Island, where the curriculum aimed to develop a "manly, Christian character, a strong physique and the power to think," in the words of early headmaster Father Frederick Luther Gamage. Housed in a massive, E-shaped High Victorian building on a forty-eight-acre campus, it was the closest thing to a traditional English boarding school that was also an easy bus ride from Queens. The gothic chapel sat four hundred. The teachers were called "masters." Freddie immediately gravitated to the cutups in his class, though he also got along with the athletes, the nerds, and pretty much everyone else.

If St. Paul's was supposed to turn him into a more studious young man, it did not have the desired effect. Freddie had tons of friends, a so-so report card, and an infectious kind of energy that made the other boys and girls want to chase after him. He was insatiably curious. He and his school friends Karl Walther or Homer Godwin or his neighborhood friend Billy Drake were always riding the train somewhere or out exploring another neighborhood. Though Freddie was a natural athlete, he wasn't much of a jock, not the football-baseball-basketball kind. He just wasn't drawn to sports with so many rules. He was definitely playful, but what he loved was boating and fishing and swimming and going off to friends' houses on the weekends, and from an early age, he devoured flying magazines.

Nothing delighted Freddie more than a good practical joke, though his friends weren't sure he would ever top the Great Hearse Caper. One day, he and Homer skipped out on school and somehow managed to "borrow" a hearse from a local funeral home. After joyriding for hours while shooting somber looks out the windows at passing cars, Homer lay down in the back. They pulled into a gas station to fill the tank before returning the vehicle to the funeral home. Just then, a car pulled in. When the other driver glanced over, Homer bolted upright and fixed him with a menacing grin.

Yikes! A runaway corpse at the Esso pump!

The look on the other driver's face was priceless, as the frightened man screeched out of the gas station, escaping the hearse and its undead passenger as quickly as he could. When they pulled the hearse out of the station, the boys forgot to take the gas pump out of the tank. *Oops.* The handle bounced loudly on the pavement as they made their getaway.

Freddie and Homer laughed all the way to the funeral home and back to St. Paul's, where the story only got better every time it was told.

While outsiders were easily drawn to Freddie, his father rode him hard. He could see that his son had leadership potential, and he wanted that potential to be realized. But while others saw him as laid-back and fun to be with, his dad saw him as unfocused or lackadaisical. His father could often be heard telling Freddie, "You need to buckle down and apply yourself." In a business as black-and-white as home construction, it took hammers and nails to make a building, not pranks and adventures. That's how my grandfather saw it, anyway. With all that native ability, Grandpa believed, all my father needed was a firm, guiding hand. And who better to deliver it than his own father?

My grandfather tried, with his trademark focus.

He dragged his oldest son to construction sites on Saturdays and urged him to stop by the office in Brooklyn after school, none of which Freddie showed much interest in. But with all those personal skills—and "Junior" tacked onto the end of his name—everyone just assumed that Freddie would outgrow this phase he was in and one day run the entire Trump empire.

Everyone but Freddie.

When it came time for him to graduate and the final grades were being tallied, his father made a generous donation to the St. Paul's capital fund. He didn't only write a check. He also brought in a pair of earth movers from one of the Trump construction companies and leveled a patch of campus land large enough for a soccer field. No one was exactly saying that Freddie wouldn't have graduated without that. But his dad's generous gesture couldn't have hurt.

Freddie never asked him to do it. It really wasn't his kind of thing. But the brass plaque left no room for confusion. "Trump Field," it said. "Presented by Fred C. Trump and the Class of 1956." And Freddie graduated right on time to rousing applause from his classmates, though I'm sure they would have clapped just as hard with or without the soccer field. That's the guy he was. No one ever said his father didn't know how to get things done, but none of that changed who Freddie was.

What all this taught him early on was to live his own life, no matter what anyone thought about it, least of all his family. Lesson one: He should avoid his father whenever possible. Also . . . offer vague answers to whatever questions were asked. Deflect—whenever necessary—about after-school antics, choice of friends, the smoking habit he picked up from his older sister, and anything else that might come up.

Just sidestep everything. The less his father knew, the less his father had to lecture him about.

Not all the Trump children had large personalities. There was also Elizabeth, the quiet middle child, who did everything she could to avoid attention. In a family of extroverts, she was anything but. She saw what happened above her. She saw what happened below her. She didn't want any of it.

Elizabeth followed Maryanne to the Kew-Forest School, but she never cut the same figure on campus. She had friends, but not too many, or too few. Her personality was often described as *nice*. The one thing she didn't want to do was stand out. As graduation neared, Maryanne and Elizabeth both chose private, all-female colleges, but the two schools seemed tailor-made to their distinct personalities. Maryanne enrolled at the academically rigorous Mount Holyoke College in western Massachusetts. Elizabeth headed south, to the foothills of the Blue Ridge Mountains and the far more genteel and very beautiful Southern Seminary College in Buena Vista, Virginia.

To each her own.

. . .

In a family that could sometimes seem like the cast of a 1950s sitcom, my uncle Donald had a role of his own.

He was the obnoxious one.

And it's true: Many of Donald's adult traits—his determination, his short fuse—first displayed themselves in his childhood. I'm not sure I can sum up his early days in a single slogan, but I think I can do it in two: "I wanna do what I wanna do" and also "That's not fair!" Both those impulses were fully apparent by the time he was toddling around the house and howling, "Nooo . . ." For the first thirteen years of his life, he seemed largely unconstrained by the limits other children lived with, and he might erupt at anyone who tried to tell him otherwise.

Donald needed a lot of attention. When he assembled an Erector Set in the basement, no one was allowed to touch it until he was done. When he was finally finished, everyone was summoned to say how amazing it was.

"Isn't that the greatest."

"Great! Theee best!"—with an accent on "theee."

Donald was already practicing for the days ahead.

So much has already been said and written about my uncle's tumultuous boyhood, I don't want to repeat all that. But there are a few key experiences in his early life that are worth recounting, meaningful moments that I don't believe have ever been adequately appreciated. I caught the very tail end of this, and I know my family well enough to grasp how the five siblings of my father's generation got formed by an unyielding father and also by each other.

A sandy-haired child in this home of privilege and wealth, Donald learned early that he could get away with things.

What kind of things? Stupid kid stuff at first. Taking toys from other children. Throwing cake at a dress-up birthday party. Refusing to eat anything he didn't want to eat. And bedtime? Forget about it if Donald wasn't ready for bed. Whenever he didn't get his way, he could be a maddening handful, especially for the exhausted maids, nannies, and babysitters who were often expected to look after him. His mother did what she could. But a lot of this behavior she just attributed to him being her "fussy one."

If anyone found any of this cute, it didn't stay cute for long.

Once he followed his two sisters to the Kew-Forest School, Donald brought that same attitude of his into the classroom. One day, he famously threw an eraser at a teacher's head, giving her a black eye. What started as impish behavior was clearly becoming more serious. The teachers said Donald was aggravating younger children in the lunchroom and in the schoolyard. He was certainly pushy . . . and annoying.

When it comes to memorable stories, every family has its greatest hits. The Mashed Potato Toss holds a permanent place at the top of the Trumps' list, a story that so encapsulates the different personalities, it was bound to be repeated for decades to come. Donald was in middle school. One night at dinner, when my grandparents were away, Donald was harassing his younger brother, Robert, and would not let up.

Poking him. Teasing him. Making fun of the games he played.

"Stop it," Maryanne snapped.

"Enough," Freddie said.

As usual, Elizabeth sat there quietly. Thinking first, commenting later. I think that's why my father liked her so much.

As Donald kept going, Freddie took matters into his own hands. He reached calmly toward the bowl of mashed potatoes that one of the housekeepers had just set on the table. He scooped a heaping handful and took aim. Then he hurled the clump of mashed potatoes straight across the table, where the soggy projectile landed squarely on Donald.

Rather than face the humiliation of his siblings, Donald jumped up and ran from the room.

No mashed potato payback.

"I think you made your point," Elizabeth said calmly to Freddie, who just smiled.

That night would feature prominently in the family lore for decades to come.

The siblings were always testing each other. There was one memorable day when Donald was being particularly obnoxious and my dad decided he had to do something. He knew how much his little brother hated snakes. He also knew that their Jamaica Estates neighborhood was crawling with garter snakes. Literally. It didn't take long to find a big one in the backyard.

It was long and slithery, but the snake was harmless. Some of us were just fine with these friendly snakes. No big deal.

Freddie brought that snake into the house. He snuck into Donald's bedroom while he was taking a bath. And he dropped the snake right into his little brother's unmade bed. Even their mother, who was down in the kitchen, could hear the screams from the dripping-wet Donald as soon as he sauntered back into his bedroom. As she came running to see what was wrong, my father was already heading back down, laughing so hard he had to hold on to the banister.

If that prank sounds immature on my father's part, it certainly was. But Donald was just the kind of child who could drive almost anyone around the bend.

One reason those get-back-at-Donald stories stand out: They were so much more the exception than the rule. Usually, Donald was the one coming out on top. Those happy moments of comeuppance never lasted long, and they certainly never changed him. He'd stomp off and sulk but, bright and early the next morning, he was right back where he had been, and most days, no one had the heart or the energy to confront or correct him, especially since my grandfather was mostly working and my grandmother battled a series of health problems when Donald was young. At the time, that made her a distant mother. The household staff was no match for the young terror's temper tantrums. His older siblings had other things to do. So when he refused to do something, there was literally no one to make him. To point out what might be obvious about this young son of privilege: Some of the other adults on the scene considered it more prudent just to step aside. His teachers tried to corral him, but they often threw up their hands. They had issued so many punishment sessions, they decided D.T. didn't only stand for detention, it also stood for Donnie Trump. Eventually, the teachers started telling themselves, "His father's on the board of trustees. What are we supposed to do?"

Maybe they really were helpless. Maybe not. But it was understandable why they might feel that way. Finally, by the summer of 1959, things had gotten so out of hand and the complaints had grown so loud, my grandfather decided he had no choice but to act.

Just in time for eighth grade, he yanked his incorrigible son out of the comfort of the Kew-Forest School and his comfy bedroom in Jamaica Estates and shipped him off to the New York Military Academy, hoping that some Army-style discipline might be just the ticket to get the stubborn boy back in line. If Donald wouldn't listen to his teachers, babysitters, or even his parents, maybe a platoon of stern-faced drill sergeants would have more luck.

A fellow Kew-Forest board member had told my grandfather about the New York Military Academy, which was founded by a Civil War veteran in 1889 and now run mostly by men who'd served in World War II. The adults there didn't believe in coddling anyone. Donald was used to threats of punishment that didn't tend to happen, and he half expected his mother to save him from this awful fate. But when she said nothing other than "good luck, let us know if you need anything," her thirteen-year-old wise guy of a son finally realized he had squandered the opening chapter of his childhood and had lost his final ally.

What a change this was going to be for this careening son of privilege! To go from the warm embrace of the Kew-Forest School to the loudly barked orders of men in khaki uniforms. To go from bustling New York City to Cornwall-on-Hudson, a tiny speck of a town sixty miles to the north, just a short drive from the U.S. Military Academy at West Point.

But off Donald went.

The school had its routines down cold. The cadets were rousted from sleep at dawn. They threw on their uniforms and marched in ranks to the mess hall for breakfast, then hurried back to their sparse rooms for inspection. Their shoes had to be shined. Their beds had to be made. Their uniforms had to be just so. Compared to the New York Military Academy, Donald's old life at the Kew-Forest School and the Trump mansion in Jamaica Estates was a day at the beach. His new school was not a place where people got away with anything. It was a place of order and rules.

And yet . . . Donald seemed to take to it with barely a complaint.

Some kids were desperately homesick. Others bristled under the iron traditions and unyielding faculty. But the kid from Queens, whom no one had been able to control, immediately began shining his shoes and his belt buckle, making his bed with extra-tight corners and hopping out of his bunk at reveille. On a few of these tasks, he needed instruction. He'd never been much of a bed maker at home. But with a small assist from some of the older students, he got his moves down and took to it all. Later, his ceremonial sword would be proudly displayed along with his matching hat (with feather) over the upright piano that his parents had never bothered to tune.

Through eighth, ninth, tenth, and eleventh grades, he moved slowly up the student ranks, from middle-school cadet to high-school sergeant. His grades might not have been anything to write home about—but he probably didn't write home anyway. He loved the energetic competition. He especially loved the medals and ribbons that were constantly being handed out. Cleanest room. Shiniest shoes. Best marcher. There were never-ending opportunities for him to excel at things he could be good at. He joined almost every sports team there was on campus. Soccer. Wrestling. Football. He really made a mark on the baseball team as a quick-footed first baseman. If his earlier life had left him in a bubble of privilege, this was a bubble too—but a different kind. A bubble where everything was laid out in front of him and his hyperaggressiveness was no longer considered a character flaw: It was worthy of another ribbon.

His mother and father visited occasionally but not too often. Mostly, they seemed pleased at the progress young Donald was making and pleased that he was mostly gone. He was certainly more polite when he was home. And on summer breaks and holiday weekends, he seemed happy to do what his brother Freddie had always resisted, tagging along with his father as they visited apartment complexes and construction sites.

It wasn't just that the drill sergeants had taught him not to complain. He actually displayed interest when my grandfather spoke about the real-estate business and its many ins and outs.

"Really?" he would say when my grandfather pointed out some unusual construction technique. "Neat."

There were times in military school where Donald may have gone overboard. When he was put in charge of the rifle rack, he cleaned the rifles so obsessively, he might actually have damaged a few. When he was given authority over younger cadets, his gung ho approach really stood out. Was he maintaining appropriate standards? Or was he enjoying the authority a little too much? That was a matter of perspective. But he was a stickler for everything. When he performed inspections, he showed no mercy. If any of the younger cadets uttered the slightest grumble, he had a ready answer for that: "Everything needs to be right." And he left it at that.

He was two full hours from Jamaica Estates, but he was still Fred Trump's son.

If Donald's progress was slow and steady for his first four years, he had a sudden lurch forward at the start of senior year. Prior to then, the highest rank he'd achieved was supply sergeant, as several of his classmates were promoted to lieutenant. But when he came back from that summer break, he was elevated straight to captain and named commander of A-Company, the most prestigious assignment a student leader could have. It surprised quite a few of his classmates, but all those years of being the eager enforcer must have impressed someone.

The story of how my uncle Donald got to military school is certainly revealing. But the story of how he got out may be even more so. Thrust into such a high leadership position, the hard-charging senior . . . suddenly forgot how to lead.

What happened? It's hard to say for certain. But as we all eventually heard, he would finish dinner and head straight to his room in the barracks, leaving it to his subordinate officers to inspect the cadets. When people asked him questions, he never answered directly. He always seemed to refer things to someone else. He rarely walked the hallways or knocked on doors of his cadets, just to check in and see what was up. As I know from the business world, that's a great way for a leader to become isolated. It was only through his subordinate officers that Donald tried to maintain the discipline he was known for.

He quickly lost control.

Within a month, a freshman named Lee Ains filed a complaint about being hazed by a student sergeant who was under Donald's command. Donald wasn't accused of being directly involved in the hazing, but school officials quickly decided that he was such an unengaged leader that his sudden hands-off style was approaching negligence. He hadn't been paying close enough attention, and here was the result. So the top student leadership was shuffled for the rest of the school year.

Donald was moved to the administrative building, where he wouldn't have much contact with other students or be expected to lead anyone. The new job was more "outward facing," as they say in the military.

Donald didn't lose any rank. He was still a captain. On paper at least, the move could even be read as one of those kicked-upstairs kinds of promotions. Any guess how Donald described it when *The Washington Post* asked him about the episode early in the 2016 presidential campaign? That's right. It was a major triumph, he said.

"I had total control over the cadets," he boasted. "That's why I got a promotion—because I did so good."

That was another Donald lesson right there: Declare victory and move on.

But whatever the complexities of his exit, the New York Military Academy gave my uncle this much: It was where he transitioned from simply obnoxious to thoroughly brash. It confirmed a key lesson his father had tried to teach him, that the world was divided into two kinds of people—winners and losers—and you always needed to do whatever it took to be on the winning side. This wasn't a place that taught a lot of nuance or was long on compassion. But those drill sergeants sure did emphasize the necessity of having clear-eyed goals.

The main one being: It's better to win than to lose. Don't stop at anything.

If Donald had a polar opposite in the family, that would have to be Robert. He was quiet. He listened. While he was probably the most talented

Trump athlete, he wasn't prone to bragging. Though not as invisible as their sister Elizabeth, he certainly never sought the spotlight. Two years younger than Donald, eleven years younger than Maryanne, he benefited from being the baby Trump. His parents were older and richer. They were that much more worn down. His older brothers and sisters shielded him from some of their father's harsher judgments and stricter demands. Things just weren't as personal with Robert.

Living amid so much uproar, he seemed to conclude that a lot of it was unnecessary. Without much fuss, he learned to accommodate. Surrounded by so many distinct personalities, he blended in. It could almost be said: He was the most normal Trump.

It didn't make him a natural leader. He didn't get the attention that his more difficult siblings demanded. But he found a quiet route to achievement that often included a soccer ball. He followed Freddie to St. Paul's School, where he was a standout on the team, getting whatever brand-name benefit there was from practicing on Trump Field. But if there were few over-the-top Robert stories to match those about Maryanne, Freddie, and Donald, that was mostly a matter of temperament and choice. Robert may have lacked the stubbornness or the drive that the Trumps were becoming known for. But compared to some of the others, it wasn't always about *him*.

As a natural consequence, whatever glory Robert was destined for in the future, it would almost certainly be the reflected kind.

And those were the five Trump children of my father's generation. Five unique personalities, all living together under my grandparents' potent influence in that big, sprawling house in Queens. Their paths would head in variety of different directions. But no matter what their futures might hold, their roles and places in the family, and in the outside world, were already beginning to be defined.

CHAPTER 4

GOLDEN BOY

He had the name, and all by itself, that name could have provided a golden path into the future for Frederick Crist Trump Jr. . . . if that had been a future he ever wanted for himself. But he never went by "Junior." He barely even mentioned the "Trump" part as he left the family home in Jamaica Estates and headed off to college. My dad was "Freddie" to pretty much everyone—his childhood pals in Queens, his fraternity brothers at Lehigh University, even his parents and siblings—they all called him Freddie. And all that time, without even seeming to try, Freddie was the Trump family golden boy.

It wasn't just the charm, the height, the lean physique or the easy, casual smile. It wasn't just the front-of-the-line position as Fred and Mary Anne's firstborn son. As much as any of that, it was Freddie's openness to all kinds of people and his unabashed cheerfulness about diving into the next adventure, whatever that next adventure might be. In the fall of 1956, when he showed up on the Lehigh campus in the historic industrial city of Bethlehem, Pennsylvania, sixty miles from Philadelphia, eighty-five from New York City, he quickly established himself as a center of gravity that others were naturally drawn to. He was having fun, and didn't you want to come along?

Whitewater rafting in the Poconos . . .

A road trip to Boston or Chicago . . .

Everyone wanted to be there. Everyone was in.

It didn't take long for Freddie to become one of the most popular people on campus. The guys liked him. The girls liked him. A business major and a natural standout in the ROTC, he got his schoolwork done *and* he always had time to hang out. Grades were not a big issue, though the fat stack of study guides at his fraternity house might have helped with that. But he never lacked curiosity. He always liked discovering things, diving into subjects just because they fascinated him. He did his own research, clipped articles, and marked up books. If they'd had "independent study" at Lehigh, he'd have probably gotten straight A's. And he definitely believed that a big part of getting a college education was appreciating all the things that happened *outside* the classroom.

If his image at Lehigh could be summed up in a single sentence, Freddie was the playful rich kid with a smile on his face . . . and not an ounce of snobbery about him. He was the kind of guy who was just as friendly with the cafeteria lady as he was with the university provost and would happily assist a confused grad student with the electric pencil sharpener in the library. "There's a lot of different kinds of intelligence," he would say with a shrug. Though he wasn't one to brag about it, he never tried to hide his family wealth. Otherwise, he wouldn't have come to campus in a shiny new red Corvette. He took trips to the Caribbean or the Bahamas each year and flying lessons at what was then called the Allentown-Bethlehem-Easton International Airport, where the U.S. Navy trained V-5 fliers during World War II. No, private aviation wasn't a big hobby with the financial-aid kids. More than once, Freddie rented a small plane, rounded up some friends, and took them on Saturday-afternoon spins above the picturesque Lehigh Valley.

That made an impression on everyone.

While Freddie was away at college, among his biggest admirers was his younger brother Donald. Sometimes, Freddie let Donald tag along when his Lehigh buddies came for fishing weekends on the Long Island Sound. "I hope you don't mind, I have to take my pain-in-the-ass brother," he'd say to his frat brothers. No one minded. In his room at New York Military Academy, Donald had a photo of his older brother standing next to an airplane.

He hung the photo with pride.

Over the years, much would be made of the fact that my father said "no, thank you" to all the old-line fraternities that dominated Greek life at Lehigh, many of which would have been happy to rush the popular Freddie. Instead, he joined Sigma Alpha Mu, a predominantly Jewish frat. He was the only non-Jewish member or one of only two, depending on whose memory you believe.

No one could make a Brooks Brother suit and a rep tie come alive like Freddie Trump could. He was both preppy *and* loose. To Freddie, the Sigma Alpha Mu guys were a lot more fun than the well-bred stooges in the stuffed-shirt frats. And if his fraternity brothers didn't have a problem with him—well, who was he to knuckle under to some ancient religious and cultural prejudice?

That was Freddie just being Freddie, and no one could argue with any of it.

Though he was raised in a casually Presbyterian household, and though St. Paul's was an Episcopal boys school, it might have been Freddie's first attempt to make his own statement to his father. Accept that armchair psychology if you want to. There is probably some truth in there. Still, there was also something else at play. The "Sammies," as the brothers of Sigma Alpha Mu were known on campus, were famous for marching to no one's beat but their own. These were Lehigh's free-thinkers, and Freddie fit right in. As their write-up in *The Epitome,* the

Lehigh yearbook, put it so succinctly: "In all phases of activities and enterprises, Sammie has shown reluctance to accept the general and the ordinary and has thus fashioned its own image among fraternities."

They were *fun*.

One thing Freddie Trump wasn't in those years was a heavy drinker. He wasn't a *non*-drinker. He enjoyed an occasional glass of wine or a couple of beers. But none of his friends detected an issue with alcohol at the time. At the Sigma Alpha Mu house, Freddie was chosen as the chapter steward, responsible for overseeing the food service and the bank accounts—an assignment that went to one of the more levelheaded, responsible members . . . never some boozehound. And by all accounts, everything remained on the up-and-up. Though Freddie loved to have a good time, it wasn't the self-destructive variety.

Had my father found the right fraternity—or what?

These were *his* guys. And they felt just the same about him. Senior year, his brothers found the ultimate way to show it. They elected him Sigma Alpha Mu chapter president, the first time in anyone's memory the honor had gone to a gentile.

Mazel tov!

August 1958. Just before the start of junior year. My father and his good friend Billy Drake slipped down to the Bahamas for a little R & R. Billy had grown up around the corner from the Trumps in Jamaica Estates. He and Freddie had been friends since training wheels. The two of them checked into the oceanfront British Colonial, one of the oldest hotels in Nassau. They hired a boat and went deep-sea fishing. They were relaxing at the poolside bar, when they eyed a couple of girls just back from the beach, who were sipping on white-wine spritzers. Billy was dressed for comfort in shorts and a T-shirt. Freddie stood out a bit more in his black slacks and busy Madras sport coat.

"Wow!" the blonder of the two said to Freddie, addressing his jacket as much as him. "Where did *you* come from? I've never seen *that* in Florida."

That got smiles all around.

It was a nice icebreaker, and the four of them began to chat. Actually, *Freddie* began to chat. He carried most of the conversation while the other three filled in the spaces with their laughter and admiration.

The girls were Linda Clapp and Harriet van Dellen, friends from Fort Lauderdale. They'd taken a boat to Nassau. Linda, the one who'd admired Freddie's jacket, had graduated from high school a year earlier, had an office job, and was hoping to catch on with one of the airlines as a stewardess—no one said "flight attendant" yet. Freddie said he and Billy had been close friends since they were kids in Queens. They all went out to dinner that night and then for a ride in the boys' rental car, which Freddie said wasn't anything like the Corvette he drove to college in Pennsylvania.

"No one gave me the Corvette," he clarified with emphasis. "I had a job at a Chevy dealer. I bought it myself."

They traded family stories. Linda came originally from Michigan, she said, moving to Florida in time for high school because of her mother's arthritis. Those Kalamazoo winters had been just too much for her. Her father owned a luncheonette, drove a truck, and took care of the mother. "Nice people," Linda said, and they sure sounded that way to Freddie. He said his father owned some apartment buildings in New York, which Linda took to mean two or three.

Before they all left the Bahamas, everyone traded numbers and agreed to stay in touch. When Linda and Harriet called the following summer to say they were driving up to New York, Freddie and Billy took the girls to places just like they'd seen in the movies. Little restaurants two or three steps down from the sidewalk. A festival where people danced in the street. Billy's parents had a beach house in Southampton. He asked Linda and Harriet if they'd like to join the boys for the weekend. On their way east, Freddie and Linda stopped at the Trumps' house in Jamaica Estates.

The house was larger than Linda had imagined, but that wasn't what struck her most. It was Freddie's mom. She was considerably taller than the petite Linda, and she seemed to look askance at the short Florida sundress that Linda had on.

"Is that what you're wearing?" the mom asked. "Well, okay. You kids have a good time."

"I don't think your mother loved my outfit," Linda said, delicately, once she and Freddie were back in the car and on the road.

He just shrugged. He didn't appear too concerned.

Everyone, it seemed, had a blast in the Hamptons. And the night before the girls headed back to Florida, Freddie and Linda agreed to meet in the city for one last dinner. But when she didn't hear from him, she called the house in Queens. His younger brother Donald answered.

"Oh, he's not here," Donald said. "He went bear hunting in Canada."

Bear hunting? In Canada? Linda couldn't help but wonder: Had there been some miscommunication? Had his mother said something to him? She told herself, *I guess that's the end of that.*

It would be a full year before Linda and Freddie spoke again. By then, she'd gotten her dream job as a stewardess at National Airlines and was being stationed in New York. She and her stewardess friend Jackie were hoping to share an apartment not too far from LaGuardia Airport. That's when Linda remembered a conversation she'd had with fun Freddie. *Hadn't he said something about his father owning apartment buildings?*

She called, and this time, Freddie answered the phone. "I'll be happy to show you some apartments in Jamaica," he said.

The one-bedroom was expensive for what National paid steward-esses, but the two airline rookies felt like they could swing the studio

Freddie showed them. There was room in the closet for their tan flight uniforms with red collars and a few sets of play clothes. What else did they need? Since Linda and Jackie tended to fly on different schedules, sharing would be fine. They signed the lease immediately.

"Can I take you out to dinner?" Freddie asked Linda.

It was at that dinner that she remembered what a great sense of humor he had.

He started checking in regularly on the two roommates. Helping them buy furniture. Showing up at Christmas with a new TV, a luxury beyond their budget. Giving them advice about getting settled in the city. There were more dinners with Linda—though no romance yet. He called her "buddy" and shook her hand when they said goodnight.

(Both my parents would later swear to this.)

Still, somewhere in there, something clicked.

The dinners got fancier. They'd take his Century speedboat out on Long Island's Great South Bay. He joked about her fear of jellyfish. She'd poke him, "Do you even know how many buildings your father has?" He bought her a beautiful watch for Christmas. That next summer, 1961, he asked what style of engagement ring she preferred. Then one night he took her to a fancy French restaurant, La Cave Henri IV, where the filet mignon with champagne sauce was $3.50 and the frog legs Provençale was $3.75. Most importantly, he pulled out a marquis-cut diamond and asked her to marry him.

Right after dinner, they went to the house in Jamaica Estates to break the news. And the reception they got? It reminded Linda of the day she'd shown up in that sundress to meet his mom. His mother was polite enough, but she didn't exactly squeal with excitement about the ring or their plans, the way Linda knew her parents would. And when Freddie's dad came downstairs, he said "hello," then turned and went right back up without saying much of anything else.

"Maybe they don't like stewardesses," Linda said to herself.

. . .

As he thought he'd made clear by this point, my dad wasn't all that excited about joining the family real-estate company. But after he graduated from Lehigh with a business degree, a second lieutenant's commission in the National Guard, and no other pressing opportunities, that's exactly where he landed, at the Coney Island office of what by then had become known as Trump Management. There were various parts to the operation. The construction side. The management side. The maintenance side. The finance side. A couple of others. The company had grown so rapidly, there were plenty of ways for a bright college grad to contribute, especially a personable young man who carried the Fred Trump name.

The way my grandfather imagined it, it would be like a one-man executive-training program. My father would gradually work his way through the company, spending time in the different areas, learning the business from the ground up . . . all in hopes that one day he might run the place. If Freddie had seemed unengaged on previous trips to the office—well, maybe that could be attributed to youthful immaturity or, who knows, maybe the kid had a hot date that night. Now that he was out of school and on his way into the work world and even had a fiancée, maybe he'd finally buckle down—that Grandpa phrase again—and, you know, start living up to his potential.

Wishful thinking, I believe that's called.

In actuality, father and son started bickering almost from day one.

My father, child of Jamaica Estates, thought the windows needed to be replaced in one of the newer buildings. My grandfather, child of Woodhaven and the Bronx, thought that was a waste of money. My father pushed for pricier kitchen appliances on a new construction project. My grandfather considered that lavish. There was a big debate about how the maintenance crew should be dispatched and which of the German-born building superintendents—they all seemed to be born in Germany—should be assigned to which buildings ... and whether shuffling them around was an energy booster (my father) or unnecessary disruption (my grandfather).

Day-to-day issues. The kinds of things that come up in any real-estate company. But all of them tailor-made for father-son tension, as the younger man and the older man both dug their heels in. My father could be petulant. My grandfather could be preachy. And each of them had a way of speaking to the other as if addressing someone who didn't know anything at all.

A tone you'd never take if you were working for a stranger. Stuff you'd never pull if you hadn't gone to work for your father or hired your son. My father figured his father would come around eventually, seeing the wisdom of his son's savvy suggestions. My grandfather figured his son would do the same, recognizing the wisdom that only age and experience can bring.

Neither happened, of course. What they did was keep getting on each other's nerves.

It's hard to fully explain what the problem was. My guess is that it had almost nothing to do with window replacement or staffing practices or the quality differences between GE and Frigidaire refrigerators. These squabbles were all about blood and history, independence and interdependency, honor and respect ... and trying to put people into boxes they didn't want to be in. No one ever spoke openly about that kind of thing in the Trump family. And my father and grandfather certainly weren't about to start now.

As the wedding grew nearer, the little asides did not let up. It was clear to anyone paying attention that some people in the Trump family did not consider "Linda the Stewardess" quite good enough, in the same way, decades later, some of the same family members would gang up on northwest Georgia native Marla Maples, Donald's second wife.

It started with my grandmother, which was strange since she herself wasn't exactly to the manor born. Linda's family were practically millionaires compared to the mackerel fishermen and subsistence farmers who were my grandmother's Scottish kin. Whatever. And soon, the little digs were also flowing freely from the tart-tongued Aunt Maryanne, who by now had graduated from Kew-Forest "mean girl" right into her new role as a key Trump-family enforcer and brutal social arbiter. Never one to hide her feelings, Maryanne disparaged Linda with a special ruthlessness, and even young Donald found occasions to pitch in. When Maryanne offered to write up the wedding announcement, she wanted to make up something Linda had no idea about, that the bride-to-be would soon be studying at Columbia University.

"Why on earth would she want to say that?" Linda asked Freddie when his sister floated the idea. Apparently, Maryanne thought her future sister-in-law could use some Ivy on her résumé.

Never mind that my father seemed to love her and clearly enjoyed her company. Never mind that she was always friendly and nice to everyone and showed up dutifully at Trump family gatherings every time she was asked. A negative reputation, once attached, is never easily shaken, and that was certainly true for Linda Clapp. *She's not good enough for us,* everyone but Freddie seemed to agree.

All of which only drove him deeper into Linda's arms.

My parents-to-be were married on January 20, 1962, at the All Saints Episcopal Church in Fort Lauderdale, which had started out as a tiny mission half a century earlier and blossomed into a vibrant congregation in Colee Hammock, one of the oldest neighborhoods in Broward County. My mom was twenty-two, and my dad was twenty-three. There was no way that Linda's mother, now in a wheelchair from her worsening arthritis, could travel to New York City, even if the family could have afforded the trip. So, Florida it was. My grandparents often spent time there in the winter. Florida wasn't inconvenient for them. And yet, Donald didn't make it down from military school. Elizabeth stayed on her campus in Virginia. But Maryanne and Robert both flew down.

The bride wore a floor-length gown of ivory faille taffeta with a pearled bateau neckline and point-to-hand sleeves. She carried a bouquet of white rosebuds and lilies of the valley. All perfectly classy. Her sister Carolann was matron of honor. Billy Drake was Freddie's best man. How could he not be? He'd been there since that very first double take in the Bahamas. Several of Freddie's fraternity brothers came down for the weekend. They still knew how to have fun. So did his St. Paul's friends. The Trumps hosted a dinner the night before. And right after the service, there was a reception with dinner and dancing at the Pier 66 Yacht Club on the Intracoastal Waterway.

The high point of the evening, after the vows? That had to be when the two dads, Linda's and Freddie's, hit the dance floor simultaneously. Everyone knew that Linda's father had dance moves. After all, he and his wife had met at a YMCA dance in Kalamazoo. But who knew the great magnate Fred Sr. was also a great dancer? Believe it or not, he actually held his own.

Then, he went right back to his table and put his stoic business face back on, lost in something he was working on in his mind.

The newlyweds left for a two-week honeymoon in Hawaii, flying on heavily discounted tickets that Linda had gotten through her job. They were back in New York by early February. They moved into a new apartment on the East Side of Manhattan, and my dad returned to his miserable job.

And that November, something really important happened.

I was born.

CHAPTER 5

MY TURN

I didn't slide into the world so much as I *stomped* into it.

I was a big bruiser of a baby, a full nine and a half pounds. As soon as my parents brought me home from Mount Sinai Hospital that third week of November 1962, I was ready to get on with things. I was hungry, I was thirsty, and I wanted to know, *What are we doing next?*

I wasn't Bamm-Bamm Rubble from *The Flintstones* . . . but close.

I talked early. I walked early. My hair was so black, one of my father's fraternity brothers got one eyeful of me and decided I looked "like a little Indian"—and, no, he didn't say "Native American." That judgment became moot one day when my hair turned blond, so blond it almost looked white.

I'm not kidding. I have photos.

When my folks returned from their Hawaiian honeymoon, they said "no, thank you" to my grandfather's offer of a family discount at one of his newer buildings in Brooklyn or Queens. New York was buzzing with the youthful energy of the Kennedy years. Freddie and Linda were eager to be in the middle of things. To them, that meant Manhattan. So they found a small, one-bedroom apartment just off swank

Sutton Place, which my dad's parents helped to furnish (including an oil-on-velvet painting that matched the newlyweds' blue-and-green color scheme). My mother bought a frisky off-white French poodle they named Deux Non. My father had never had a real pet before, not counting that stray garter snake he'd snuck into Donald's bedroom. The Trump house had always been a pet-free zone.

And they dove right into the young marrieds' version of city life. The little cafés on Second Avenue. Fun nights at the Copacabana, where the décor was Brazilian but the cuisine was Chinese and the headliner might be Sammy Davis Jr. or Sam Cooke. Once I came along, my mother left her airline job to care for me full-time, pushing my stroller around the neighborhood while I kept trying to climb out. Every Sunday and sometimes Wednesday too, my parents packed little me in the car and drove to dinner at my grandparents' house in Queens, which my father told my mother was just this side of mandatory and she considered a bit much.

"You're grown now," she reminded him, not too subtly.

Soon enough, the three of us flew to Fort Lauderdale in my father's first airplane, a secondhand Piper Comanche 180, to show *it* and *me* to my mother's mom and dad, Mary Louise and Gerald Clapp, though everyone called her father "Mike." He was such an aviation buff, he used to park his car near Broward County Airport to watch the planes landing and taking off. (Years later, he and I would do the same. He was also a pilot.)

I'm not sure which one my grandfather got more delight from—me, or the plane. They decided I was cuter, but the plane was pretty cool too. No one mentioned the plane to my *other* grandfather in New York. As my dad told his sister Maryanne: "He would never understand," most likely dismissing the entry-level airplane (sticker price, $21,250, which my father paid himself) as a rich kid's toy.

After eighteen months as a family of three, that Manhattan one-bedroom was feeling awfully cramped. My parents agreed the time had probably come to take my grandfather up on his offer and move to Queens.

Which, looking back on it now, might have been the last time the two of them fully agreed on *anything*.

We landed in a two-bedroom apartment in a nine-story, doorman building on Highland Avenue, about a mile from my grandparents' house. Though the architectural style was Red-Brick Nothing Special, the building did have some charm. The open-plan apartments were laid out for modern living. The south-facing views from our top-floor unit went all the way to Kennedy Airport. And the lobby? It was designed by Morris Lapidus, best known for the snazzy lounges at his mid-century-modern Miami hotels. It wasn't the East Side of Manhattan, not by a long shot. But like many Fred Trump buildings, ours had its little touches and a fancy-sounding name. It was The Highlander. The Belcrest, The Saxony, and The Sussex were all nearby, each with its own capital "T." If you went strictly by building name, you might think you were in Merrie Olde England, though once you opened your eyes, there would be no mistaking: This was Fred Trump Sr. Country. This shiny jewel was surrounded by workaday Jamaica, Queens.

We settled right in.

Though I was officially Frederick Crist Trump the Third, my father's fraternity brothers could not help themselves from weighing in on little me. It was one of them who announced, "He's not a Fred, he's a Fritz," which quickly devolved into "Fritzie," and damned if the nickname wouldn't stick with me all the way to grade school. With my rosy cheeks, bright white hair, and barrel-chested way of walking, I guess I did look like a kid who might show up on the F Train in lederhosen, but I hated the nickname from the time I was old enough to have an opinion. And my father's mother—I called her Gam or Gammie—had her own spin on all that. To her, I was "Fred C.," though with her

Scottish-Gaelic Western Isles accent, that sounded maddeningly close to Fritzie. So, I was probably doomed either way.

Such were the burdens of my 100-watt coloring and our Trump/Drumpf heritage.

Pulling my father into the family business was turning out to be just as terrible a disaster as anyone could have predicted.

I'm not sure why my grandfather didn't find a way to reorient things. Stubbornness, I suppose . . . and the ancient fantasy of one day handing the reins to his number-one son, however ill-suited his firstborn son might have been for that role. For his part, I guess my father was still trying to win his father's approval, which my grandfather offered stingily or withheld entirely, depending on his whims and the time of day. Keeping others off balance, including his son, was a classic Fred Trump maneuver. I think my grandfather wanted my father to succeed the way he had, and not the way my father wanted to succeed. Sadly, my father put up with it for much too long, coming home every night and seething about it, while letting the entire experience slowly ruin his life.

A lot of the worst of it centered around Trump Village, the family company's most ambitious project yet. Built in 1963–64, it was a $70 million, seven-building, 3,702-unit apartment complex at the old Culver streetcar terminal, a quick stroll from the Coney Island boardwalk. This time, architect Morris Lapidus hadn't just designed the lobbies. He had overseen the whole development. Trump Village was also the first (though definitely not the last) project to carry the Trump name, an idea my father pushed and his father had always been reluctant to implement. My grandfather didn't like bragging in public and for the most part did not slap his name on things.

Did my father create a monster with that branding suggestion of his? Likely, he did. He'd majored in marketing. It was one of his fortes. And later, of course, his younger brother would run away with the idea. Before you knew it, we'd have Trump Tower, Trump University, Trump sneakers, and Trump Bibles . . . and no one, not even in our family, knew what might be emblazoned with our name next. There was never any vote on the matter.

The Trump Village financing was positively byzantine for its time, another shade of things to come: a public-bond issue through the New York State Housing Finance Agency, a giant tax exemption and future tenants funneled through the Mitchell-Lama Housing Program for middle-income renters. There were so many things to go wrong and so much to be disappointed about, and the hard feelings started when my grandfather insisted that his oldest son move his family to Brooklyn so he'd be right there on site.

My dad loved Brooklyn. Fishing in Sheepshead Bay. Going to the clam bars. Driving the borough's distant neighborhoods for the adventure of discovering something new, usually to do with boats or water. But that didn't mean he wanted to baby-sit a real-estate project.

He said no.

What my father really loved to do was to fly.

He loved flying almost as much as he loved boating and fishing, maybe even more so. From the moment he started taking flying lessons in Pennsylvania till his first solo flight over the Lehigh Valley till those glorious days when he got his private pilot's license, his instrument rating and all the steps that came next, he always got a special thrill from sitting in a cockpit, his hands on the yoke and nothing but blue sky ahead. Heck, he even liked making weight and balance calculations and filing his flight plans—anything that got him into the air.

Looking back, I don't know exactly what it was that pulled him to the sky. I'm not sure he knew. The distant horizons. The harmonious machinery. The beauty and the solitude of it all. Some of the same things, no doubt, that he liked about being on the water. In a boat or in a cockpit, it wasn't so much about going somewhere. Once you were flying or boating, you were already there. It was a love of adventure he would eventually pass down to me, our special way of spending quality time together and being *somewhere else,* where the horizons were distant and a whole different set of rules applied. Or maybe it was just that his father wasn't there. Whatever combination, as little as he felt drawn to New York real estate, that's how much my father loved to boat or to fly. He'd been on solid ground. He preferred the water or the sky.

In December of 1963, he shocked everyone, including my grandfather and my mother, by announcing he was leaving the family company. He'd been accepted into the TWA pilot training program. He was going to *fly.* While my mother and I stayed behind in Queens, he flew out to Kansas City for training. He'd found what he loved, and he was off to learn everything about it that he possibly could. The days were long. The standards were high. All the trainees were under constant pressure. It was during that time in Kansas City, from what I've been able to piece together, that my father's drinking first got out of hand. Scotch whisky mostly. Cutty Sark was his brand. When he drank, he often started with a beer, then started pouring the hard liquor. Dad was newly married, had a son he loved, and was finally on a career path that suited him. What many people don't recognize is that the triggers to drink can be a lot of things, even happy times. Some of the others in the training program noticed that Freddie sure was hitting it hard. They'd all go out to the bars together after a day of classwork and simulations, and he was almost always the last to head home. Some mornings, he didn't look so great. Was it lingering frustration with his family? Was it fresh pressure to succeed? Was it just that he was away from home with free evenings? Who knows. But everyone agreed he was drinking more than he should, especially for someone who wanted to fly commercial airliners. There's not a lot of room for error there.

Mom, I think, sensed she was needed and flew out to Missouri, determined to help in any way she could. She convinced my father not to go out so much. They spent long nights studying, using flash cards he'd put together. Mom was supportive, and insisted he was going to do well. And he did. TWA assigned him to one of the airline's more prestigious routes: Boston to Los Angeles. For this part of his training, he was sent to Massachusetts. He rented an old captain's house, overlooking Marblehead Bay on Boston's North Shore. Six months after his training started, he was co-piloting two hundred passengers across the country.

These were great, hopeful times for my parents. Mom and Dad were happy. Marblehead, like a New England Montauk, had a little village green. There were young parents and small children, and my folks felt right at home. My mom and dad rented a tandem bike one day and put a little seat on the back for me. Part backseat driver, part pretend co-captain, I rode through the village with my parents, the wind rushing through my bright white hair. No bicycle helmets then.

They bought a boat. A very small boat that my parents painted, then stenciled with the name "Huggy Bear." They couldn't go far in that boat, but they did take it into the bay to watch as the owner of Hood Dairy trained for the America's Cup. Dad's personality shone, and everyone seemed to love being around him. Mom and Dad had company almost every weekend. Loose, enjoyable get-togethers.

Then, one weekend, Donald and Robert came up.

They didn't ask to fly in a plane my father was piloting. They had no interest in joining him on a fishing trip. So what sparked the visit? What were they doing there? Soon enough, that became clear.

They'd been sent by their father to retrieve their older brother and deliver him back to Queens. "This is ridiculous," Donald told him. "You're wasting your time."

Donald passed along a comment their father had supposedly made, saying airline pilots were no more than "flying bus drivers."

Is that what did it? Was it pressure from the family? Was it some doubt inside my father's head? Was it the lingering grip of the alcohol? I can tell you this much: My mother tried. But in the end, it was the booze that grounded my father's high-flying dream. Before he was a full-fledged pilot, TWA sent him home. He was back in New York in time for Christmas 1964.

He tried to catch on at a couple of regional airlines. Nothing stuck there. He explored the idea of opening an employment agency. No-go there. And soon enough, the sad and inevitable happened. He was back at work in the family business and not enjoying it one bit more than he had before.

At least things were staying interesting at home. In May of 1965, when I was two and a half, my sister, Mary, was born. I was thrilled to have a baby sister. We shared a room for a couple of years, then Grandpa Fred let us bust into the apartment next door so we could have a third bedroom. Our block was teeming with children. We spent hour after hour running up and down the sidewalks, yelling our lungs out and crossing Highland Avenue to Captain Tilly Park, though no one called it that. There was a pond in the park, and years before we got there, the pond had had what looked like the silhouette of a goose neck at the far end. Though the goose neck was ancient history, replaced by trees, bushes, and tall grass, for us it was always: "Hey, Mom, can we go to Goose Pond Park?"

"Just be home for dinner."

People in other parts of America might think it strange to grow up in New York City. But for most New Yorkers, the city quickly divides itself into little slices, and it's not all that different from living in a much smaller town—except for the superior mass transit and the strongly held belief that no other place could possibly be half as good. Clearly, bashfulness was not a trait I was going to learn from my family or my city.

Our neighbors were teachers, civil servants, salesmen, office managers, and small-business people . . . all white. We had Irish, Italians, Germans, Poles, a few Jews. Not any Blacks or Latinos and not too many Asians either. Not then. Over the years, racial steering would become a point of bitter controversy at some of my grandfather's buildings and the subject of a sweeping Justice Department civil-rights complaint.

The residents certainly knew what was going on. In fact, the singer Woody Guthrie, who lived in a Trump apartment in the 1950s, wrote a song called "Old Man Trump" about the discrimination he witnessed:

I suppose that Old Man Trump knows just how much racial hate
He stirred up in that bloodpot of human hearts

But growing up when I did in the middle and late 1960s, it all felt normal to me.

Isn't that what it's like being a kid? You know what you know, and you don't have much to compare it with. This little patch of Jamaica was my world and where my earliest memories are. What wasn't to like? After a short stint in nursery school on Midland Parkway, the street where my grandparents lived, I started at the Kew-Forest School, the same small college-prep academy where my aunt Maryanne, my aunt Elizabeth, and my uncle Donald had gone.

After Donald's abrupt departure for a stint in military school, and with my grandfather still on the board of trustees, the teachers and the staff braced themselves for the latest Trump to arrive. It's fair to say they made sure they were ready for me. All I knew was I wouldn't be telling anyone about "Fritzie." From the first day of kindergarten, I was going to be Fred.

• • •

Everyone thinks of the Trumps as a big, sprawling family, and rightfully so. But not in my generation. Not yet. For much of my early life, I had only one cousin. There was no Donnie, Eric, or Ivanka. Certainly no Tiffany or Barron. Not anyone but cousin David, who was two years older than me.

My aunt Maryanne was married at the time to a guy name David Desmond Sr., who got the exact same treatment from the Trump family that my mother had. Only with him, Maryanne was obviously not the one leading the charge. It was Uncle Donald. Still, it was all the same: *How could she marry this guy? What a loser! He's not up to our level.* If Maryanne gained any realization or empathy from that experience, she never let on.

Her son, David, and I were close friends from the time David was five and I was three. I'm pretty sure I was David's *only* friend. He was super-smart, and he let you know it. If he didn't, his mother would. But I don't believe many other kids ever came over to play with him, and if he ever had a sleepover at someone else's house, I never heard about it. But David was my cousin, and I liked him. We both loved soccer. We loved teasing each other, and we were always back and forth between each other's apartments.

They lived six blocks from us in another of Grandpa's properties, The Coronet. It was always a little uncomfortable going over there. I can still see Maryanne and David Sr. sitting in their white bathrobes in matching club chairs, smoking cigarettes, and plowing through *The Wall Street Journal.* This was after my aunt had earned her master's from Columbia University, but before she stopped being a full-time mom and homemaker and enrolled at Hofstra law school. I'd say hello and go directly into David's room, which was always a mess. The air conditioner would be blasting to help with his allergies. He had one of those little white Vicks inhalers in his nose. I remember often thinking, *I'm glad I'm not an only child.*

By comparison, I was the rambunctious personable guy, though a lot of people might have felt that way hanging around with David. I didn't get all-A's in school or even all-B's. I didn't always pay attention. I acted up sometimes. Not Donald-level acting up, but making funny comments in class and occasionally forgetting to do my homework. That kind of thing. If someone had taken a poll of my first-, second-, or third-grade classmates and asked, "Who's the class clown?," no question that all the fingers would have turned and pointed at me. I knew how to make people laugh and I understood early: If you can get people laughing, they can't help but like you. And let's be honest: I rode that strategy far past third grade. I balanced my deficiencies by excelling in other ways. I had tons of friends, people I would stay close to for the rest of my life, and I had sports. I walked with confidence into the schoolyard and, as we inched into organized athletics, my energy and physicality—*Bamm-Bamm*—would help me thrive there.

Maybe because he was such a kid at heart, my father was what I would call a natural dad. He loved playing on the floor with Mary and me. He was always saying, "Come on, you wanna go to the park?" On any given weekend, he had somewhere we should go. To the beach. To some different neighborhood. To see something we'd never seen before. The same infectious exuberance he'd had for his friends in college, now he had for Mary and me. He could hang out for hours with either or both of us and never seem to get bored. In one of my earliest memories, my mother is trying to feed a fussy Mary, who keeps turning her head away. My father comes into the living room and says, "You want me to try?"

"Sure," my mother answers. "All yours."

"I'll take care of it," he says confidently as she hands over first the baby and then the bottle. And he does. He sits on the sofa and cradles his daughter, who stops crying. Soon, she is guzzling the milk from the bottle.

"There you go," my father says cheerfully as he hands Mary back to my mom.

I guess my mother could have felt jealous, but that wouldn't have been like her. She felt grateful and relieved. My dad really seemed to be enjoying fatherhood.

Mary was the greatest little sister I could have had. She was smart. She was feisty. She loved sports. For her sixth birthday, I gave her a catcher's mitt, and she was absolutely thrilled to receive it.

How many little sisters would be thrilled to get a catcher's mitt?

My sister had a temper. Even little things could set her off, especially if she felt like she wasn't getting her due or she thought someone else was being mistreated. Both of us got social consciences from our parents, who believed that people from privileged backgrounds had a special responsibility toward others. Mary felt that at least as strongly as I did—and more emotionally. She was independent and driven and had a steely will about her. When she wanted something—look out. Don't get in Mary's way. And whatever was happening around us, we always had each other's backs, and that made us close in a way that nothing else could have. She was always there for me when we were little, and if anyone messed with Mary, they were messing with her older brother too.

One sign of how much I loved my little sister? I let her call me "Fritz" long after I succeeded in steering almost everyone else away. I still hate the nickname, and I still let her call me that.

Mary followed me to the Kew-Forest School, two grades behind. If I was the class clown, she was the scholar-athlete. She loved to write. She brought home excellent report cards. And she could also dribble a basketball. Though I was a boy and more than two years older, it was still fun to compete with her, and she loved a well-played prank at least as much as I did, especially if it was on me. One day, when I was around twelve, she out-Trumped me on one of those pranks. She knew I liked sunglasses—and for reasons far more than looking cool. They kept my sensitive blue eyes out of the sun so I could actually see. Anyway, she and one of her friends swore they'd buy me a pair of sunglasses. Ones I really, really wanted. But I had to do something first.

"Okay," Mary said, "you gotta drink from the toilet, and we'll get you those sunglasses."

I must have flushed that toilet a thousand times and cleaned it a few more than that. Then, in front of Mary and her friend, I carefully dipped a paper cup into the water and down the hatch it went. They both looked shocked, then started laughing so hard, they almost started to cry. And to this day, I still haven't seen those sunglasses.

I made big-brother mistakes with Mary. I know I did. One of them still feels as fresh as yesterday.

It was my thirteenth birthday. As I came home from school, Mary was standing near the door with a smile on her face and a small box in her hand. It was a ring. Gold, as I remember. She stood there so excited as I opened the box. I took one look at it and said, "I am never going to wear that thing."

I didn't wear rings, I didn't like wearing jewelry of any kind. It got in the way when I was playing sports. But I might have broken her enthusiasm with that comment. I saw the ring and forgot to see the gift.

To this day, I would like to take back that moment. Okay, maybe I wouldn't be wearing that ring right now, but I still feel bad about what I said.

Big-brother error.

If anyone in our family was bound for academic glory, it was Mary, who'd go on to the Ethel Walker School, a boarding school for girls in Connecticut, and three top universities, Tufts, Columbia, and Adelphi. Good for her. Even as a little kid, I think I understood that those were doors I probably wasn't going to darken, but I could still cheer for my sister each time she walked through another one.

We both got loads of individual attention at Kew-Forest. The entire school, kindergarten to twelfth grade, had 220 boys and girls. In a school that tiny, everyone gets a clear identity. And some of the Kew-Forest teachers were truly inspiring. Against all odds, I became a passionate reader. I started with *Charlie and the Chocolate Factory* and *The Wind in the Willows* and I just never stopped. Before you knew it, I was diving into *The Caine Mutiny, Fahrenheit 451*, and *Jaws*. Then, it was on to *1984* and *Brave New World*. Inside and outside my family, I became known as "a reader."

My uncle Donald wasn't much of a reader unless you counted newspapers. And the books in my grandparents' house were scattered here and there. School texts. A set of encyclopedias. Whatever the kids brought home. But I wasn't the only member of the Trump family who liked to read. Both my dad and mom were big readers. Dad was drawn to discovery, adventure, and entrepreneurial spirit, finding what he liked, especially flying and boating books, and searching for the right career. I remember him diving into *The Godfather* series and *Serpico* and biographies of W. C. Fields and Abbott and Costello. He was convinced that most comedians led tragic lives. "Comedy was a release for these guys to bury the pain," he explained. Mom enjoyed fiction almost every night before bed. The Queens Public Library was an important place to her.

Maryanne was a reader. So was her son, David. As for me, I started, and I just never stopped. And now that I was "a reader," I noticed other kids asking my opinions . . . about all kinds of things.

"Is Tom Seaver the best Mets pitcher ever?"

"Obviously."

"Is the Vietnam War a bad idea?"

"Yep."

"Football or soccer?"

"Soccer. People play soccer all over the world . . . and they call it football some places."

Soon, I was displaying actual leadership skills. The Kew-Forest teachers encouraged all of that. They were caring, dedicated people, and they gave us all a sense of belonging no matter how complex or chaotic our home lives might be. People didn't use the term "safe space" back then. But Kew-Forest was a safe space for a lot of people.

Half my childhood, it seemed, unfolded at my grandparents' house.

Dinners once a week when I was little, and every major holiday. When Maryanne married her husband and converted to his Catholic faith, it was back to the house for fish on Fridays. Just Maryanne converted, but we all got a Friday fish fry out of the deal. Riding my bike over there to drink Cokes in green bottles with Gam. Endless hours in the backyard kicking soccer balls with cousin David and Uncle Robert. Sleepovers that allowed me to witness something that I don't think many people in the world ever got to see: My all-business grandfather in the kitchen at dawn, standing in his plain white T-shirt at the stove, pouring pancake batter into a sizzling iron skillet and carefully stacking our breakfast *just so* with extra pats of butter.

"Try these," he'd say proudly.

I don't believe my grandfather ever cooked anything else in his life. Not that I saw, anyway. But let it be said: His pancakes were warm and fluffy, two words that were rarely if ever applied to the real-estate titan Fred Trump. The rest of the day, the rest of his life, he resumed his role as stern, demanding, work-focused patriarch, even or maybe *especially* at home. But the pancakes were really, really good. I can't deny that.

As far as the post office was concerned, my grandparents' neighborhood was just another part of greater Jamaica. But to anyone who lived there or wished they did, Jamaica Estates was a lavish suburban enclave smack in the middle of some less-desirable areas of Queens. Compared to our apartment, compared to *anyone's* apartment, their house on Midland Parkway was a bona fide New York City mansion. Because my grandfather was a builder and he wanted everyone to know it, he poured his heart and his checkbook into renovating and updating that beautiful home. The white pillars out front. The slate-and-brick stairway leading up to the main entrance and its two sets of double doors. The kitchen wasn't huge, but it was stocked with up-to-the-minute devices and appliances: an automatic ice maker, a professional deli meat slicer, a blender with a motor that could have come off an airplane—none of which we had in our apartment. And always, a huge supply of ice-cold Cokes, which I loved almost as much as Gam did and helped myself to whenever I felt like it. I don't know what it was with Gam and Coca-Colas. She must have been the Coke-drinking champion of Queens, guzzling her favorite beverage from early in the morning until late at night.

There was no kids' table at my grandparents' house. We all sat together for dinner at a glass-top table with a wrought-iron base in what they called "the breakfast room," which was a strange thing to call it since no one ever ate breakfast there, just lunch and dinner. The room looked out over the backyard. In summer, the sun streamed in through the trees.

We all had our set places and our set roles. I was next to Grandpa, where he could easily correct my table manners and opine on this or that. Mary was next to Gam. The two of them seemed to have a secret language as they traded knowing glances all through the meal. Grandpa stacked phone books on the chairs of the three grandchildren, David, Mary, and me, so we could sit at the same height as everyone else. Oh boy, was it a big deal when you got down to just one phone book. At that table there was a place for everyone. I still have my grandfather's voice in my head, reciting his favorite rhyme:

"Elbows, elbows off the table.

"This is not a horse's stable,

"But a first-class dining room."

And he definitely believed in the *first-class* part. If it was a meal, my grandfather wore a tie for it. If it was worth eating, it was served on nice plates. And the "it" was inevitably some version of beef, potatoes, and vegetables. (Yes, Donald came honestly by his cuisine of choice. That was "dinner at the Trumps'.") My grandfather, not my grandmother or anyone else, was the keeper of standards in that house. We always started with a quick grace.

"Come, Lord Jesus. Be our guest. Bless this meal, which thou has given us."

Then everyone: *"Amen."*

Grandpa quizzed the children and the grandchildren. "What are you learning in school? . . . What did you do today? . . . Can you spell Mississippi backwards and forwards?" And you'd better have answers. I was never sure how closely he listened, but there was one thing you couldn't say when my grandfather asked what you'd been up to.

"Nothin'."

That was one answer that didn't fly with my grandfather.

"What do you mean, *Nothing?*" he'd fire back.

Mostly, what my grandfather liked to do at those family dinners was express his opinions. About the city. About current events. About something he'd heard somebody say. On any of those subjects, he could go on for quite a while. And he declared those opinions with a kind of adamance that made even his grown children nod along. No one wanted to risk setting off Grandpa, including my father, who mostly just sat there. He would happily let the conversations fly right over his head.

After dinner, we might retire to the "library"—and yes, the quotes are intentional. The "library" was my grandfather's favorite room in the house.

There were no books in this library. No novels. No biographies. No histories. Not even any Reader's Digest Condensed Books. Just the Yellow Pages and the White Pages. That was it. Those were the only books in the house. My family still jokes about that to this day. There was a black dial telephone on the table next to his chair and a television in a heavy wooden cabinet across the room. My grandfather didn't have a dedicated home office. The library is where he held forth after dinner and where he kept working after he was home for the night. I'd sat in there on many nights while my grandfather made calls to his employees and buildings. Checking on things. Ordering supplies. Putting out little fires. Fielding issues and complaints from his tenants and employees. My grandfather's workday was almost never done.

Sometimes, he identified himself on the phone as Fred Trump. Sometimes, not wanting people to know who was calling, he used different names, a technique his son Donald would pick up years later while talking to reporters and praising himself. ("Hi, it's John Barron.") All that happened in the "library."

It was at those extended family dinners that below-the-surface issues had a way of quickly blowing up. Some disagreement in the office. Some problem Donald was having in school. A sarcastic comment about someone's outfit or life choice or friend. At my young age, I didn't always grasp the particulars, but I knew the tension was usually thick enough to cut with one of Gam's dull butter knives.

Holidays were always a big deal. Christmas, Thanksgiving, Easter, Mother's Day—those were command performances for the grown children and the grandchildren both, whether we were excited about being there or not. Sometimes, my sister and I grumbled about going. It didn't matter. We went. As time went on, my father grumbled too. I'm sure he felt caught in the middle when my mom said she'd like to have a family holiday with *her* parents in Florida. It was easier for Donald, Robert, and Elizabeth. They just came downstairs. And the family combination could quickly turn combustible. It didn't take much.

Those frequent family get-togethers were especially hard on my mother. All my mom could do was nod demurely and pretend she didn't notice the digs.

I really don't think it was anything my mother *did*. It was who she was, and the man she married. For her, the condescending comments never let up. Every time we went to my grandparents' house, someone was sure to say something disrespectful to my mom. It started from the minute we walked in the door. First, they would ignore her. Greeting Mary and me with hugs and kisses. Joking around with my dad. And acting like my mother wasn't even there. Soon, my dad and his brothers would be deep in conversation about real estate or sports or something else that was sure to leave my mother out. Then, someone, usually though not always Maryanne, would drop a little stink gas into the dining room. It would start innocently enough, recalling a family vacation my mother hadn't been on or asking about a beloved old friend whose name my mother wouldn't recognize or mentioning how important college was. Then Maryanne would glance at my mother and sniff disdainfully: "Oh, you wouldn't know about that." Other times, Maryanne just wouldn't talk to her at all. And the man who'd brought her in and should have been looking out for her was already at odds with his family and not in a strong position to stand up for her, even if he'd tried, which as far as I could tell he rarely did. It wasn't a secure place when my mother first came around, and it would only get worse as the years went by.

Two things that weren't often discussed at the dinner table: news and politics. Especially some story in the media that might have gotten under my grandfather's skin. That was left for other times and other rooms. These were *family* dinners, and the talk was *personal.*

It was all so weird and so unnecessary, but I never remember a carefree holiday dinner at my grandparents' house. There was always *something.* And the tension could just as easily turn on *me.* One Christmas, just before we left the apartment, my mom got a call asking us to stop for Cokes on the way. Gam had run out, it seemed, and that was nothing short of an emergency. On the way to the house, we found the only open bodega on Hillside Avenue and 169th Street. I was sent in to get the Cokes. But all they had was Pepsi. Not sure what to do but not wanting to return empty-handed, I bought several half gallons of Pepsi. When we walked into the house, I began to explain how only one store was open and all they had was Pepsi and . . . but the minute I got to "Pep—" all hell broke loose.

"Pepsi?" The burning look said it all.

"Has to be Coke. Only Coke."

"That's ridiculous. How could you bring Pepsi?"

And I swear, they weren't only teasing me. This wasn't some kind of shtick. They were *mad* . . . and blaming me. Nothing I could say could dissuade them. It seemed like everyone stayed angry all the way through dessert.

I liked going over there when it was only me. Riding my bike from our apartment. Not calling first. Just showing up. Hanging with Uncle Rob, who wasn't old enough yet to feel like a grown-up. Visiting with Gam.

Grandpa was always at work, so the house would mostly be empty, other than a maid pushing a vacuum cleaner or someone else asking if I was hungry and wanted something to eat. And the yard was always calling. I could spend hours out there, often with David, sometimes alone. Dribbling the soccer ball. Dodging make-believe opponents. Forever throwing a baseball up in the air. Catching it behind my back. Becoming an athlete, one small move at a time.

That was the fun part. Those family get-togethers, at the holidays especially . . . not so much.

One saving grace: We never stayed long.

Nobody minded the quick in and out. It was actually efficient, almost a family trademark. Some families sit for three-hour marathons, relaxing over lengthy conversation, coffee, and dessert. Not the Trumps. My grandfather didn't have that kind of patience, and neither did any of his children. He would stand at the door and "greet us out."

Sit by one, out by two. That was the schedule. Eat and be done with it, including cake. Maybe we'd sit and talk for a few minutes after dinner. But soon enough, everyone was standing and saying their thank-yous and goodbyes.

As quickly as we'd arrived, we'd all be gone.

Once we got home, a whole new psychodrama would unfold. My mother would blame my father, saying he hadn't stood up for her. My father would blame my mother, saying she should have stood up for herself. (Though on the occasions when my mother tried, it only made things worse. You couldn't argue with Maryanne any more than you could reason with a feral cat. Empathy wasn't a language spoken at that table.) As my parents traded barbs, Mary and I would go into our bedrooms and shut the door, hoping not to hear the fighting. I tried in small ways to shield my little sister from this. It just wasn't possible. My mom could always find some way to goad my father some more, from the largest to the tiniest things. It's the little ones I remember most.

One day, my father was gazing at himself in the mirror, tracing his big, caterpillar eyebrows, a physical trait he shared with most of the males in the family, including me. (Grandpa used to carry a special comb in his pants pocket to tame his runaway brows.)

"Oh, my eyebrows, they are so sexy," my father said with a laugh.

My mother shot him the most disdainful look. "No one thinks they're sexy."

And I was just sitting there, thinking to myself: *Oh, Mom. Did you really have to say that?*

What I felt was *squeezed.* Squeezed in all directions.

While I tried to ease the tension and mediate the disputes, Mary tended to retreat inside herself. She became as big a reader as I was, and I was happy to see that. Reading for her was a place of refuge just when she needed it most. My parents would be arguing in the apartment and Mary would have her nose in a book. Each in our way, both of us needed to escape from the noise.

I spent far too much of my youth mediating between the adults in my life, something no child should ever have to do. But I felt like I had to. Between my mother and my father, who were constantly arguing. Between my father and my father's family. Those undercurrents from the workday could turn into daggers with one stray comment.

I might as well have tried to bring about world peace.

That's a lot for a kid to navigate, and I didn't want to navigate any of it. I just wanted to make sure my sister was okay, skip dinner, and go outside and kick a soccer ball. Neither Mary nor I had any idea how to fix what was broken. Where was the joy in that?

There was less and less of it for this protective son.

CHAPTER 6

THE MISSING

In some families, the kids can't wait to get out of the house and on their own. Finish high school, go off to college and never look back, heading off wherever life takes them, which could easily be far, far away.

That wasn't the Trumps.

Part of this, I am convinced, had to do with my grandfather's business—how successful it was and how many family members found places for themselves there. Clearly, some of it also had to do with his domineering personality. Even the children who might have craved their independence—see my dad on this one—often had trouble getting out from under Grandpa's thumb. All those return trips to the big house for dinner demonstrated something. My father and his siblings might have looked like adult men and women, but the little birdies all flew home to the nest.

What was it my mother said? Oh, right: "You're grown now."

The ones who were away at college all came home frequently for the weekend. All those childhood bedrooms never stayed empty for long. Holidays were a given. Summers too. For my dad, that meant a lot of time boating and fishing on Long Island, often with his fun-loving

Lehigh fraternity brothers or his old pals from St. Paul's. For Donald, it meant eagerly riding around with his father to construction sites and long stretches in the summer working at his side at the company head-quarters in Brooklyn. If my father had to be dragged into the family business kicking and screaming, Donald made clear, even as he was still saluting his teachers at New York Military Academy: He was leaping in with both spit-shined shoes.

His main question now that he'd become a military-school up-at-dawn kid? "How early can I come in?" But first, Donald had to get through college. Actually, let me rephrase that. First, he had to get *into* college.

With dreams of his own real-estate career in New York City, Don-ald thought what he needed was a degree from a fancy college, some-thing that would clearly set him apart from the others he would run into in Brooklyn and Queens. A brand-name degree, he hoped, would be part of his ticket to the big time.

My father told me exactly what he'd done to help his little brother, laying out the story in precise, head-shaking detail. As high-school graduation neared, Donald could see himself attending an Ivy League college. My dad knew immediately what a reach that would be for someone with Donald's spotty academic record. Donald was coming out of a high school that was second to none in stern discipline and marching techniques but not exactly known for its academic rigor.

That's where my father stepped in.

He made no promises to his eager younger brother, but he said he'd try to be helpful. He might know someone. My dad, it seemed, almost always *knew someone.* This particular someone went all the way back to early childhood. His best friend from Jamaica Estates, Billy Drake, had graduated from Cornell, and Billy's father, William Drake Sr., was a prominent Manhattan attorney who'd graduated from Columbia University and Columbia Law School. And when my dad asked, Mr. Drake said he'd be happy to write a letter for young Donald.

Mr. Drake delivered. His letter made Donald sound like quite a promising young man, a real leader for the next generation. But given the rest of Donald's file, there was only so much one letter could do. He didn't get into any of his aim-high options, including the one he was really hoping for, the Wharton School of the University of Pennsylvania. That's how Donald ended up at his safety school, the one that accepted him, Fordham University in the Bronx. Nothing wrong with Fordham. A fine Jesuit university, it would give Donald a chance to polish his record for a possible transfer application. But it wasn't quite Penn, Columbia, or Cornell.

Midway through his sophomore year at Fordham, Donald was itching to try again. He still thought a big-name degree could be just the ticket he needed. And again, he turned to his older brother for help. Of course, my dad *knew someone.*

This time it was Jim Nolan, one of his closest friends at St. Paul's, who had gone to work in the admissions office at Penn. Jim and my dad had been tight. Jim had spent lots of time at the house in Jamaica Estates. He didn't have much memory of his friend's little brother, but he said he would try to be helpful if he could. The first step, Jim said, was to set up an on-campus interview.

The truth was, Penn wasn't *that* hard to get into in the mid-1960s. Nothing like today. They accepted close to 50 percent of the applicants, an even higher percentage of the transfers. But Donald hadn't made the cut last time, and he knew he needed every extra boost he could get now. My grandfather understood that too. This was not going to be easy.

My grandfather flew into action. Suddenly, he was the can-do Fred Trump. His kid was trying to crack the Ivies. This time, he wasn't leaving anything to chance.

My grandfather went with Donald to the on-campus interview. He chatted up the admissions staff, mentioning several of his projects in New York City and his longstanding belief in business education, making sure everyone knew exactly who Fred Trump was. Since Jim was the only admissions officer to interview Donald, it was his job to give the application a rating. No one in the family knew what that rating was. But it was high enough that, this time, with a firm assist from his older brother, Donald got in.

It took a full family effort led by my dad and strong hints from my grandfather of donations to come. But . . . *mission accomplished.* Donald was going to Penn.

Decades later, he would declare that the Wharton School at the University of Pennsylvania was "the hardest school to get into, the best school in the world." That wasn't close to true. He called it "super genius stuff." Again, a stretch. But it was a great school, and it had the name. And he would never hide the role my father played in getting him in.

Over the years to come, Donald would mention that to me several times. "Your father was very helpful getting me into Wharton," he said. "Wouldn't have happened without him."

I remember that so clearly because, for Donald, giving credit like that was *so* rare.

When the first Selective Service draft lottery was held in December 1969, I had just turned seven, and I had a front-row seat. I spent that dicey night at my grandparents' house with one of the potential draftees—an especially jittery one.

My uncle Donald.

He was eighteen months out of Wharton by then and twenty-four years old, a healthy, six-foot-three-inch, single, childless American male, living in his parents' house and toiling away in the family business.

There was a term for guys like that in 1969.

Draft bait.

Donald was just the kind of person that the sergeants in the U.S. Army recruiting command wanted to fit for fatigues, send off to boot camp, and promptly ship to Vietnam. In fact, he was an even more attractive prospect than most. Having spent eighth grade to senior year at New York Military Academy after crossing his father's invisible line, he already had some basic grounding in military practices. He knew how to march. He knew how to clean a rifle. There was clear photographic evidence of this: lots of pictures in the Trump family albums of the sandy-haired boy in a snappy dress uniform and a shiny, brass belt buckle.

He had the posture, that's for sure. Chest out. Shoulders back. That stare-down-the-enemy look in his eyes.

Donald *really* didn't want to go to Vietnam. That much was clear to me, even as a seven-year-old. And he didn't think he had to. "It doesn't make any sense," I remember him saying at dinner one night about the prospect he could be drafted. "It isn't what I'm focused on."

At seven, I didn't know all the dates and details of what had happened already, but everyone else in the family seemed to. Donald had registered for the draft in 1964 when he turned eighteen like all American males were required to. As a Fordham freshman, he'd applied for and been given a college-student deferment. Those were still fairly easy to get in 1964. He renewed the deferment three times, once while he was still at Fordham and twice more after transferring to Penn. But as soon as he graduated in May of 1968, it was a whole new day for my uncle Donald. The draft landscape immediately changed.

Danger zone.

That July, his draft status was reclassified as 1-A, putting him right where those recruitment sergeants wanted him, at the front of the line for compulsory service in Vietnam. The national need was great.

President Lyndon Johnson kept expanding the U.S. presence in Southeast Asia. Nearly five hundred fifty thousand American troops, most of them young men, were already engaged in the conflict. And the Pentagon was asking for more.

My grandfather told Uncle Donald not to worry. They would figure something out.

That's when the two of them sprang into action, though as usual, my grandfather was the one doing most of the springing. The strategy? Relying on the same mix of technical know-how, personal connections, and can-do spirit that had always defined Fred Trump and turned him into one of New York's mega-builders, not to mention a domineering family patriarch and the closer on Donald's dream of an Ivy League education. As my grandfather had learned fighting community groups, zoning officials, and city councilmen with their hands out, there was always a way to get things done if you knew how to play the game. And my grandfather was excellent at playing the game.

"I have an idea," he said.

And it was a brilliant one, in a Grandpa Trump kinda way.

The move involved a podiatrist who rented space on the ground floor of the Edgerton Apartments in Jamaica, a Fred Trump building. After a call from my grandfather, Dr. Larry Braunstein wrote a letter saying Donald suffered from bone spurs, an ailment so severe that this otherwise healthy twenty-four-year-old male could not possibly serve in the United States military.

Bone spurs?

No one in the family had ever heard of Donald's bone spurs.

No one had ever seen him hobbling. No one had ever heard him complain. About other things, sure, but not about bone spurs. And hadn't we all heard about his triumphs as captain of the New York Military Academy baseball team, where his extraordinary on-field talents got him scouted by the Boston Red Sox and the Philadelphia Phillies?

No mention of bone spurs there. And yet these purported bone spurs, confirmed by my grandfather's tenant, had just pulled Uncle Donald back from the edge of some rice paddy in Vietnam.

Or as Donald would put it later in an interview with *The New York Times:* "a very strong letter on the heels" had kept him from being drafted.

That letter worked exactly as it was supposed to. It provoked a crucial change in my uncle's Selective Service classification, from a 1-A ready-to-go to a 1-Y medical deferment, meaning he was qualified to serve only in the case of a dire national emergency.

A high bar that even the Vietnam War hadn't yet hit.

This small favor from a tenant to his landlord was a very big deal. It got my uncle through a high-risk period when he could easily have been drafted. As thousands and thousands of other young men, many from places like Queens, went off to serve their country, Donald had a get-out-of-war-free card. Years later, when his political enemies would call Donald a "draft dodger," this is what they were referring to. He was on the verge of being grabbed. The bone-spurs diagnosis let him sidestep (no pun intended) this dicey time.

So, would it be a permanent reprieve? That was the next question he would have to confront.

Bone spurs could always heal, especially with the help of a good podiatrist. The doctor might move and not need to curry favor with his landlord anymore. At a difficult time like this one, nothing was guaranteed. The pencil pushers at the Selective Service System could always seek a second opinion from an independent military podiatrist, someone who wouldn't be as quick to detect bone spurs as Grandpa's tenant had been. But with the doctor's diagnosis, Donald won immunity just when he needed it most.

As the months rolled on and the war kept raging, the national frustration only intensified, as the Pentagon's demand for more soldiers continued to rise. Antiwar protests were erupting across the country, and not just on college campuses and in major coastal cities anymore. Americans had grown fed up. Lyndon Johnson decided not to seek reelection. Richard Nixon was in the White House now. And the Selective Service System faced a growing wave of complaints about favoring the wealthy, the educated, and the well-connected, young men like Donald Trump. By late 1969, the people in the Nixon administration came up with what they hoped would be a less biased approach and a more popular plan.

A draft lottery.

The old classifications would still carry some weight. But now, every birthday in the year would be given a code number. Three hundred and sixty-six of them. Don't forget Leap Day. The code numbers were written down on slips of paper, which were sealed in little capsules. All those capsules were shaken in a shoebox, then poured into a giant glass jar. Therein lay the fate of 850,000 American men born between 1944 and 1950, including one Donald John Trump of Queens, New York, date of birth June 14, 1946.

A high number meant you were probably safe from serving. A low number meant you'd better kiss your girlfriend goodbye and start packing your duffel bag. I knew Uncle Donald still dreaded the idea of packing any duffel bags, despite his often professed love for military school. But there was just no telling how much weight that bone-spurs excuse would still carry once the new lottery was complete. It was high-drama time again. And the big night finally arrived.

December 1, 1969. A blustery, overcast Monday in New York City. We were having dinner that night at Gam and Grandpa's house in Jamaica Estates. It was already dark when my mother, my father, Mary, and I arrived. Uncle Donald was there. And so was Aunt Elizabeth. Robert was away at school. What we didn't know until we arrived was that the long-awaited draft lottery was being held that night, and it was being televised.

Dinner at my grandparents' house was never a relaxed affair, as mentioned. But there was an added reason for tension on this particular Monday night. I could detect something was different as soon as we stepped past the four white columns on the porch and went inside.

Donald was pacing. My grandfather kept checking on him. My grandmother tried to make small talk with Mary and me. But even she seemed distracted. I'm not sure how much she was listening when we tried to answer her questions about how we'd spent the weekend. Of the 850,000 American men whose lives hung in the balance that night, I'm sure many of them felt the same jitters that Donald did. He was pacing like a tiger who didn't want to step into a cage.

It wasn't anything he said exactly. It was how he looked at me . . . or didn't. Mostly, he just seemed off in another world somewhere.

Dinner was done within an hour, like it usually was. Then, my grandfather said, "Let's go into the library." While Donald continued pacing, my grandfather turned the TV dial to Channel 2, where the regularly scheduled broadcast of *Mayberry R.F.D.* was interrupted by a live feed from CBS News Washington correspondent Roger Mudd at Selective Service headquarters.

"Good evening," the reporter whispered in a tone usually reserved for golf matches. That only added to the seriousness of what was ahead. "Tonight, for the first time in twenty-seven years, the United States has again started a draft lottery."

Alexander Pirnie, a congressman from upstate New York, selected the first number, which corresponded to September 14, exactly three months *after* Donald's birthday.

Whew!

Men who were born on September 14 would therefore now be first in line for the draft. Then came April 24, December 30, February 14, October 18, and on and on and on. All misses. As the birthdays kept coming, other congressmen stepped in. We all sat around my grandparents' library, hardly saying a word as the numbers came and came and came some more.

My grandparents exchanged small smiles when number 245 was assigned to August 26, Uncle Robert's birthdate. He was away at Boston University and had a 2-S student deferment. But if he got kicked out or quit school, at least his number wouldn't be a bad one.

With each new number chosen, Donald let out another sigh of relief.

Donald's birthday, June 14, wasn't chosen until 356th, meaning that even if his "bone spurs" somehow failed him, he was still highly, highly unlikely to serve. In fact, the letter from his father's foot-doctor tenant had done exactly what it was supposed to, protect my uncle when he was at highest peril, buy him some time just when he needed it most.

That may not rank among my grandfather's greatest public achievements. But it sure did do the job of running interference for his middle son, and it opened up a place in the U.S. Army for another young man who didn't have a father as crafty as Fred Trump and would now be filling those boots in Vietnam.

I felt relieved for my uncle. I think everyone in the family was. He seemed to feel great relief as well, like he had dodged a bullet. And who was I to question that? I was already a regular news watcher at seven years old, but it wasn't like I had my own foreign policy. I had no clear view about who should join the Army and how they should be chosen. My uncle was happy, so I was happy. That was about it.

The war kept raging for several more years. And so did the debate over who should serve. The lottery brought some fairness to the equation, but it wouldn't please everyone, and it certainly didn't end the disagreements over privilege and service and unequal burden-sharing. Growing up in the Trump family, I had already picked up the idea that life wasn't fair.

So why did that story not end when it was supposed to? When I could be happy for my uncle and just move on?

The vivid memory of that moment was something much more.

There was a girl I knew in school. Not well. She was a couple of grades ahead of me. But I knew her. One day, I heard she was selling POW/MIA bumper stickers. A couple of my friends had them.

"You Are Not Forgotten," the red-and-white stickers said.

"That's weird," I said to one of my friends:

Back then, anything we didn't understand, we thought was *weird.* "I didn't know she was interested in politics. I don't know why she's doing that."

My friend gave me one of those looks that said "clueless" and shook his head. "Her father is MIA in Vietnam," he said.

I knew enough to know what MIA meant, Missing in Action, and I couldn't imagine too many things that would be worse than that, having your father missing in action in Vietnam.

Just thinking about my own dad ever being missing—that terrified me.

I felt sad for her and embarrassed for me. The next day at school, I bought one of her bumper stickers and told her, "I hope they find your father. I will be thinking about him."

"Thank you, Fred," she said. "I appreciate you saying that."

I really did mean it, and I couldn't get this girl out of my mind.

It was only after I was heading home that afternoon that the rest of the thought occurred to me.

I suddenly recalled the night in the "library" at my grandparents' house, in that room with the Yellow Pages and the White Pages and no other books, just a TV in a large, heavy wooden cabinet and a black dial telephone. I remembered Donald being so nervous and then so relieved when he got that good number in the lottery.

As for me, all I could think about—and to this day—was that a girl I knew had a father who was missing in action in Vietnam. He would not be forgotten.

CHAPTER 7

LOSING IT

Things didn't get much better for my dad.

As the screws kept tightening in the office, he brought all that pressure home. Pretty soon, he wasn't just seething. He was flying off the handle in the kitchen and drowning his feelings of frustration in massive quantities of Scotch.

He blamed my mother for reasons that made no sense, and he didn't hide much of it from Mary and me. My charming, talented father was losing control, and he didn't know what to do about it. Even TWO Non, our new dog, wasn't enough to calm him. Only the Cutty Sark seemed to have that effect, and not for long.

My parents fought a lot, often at high volume and often about alcohol . . . and my father's consumption thereof. As long as I live, I will never shake the memories of those mammoth fights. My mother saying my father drank too much. My father saying she should mind her own business. My mother saying maybe she would if he drank less. My father saying maybe he'd drink less if she quit hounding him. Even as a little kid, I could tell that neither one of them was making much progress.

I was lying in bed one night, trying to fall asleep. Suddenly, I could hear my parents arguing again. The walls muffled their words, so I could only guess the topic. My father's drinking, probably. I could feel the growing intensity. My mother's voice sounded just as angry as my father's did.

As I lay there in the darkness of my bedroom, I felt what thousands of other kids have felt before me, the insecurity of parents at odds. I went from hurt to angry to scared.

Mary was in her bedroom. I didn't know what she was hearing, if anything. Then, the thought occurred to me: Maybe I should just run into my parents' room. I could tell them I was trying to sleep. I could ask them to please be quiet. I could say, "Don't you know I'm hearing all this?"

I didn't do any of that, of course. Kids seldom do. But here I am half a century later, and I can still hear those muffled voices and still feel the shivers I felt that night. I felt bad for my parents and bad for me. My sister and I didn't deserve it, and neither did they.

One weekend when my parents were away somewhere and I was about seven, I spent Friday night with the Gelusos. They were our neighbors. They had a small house across the street from our apartment building. Mr. and Mrs. Geluso had five children, and Mrs. Geluso's father, mother, and grandfather also lived there. The Geluso girls sometimes babysat for Mary and me. When one of the older daughters got married, she and her husband moved in upstairs. There was always something going on at the Gelusos' house. The plan was that, after staying there on Saturday night, I would spend the rest of the weekend with my cousin David.

Early evening Saturday, Aunt Maryanne arrived.

"Let's go, Freddy," she said.

It wasn't like me to talk back to one of my aunts or uncles, especially not Aunt Maryanne. But I found it in me somewhere.

"I'm not going," I said. "I want to stay here."

And I meant it. I'd been having so much fun, I wasn't sure I ever wanted to leave. In twenty-four hours at the Gelusos', I didn't detect a whiff of tension or liquor in the house. It was loud and active and busy. But as far as I could tell, they all got along. I'd never experienced anything quite like that before.

No one was yelling like in our apartment. Nothing was weird like at Maryanne and David's. There weren't any undercurrents like at my grandparents' house. Mrs. Geluso always seemed to have a loaf of homemade bread in the oven and a giant pot of sauce on the stove. They had a little backyard. On the other side of that yard were their friends the Signorellis, and everyone was going back and forth. Music was playing all the time. "Cracklin' Rosie" by Neil Diamond is the song that sticks in my mind. It wasn't like we actually *did* anything. But there were all these people, enjoying each other's company, having a wonderful time. I'm not saying the Gelusos were a perfect family. I'm sure there's no such thing. They probably had their issues like anyone. But I knew this much after one night of staying there: They couldn't have been any more different from the Trumps.

I got my wish, and stayed there until my parents got back on Sunday night. Things kept swirling at home.

One night, my mom and dad were having another one of their arguments. My dad was drunk. Again. My mom was expressing her displeasure at that. Again. By this point in their marriage, neither one of them was showing much restraint.

My parents were in their bedroom. Mary and I were in my bedroom with the door open. We could hear the rising argument. This one sounded extra serious, like my mother was trying to contain the situation and not succeeding. Then, my mother came into my bedroom and announced firmly, "Come on, we're leaving."

Apparently, at some point in the argument, my father was cleaning his old military rifle. I had no idea if the gun was loaded or not, or any other details. But I could see the fear in my mother's eyes. When Mary and I delayed a moment, not sure what was happening, she said firmly: "Come on." The three of us went down to the garage, got in the car, and drove to the house of one of my mother's friends, where we all spent the night. And when we went back home the next morning, my mother never mentioned any of that again.

I believe that night may be the reason I've never liked guns. To me, they always felt like trouble. I had friends who loved to hunt. Not me. My younger cousins would eventually become avid hunters. Not me. I loved to fish and go to the beach and be on the water and be outdoors, but none of that required firearms. From that night forward, guns would never be my thing.

If my parents weren't arguing about my father's drinking, or the way my father was or wasn't standing up to *his* father in the office, they were probably arguing about Montauk. My father had always been drawn to the water (along with the sky), and Montauk was a picturesque fishing village at the eastern end of Long Island. They bought a small cottage in town. He loved going out there, which sometimes meant he could spend all day fishing and drinking while my mother stayed at home with two little kids. But we often went out together. Mary and I adored being there. My mother, not so much.

It might have looked idyllic from the outside. There was a beach. There was a boat and a place to dock it. We belonged to the Deep Sea Club, which also had dinner and dancing and an A-list membership. The clubhouse had been a speakeasy during Prohibition. In 1930, New

York mayor Jimmy Walker supposedly jumped out of a window at the club to escape a gambling raid. There were stories that at one time the club also housed a brothel. And now they had Trumps as members. I wonder how my great-grandfather would have felt about that. But for my parents, Montauk was no escape. It was just something else for them to debate.

And believe me, they did.

The summer I was seven, my father said to me: "You're going to camp on Cape Cod." I wasn't quite sure what that might entail, even after my father mentioned sailing and hiking and sleeping in a cabin and sitting around a campfire at night. But I got so homesick the first night I was there, an assistant counselor carried me to the office in the driving rain. They got my mother on the phone, who told me calmly, "Go back to the cabin. Camp will be fun."

I went back, and she was right. For me, Cape Cod Sea Camps in Brewster, Massachusetts, would become the happy place I could go every summer and just be me. It was an old-school summer camp with a world-class sailing program and a longtime military bent. We wore gray shorts and white T-shirts and never stopped having fun. The senior counselors were in the Army or Navy Reserves. We marched after dinner and got reviewed, and that might sound awful, but the way they did it, it was really fun. As Vietnam heated up and some of the older campers started wearing long hair and having opinions, the military traditions would get harder to maintain. But I had a blast at camp from my second day as a camper. Camp was where I learned I could be a hell of an athlete. Camp was where I kept building my confidence. Camp was where I learned all kinds of new things. The only problem with camp was that it ended as the summer did, and the time eventually came to say goodbye and go back home.

When I got home, both my parents were in the apartment. They welcomed me back with a plastic Best Camper trophy. I left to go play in Goose Pond Park with my friends, who I'd missed while I was away for the summer, and I took the trophy to show them. When I came home from the park, my dad wasn't there. It was after dinner that my mother told me: "Your dad and I will be getting a divorce. Your dad won't be living here anymore."

I tried to hold back my tears, but I couldn't hold them back for long. I didn't know how to feel. This was all new to me, but I knew I felt very sad. As I walked back to my bedroom, I realized my life would change forever, as would the lives of my mom and Mary. I learned later that my parents had been talking about getting divorced for the past five years, ever since I was two years old. The first time had gotten sidetracked when my mother got pregnant with Mary. The idea had been on and off ever since. But now it was real.

My mother made it sound like a lot of things wouldn't change. She and Mary and I would keep living in the same apartment. My dad was getting his own place. But we would spend time with him once he settled in, and he would also come over to visit with us. Mary and I would keep going to school at Kew-Forest like we always had. I could go back to sea camp on Cape Cod the next summer if I wanted to, which I certainly did. I could keep seeing David and hanging out at my grandparents' house and go to Goose Pond Park and do all the stuff I had always done. There would still be a lot of family dinners at my grandparents' house in Jamaica Estates.

"The bad news?" my mother said, letting a moment pass before she answered her own question with what sounded like a sigh of resignation. "Your father's parents say I should keep going over there with you guys for dinner."

My poor mom.

• • •

The truth is my mother was right about all that. Things really didn't change that much for Mary and me. Yes, we started spending time with my dad at his new apartments—apartments, plural. He never stayed anywhere for long. And the part about my grandparents' house? Once my parents separated, it seemed like I was over there more than I'd ever been, seeing my grandmother and spending time with my uncles Donald and Robert, both of whom were still in their early twenties and living at home.

Robert was my cool uncle.

Ten years younger than my father, he was a lean, dark-haired athlete who was more like an older brother to me, definitely cooler than Uncle Donald, who mostly talked with his father about real estate. Uncle Rob seemed to love nothing more than going out into the yard and kicking a soccer ball with me.

I couldn't have had a better coach or a kinder influence.

He was captain of the men's soccer team at Boston University and also the team's MVP. He knew his fake crosses and could show me how to execute them. When he was home from college, which was often, he spent every holiday and all summer with his family in Queens. As the youngest, he had siblings with their own busy lives. I think he was happy for my company and liked it when I came around. And if he sometimes felt imposed upon, he never let on to me or made me feel anything but welcome being there.

Everyone needs an Uncle Rob early in life.

I think he also understood that things had to be a little tense for me as Freddie and Linda's son. He was well aware of my father's drinking. He'd witnessed my parents' fights. Now with the breakup, I don't think he wanted me to feel adrift. We never talked directly about any of that. He didn't try to be my therapist. None of that would have been very *Trump*. But I could ask him questions about the family, about my friends, about other things I was confused about. I could tell him stuff and know he wouldn't blab it. In those days, he was generous with his time and comforting with his encouragement. He was a good guy and a good friend, and I guess we did share some things in common that he didn't share with anyone else in the family. I don't think he was kicking many soccer balls with his work-focused dad or either of his older brothers. Though I was just a little kid, he seemed happy that someone in the family looked up to him. Being the baby brother of Maryanne, Fred, Elizabeth, and Donald must have had burdens of its own.

Which didn't mean Rob couldn't be provoked, especially by his immediate older brother. One day, Rob, Donald, and I were sitting on the sofa in the library. The TV was on, and my mother was sitting nearby.

Donald said to me: "Hey, Fred. Hit Rob."

"Really?"

"Yeah, hit Rob. Just hit him."

I don't think Rob was paying much attention. I'm sure he wasn't expecting what happened next. But I shrugged and said, "Okay," and I punched Rob in the arm.

Rob didn't say anything, but he definitely looked surprised. Then, he wound up and slapped me across the face.

Hard.

I couldn't believe he'd just done that.

Honestly, it was like a *Three Stooges* episode on the library couch. The Three Trumps. Everything but the clanging bells, the *boing-boings,* and the nose twists.

Donald thought the whole thing was hilarious. He was laughing so hard, he had to catch his breath.

I'll tell you who didn't think it was funny, besides Rob. My mother didn't think it was funny at all. Though she wasn't normally one for explosive anger, she blew up at that.

"How could you do that?" she demanded.

I wasn't sure which of the stooges she was talking to. All three probably. And you couldn't say we didn't deserve her ire.

To me, that was such a part of growing up. Hanging out with my father's younger siblings, who could be every bit as immature as me. I'd get over there anyway I could and let myself in. "Where's Uncle Rob?" I'd asked my grandmother or whichever member of the household I ran into first. He'd lumber down the stairs in his shorts and BU T-shirt. We'd head outside and hit some baseballs in the backyard or kick the soccer ball again.

This couldn't last forever. I understood that. And it didn't.

One fresh June morning, I showed up at the house and asked my usual "Where's Uncle Rob?"

"He's working," I was told.

"What do you mean *working*? It's the summer."

"Yeah, he works in the summer."

And that was that.

Spending time with Uncle Donald wasn't quite the same kind of low-key fun. With Donald, almost everything had to be a competition.

One day, he and my cousin David were playing catch in the yard. Just a friendly game of catch between an uncle and his nephew. That's what David thought, anyway. But as the baseball went back and forth, Donald started throwing harder. And harder. And harder. Until he was firing rockets at his nephew, as hard as he could.

David definitely wasn't enjoying it. I don't think he understood what Donald was trying to do or why he was doing it. And as the balls kept flying, Donald kept laughing out loud. No one had ever enjoyed a game of catch as much as Donald seemed to be enjoying this one.

Then, he hauled off and threw one more fastball. This one hit the tip of David's glove and bounced off his forehead, sending my cousin straight to the grass. As David fell, the ball landed on his stomach, before plopping with a little thud to the ground.

Maryanne came running over, steaming mad.

"What are you doing?" she yelled at her brother. "He's just a kid."

As Maryanne walked David into the house in search of a dishrag and some ice cubes, Donald wasn't apologetic at all.

"That's what the glove is for," he said.

That was Uncle Donald. To him, a win was a win was a win, whether or not the other person even knew the game was on. There was nothing that couldn't be turned into a competition and nothing more satisfying than yet another win. And for Donald to be the winner, someone else had to lose.

Even if it was his nephew.

That weekend, I happened to be staying at my grandparents' house because my mother was away. That night, Donald and I were in big, black leather studded club chairs in the library-that-had-no-books. We were watching TV together. It was raining and thundering outside. A perfect night for *The Twilight Zone*. And this episode was one of the best ever, "Time Enough at Last."

Burgess Meredith—the Penguin from *Batman*—is a bank teller who really loves to read. That's all he wants to do. Read, read, read. He's in the bank vault one day on his lunch break, reading of course, when the room begins to shake around him. The world has blown up, and human life as we know it is destroyed. But as the lonely book lover wanders the empty city, he starts to think maybe this isn't so bad. Now, he'll have more time for reading. At the deserted public library, he loads up on books that he can read for the rest of his life. But when he leans down to pick up another one, his Coke-bottle glasses fall off and shatter. Now the man who loves to read can't read anymore.

Sitting next to Donald in that big leather club chair, that was a really nice moment.

"You ready for bed?" he asked me. "We can play catch in the morning."

Clearly, I needed to train up for the fastballs that would soon be coming my way.

CHAPTER 8

SINGLE AGAIN

W hat kid wants to watch his parents dating again?

    I know I didn't. But there it was, just as uncomfortable as I imagined it would be. My father was keeping company with a woman who lived on the third floor of The Highlander, making my mother say to herself: "Gee, I wonder how long *that's* been going on . . ."

As a single mom with two young children, it wasn't easy for my mother to have a grown-up social life, and I admired the fact that she really tried. She had a sunny personality, and people liked her. Away from the pressures of life with my father, she blossomed a bit. Some of her dates were memorable. One—I kid you not—was a one-armed banjo player. I'd never met a one-armed banjo player before . . . or since. But he came up to the apartment and was a really fun guy. It was the early 1970s, and it just so happened I'd been learning to play the banjo.

My mother really liked another guy who was an Alitalia pilot. He was a friend of our doorman. The pilot took me to Kennedy Airport one day to look at a new 747. I couldn't believe how huge the plane was. "It's like flying a house," he told me. One morning, as Mary, my mother, and I were leaving our building for school, the doorman said to my mom: "Oh, we just got news. He died in a car crash in Italy."

That came as a real shock for my mom. I didn't know if that guy was going to be *the* guy for my mother. But I knew he was someone she cared about.

Having an ex with such an armload of issues, my mom took on the day-to-day child-rearing responsibilities. But she was still dependent on my father and his family, who owned our apartment and were still paying the bills. My mother had stopped working as a flight attendant before I was born. It wasn't like she was going to spring into some new high-paying career.

Though she tried to rise to the realities of her new situation, I'm not sure it ever bought her much relief from my grandparents' condescension. They knew my dad's limitations as well as anyone did. They certainly knew who was picking up the slack now. But for all my mother's efforts to raise their two grandchildren, Gam and Grandpa never really did credit my mom.

My father came with us for some family occasions, but not that first Easter. It was just my mom, Mary, and me, driving up to my grandparents' house right on time for a 1 p.m. lunch. Something didn't look right. As we pulled into the driveway, my grandparents were getting into my grandfather's dark blue Cadillac.

"Hey," my mom asked. "Where are you going?"

"Oh," my grandfather said, as if everything were normal. "We're going to Easter lunch."

Easter lunch?

My mother froze with her hands on the wheel. Her words rolled through the car, loud enough for only Mary and me to hear: "Oh-kay, and we weren't invited?" And it wasn't just the two of them. It turned out they were all going to a restaurant for Easter dinner—Maryanne,

Donald, Elizabeth, even Robert, the whole family—just not us. If my grandmother thought this was odd, she didn't let on.

It was probably for the better, even though I was hungry for a nice Easter dinner. But I understood immediately that my mom took it as a sign of exclusion, a sign of unwelcome, a sign of we're-going-but-you-can't. For all of us, there was a growing sense of being pariahs in our own family, second-class citizens, like we'd been judged and we'd clearly fallen short.

We went home, where Mom did her best to make it a happy Easter for Mary and me.

My mom was strict in her role as single parent, stricter than I remembered her before the bust-up. She drove Mary and me to school every morning. She made sure we kept up with our studies and constantly quizzed us about our homework. She seemed to keep an extra eye on the friends we were hanging around with. And she emphasized the importance of helping those less fortunate and giving back to the community.

She'd always liked doing volunteer work, and if anything, now she was doing even more of it. She served twice as president of the Women's Auxiliary at Booth Memorial Hospital in Flushing, where my father's grandmother, my great-grandmother, had spent her final days in the affiliated nursing home. There were afternoons that my mother would pick up Mary and me from school and drive us back to Booth, where we did our homework while she led fundraising meetings.

It was impressive watching her do all that. Frankly, I was proud of her.

But when she and my father had any kind of interaction, everything was tense again. He could fly off the handle at a moment's notice. She could get her feelings hurt. It wasn't that they wanted to argue less now. It was that, living apart, they simply had less chance. And for Mary and me, things could always erupt at any time.

• • •

Not every weekend, but many, Mary and I packed a few things and went off to spend time with our father at his latest apartment. He started out in a dark, basement-level one-bedroom in Ridgewood on the Brooklyn-Queens border. My dad kept live chickens in the backyard and built a little platform so we could get a peek out to the street. That place was bleak. Then, he moved into a larger unit with all-white walls in a classic immigrants' apartment building my grandfather owned near Sunnyside. This one had a wonderful mix of ethnic groups, a huge pool, and a park across the street, where Mary and I both played in the sports leagues. That apartment was a whole lot cheerier than the first place.

My dad always wanted to know what we were up to and how we were doing, though he often fell asleep hours before Mary and I did, sometimes as early as eight o'clock. He was drinking—Scotch mostly— and I think he was having some trouble adjusting to his new, single life. Gradually, though, my father's energy seemed to return, and we started going out and doing stuff. I'd say it took us all a little while to get used to the new arrangement.

One Friday afternoon, my dad came to our apartment to pick up Mary and me, and I didn't want to go. It was the Gelusos all over again. My mother was dating a guy who had promised to take us bowling on Queens Boulevard. That sounded like a lot more fun.

I felt like I needed a break. I didn't want to be the kid in the middle between his two squabbling parents. I didn't want to be the Henry Kissinger of Highland Avenue, moderating like a diplomat. I wanted to go bowling instead.

And I could think of even more reasons than that. The alcohol made him moody. He was prone to fits of anger over stupid little things. Driving with him could be terrifying, especially in the backseat when my sister was also in the car. You never really knew how steady he'd be behind the wheel. Young as I was, I could already see his life wasn't heading in a positive direction. There was just a lot of tension in the air. All of which is to say I shouldn't have sent my two-and-a-half-year-younger sister over there alone.

I knew the second I did that that Mary was going to hate me for bailing at the last minute. And when she got back, she really let me have it.

"That wasn't fair," she said. "You can't make me do that alone."

I felt awful about it and promised I wouldn't abandon her again. As far as I can recall, I never did.

My mother dated a lot of nice guys, who all seemed to like her. I got to know several of them pretty well. And she seemed serious about a few of them. But for some reason, the relationships all fizzled out. As I noticed that happening, I started to wonder what the issue was. It dawned on me that *Mary and I* might be the problem. Nothing about the kind of kids we were or how we behaved. It was just that this was the 1970s, and a lot of guys my mom's age weren't looking to get too serious with a woman who was raising a couple of kids.

I felt bad about that. I wanted my mother to be happy. I certainly didn't want to stand in her way.

"Baggage." I think that's what people would call Mary and me.

My father had a gazillion issues, and in hindsight, people always tend to focus on those. To this day, they only want to talk about the bad times. But I have to say that, even at his low points, he could still be a wonderful dad. He never stopped taking me boating and fishing, two things I've never stopped loving. Later, he would get me interested in flying. People can say whatever they want to about my father. I never had a second of doubt about his love.

One memory stands out—not because it was crazy or bad but because it was so normal. He, Mary, and I drove out to Montauk and spent the weekend at the Snug Harbor Motel & Marina on Star Island Road, an old-time fishermen's haunt. We rented a boat for a trip across Gardiners Bay to Shelter Island, where my friend Michael Siegel's family had a house. We pulled up on the beach, picked up Mike, and went weak fishing.

That's what they're called, "weak fish." If you yank too hard on the line, you will literally yank their heads off. As my father kept saying, "Easy does it with weak fish."

As in life too.

We spent the night before with nautical charts from Montauk to Shelter Island, mapping our route along the buoys with two metal rules and a navigation system called "parallels." We spent all day out there. It was wonderful, and we didn't catch a single fish. I think my father loved those outings as much as we did, and we had many of them.

He took us to pro wrestling at Madison Square Garden and, for the really gritty stuff, Sunnyside Garden Arena in Queens. College basketball. Roller derby. We'd park the car at Queensboro Plaza and take the train into Manhattan with whichever of my friends we'd rounded up. Just like when he'd been in high school and college, my dad was still the leader of the pack. When he was good, he was great. And most of the bad stuff, he mostly managed to keep to himself. Mostly.

I knew what a painful experience he was having at work. I knew how tense things were with his father and, increasingly, his younger brother Donald. I knew my father didn't have the drinking under control. No one seemed all that concerned with sheltering the children from those truths. But strange as it might sound now, he still made Mary and me—or maybe I should just speak for myself here—he still made me feel loved and part of him in his own way.

• • •

Mom had her own adventures in mind for Mary and me. She thought it might be fun for the three of us to drive out to the Ohio State Fair, not far from where one of her closest friends from high school now lived with her family. That sounded like a blast to us. We'd never been to Ohio before. I'm not exactly sure how it happened, but my grandfather heard about the trip, and he called my mother.

"Oh," he said. "That's a long drive. It's better to fly." And he bought round-trip tickets to Cleveland for Mary, my mother, and me.

There were times he would really come through for us. Yes, my grandfather could be gruff and businesslike. But sometimes when you weren't expecting it, he could also be really nice. We had a great time with my mother's friend and her family. And when I stared at the map and realized exactly how far Ohio was, I was especially grateful to my grandfather. Flying for two hours was a whole lot more fun than five hundred miles in a car.

My mom also took us to Washington. We rode Amtrak down for a couple of days of touring the capital and seeing the sights. Before we left, my grandfather gave me a five-dollar bill.

That visit took one unexpected turn.

I was standing by myself in front of our hotel. Mary and my mom were still in the lobby when two boys about my age came up to me.

"Gimme your money," one of them demanded.

"I don't have any," I answered, fumbling for a response.

"Gimme your money," the other one insisted.

Of course, I remembered the five-dollar bill Grandpa had given me. It was still in my front, right pocket. I suddenly thought, *I can't go home without my grandfather's money.* I didn't waste another second. I slugged them both, hard in the stomach. They didn't fall to the ground, but my punches definitely stunned them, as I ran back into the hotel. They never got my fiver.

When I told Grandpa about that later, I don't think he liked the idea of me brawling with Washington muggers. On the other hand, I believe he took pride in the fact that I was tough enough to hold on to the money he'd given me.

The divorce and the aftermath were having an impact on me. I was becoming more and more of a handful in school—enough that people noticed. Dragging my feet on assignments. Making funny comments, loud ones, in the middle of class. Finding every opportunity to call attention to myself. I don't know if I was acting out because of the disruption in my home life or I was just being an adolescent jerk. Maybe a little of both. I know my mother was getting complaints from my teachers. She finally decided she needed to call in reinforcements. Since she didn't feel like she could turn to my father, she sought out the next best thing.

His two brothers.

"I need your help with Fred," she said one day to Donald and Robert, when I was twelve. "He's getting to a tough age, and I don't like the way things are going." She never said so directly, not to me anyway. But I think she feared I might be heading down some of the same paths as my father, the talented, likable guy whose life took a couple of wrong turns.

I wasn't anywhere close to that, not yet. But I guess she could see signs and they worried her.

Unlike Uncle Robert, Donald hadn't shown all that much interest in me. But this time, he rose to the occasion. I was around the same age Donald had been when Grandpa had shipped him off to New York Military Academy, and he must have had that inglorious day on his mind.

He and Rob took me up to my grandparents' bedroom. They shut the door so we could talk in private. Donald had a sour look on his face, and he took the lead.

"Listen, pal," he said sternly. Donald was still single and childless, so this was a bit of a put-on. He wouldn't marry Ivana until 1977. "You better straighten up or you'll be on your way to military school."

He didn't have to say he was speaking from experience. I already knew that. He just wanted to get downstairs for dinner. He didn't want to deal with me anymore.

"I mean it," he added.

"Yeah," Uncle Robert agreed.

I'm still not sure if that was just Donald talking or whether my mom specifically planted the military school threat, asking him to deliver it to me in a way that I might listen. She'd never raised that scary prospect before. I certainly didn't want to help it become a Trump family tradition.

And I have to say, Donald's words had an immediate impact.

"Oh, shit," I said to myself. "I don't want . . . *that.*"

All the dreadful implications went rushing through my brain: *I'll have to leave my school. I'll never see my friends again. Some guy with a crew cut will be yelling at me. This won't be "fun" military stuff like at Cape Cod Sea Camps. God knows what horrors might be waiting for me. I'll have to wear a uniform. Will there even be any girls?*

After that, I tried to straighten up. I made a stronger effort to pay attention in the classroom. I didn't talk back to my teachers . . . *as much.* And I had to give Donald and Robert some of the credit. I can only imagine what they told my mother after our conversation. There was one other development at the time. David told me that he'd be going that summer on a teenagers' tour of Europe.

That sounded awesome to me.

I asked my mother if I could go. She didn't say yes. She didn't say no. But if this was going to happen, I could tell, I couldn't wait for my mother to nail it down. In an impressive blast of youthful independence, I called for an application, and I completed it. I went through the interview process. I gathered the letters of recommendation that the program required. I asked my geography teacher, Mr. Kimball, if he would write one. I knew I'd been a pain in his class, but he wrote a very nice letter for me, making me sound maybe a little better than I was.

And then my mother spoke to the program director.

"Well," the director said, "he's thirteen. I don't think we've ever had anyone that young before. But he sounds like a mature young man." *Thank you, Mr. Kimball.*

The bottom line: They decided to let me join the summer tour.

The trip was great. David and I had a blast together. I got to hang out with a bunch of older kids. We saw churches and museums and old buildings, places I'd only read about or seen pictures of, and we got to climb 674 of the 1,665 steps in the Eiffel Tower, which was as far as they would let us go. And right at the start of the new school year, I began acting up in class again.

Mr. Kimball did not appreciate it.

"Mr. Trump," he said to me. "You know, I wrote you a very nice letter, and I meant it. This is the way you repay me?"

Damn it, I thought. *Mr. Kimball is right.*

And that's what it took. Deep down, I think, despite some questionable role models, I wanted to be the best person I could be. I really started shaping up, way better than before. My grades would never be phenomenal, but I actually buckled down like everyone had been telling me to. Great teachers are worth their weight in gold. Many thanks to Mr. Edson, Mr. Heredy, Mr. Quinn, and others. In junior high, Mr. Quinn assigned great books for us to read: *The Grapes of Wrath* by John Steinbeck, *To Kill a Mockingbird* by Harper Lee, *The Catcher in the Rye* by J. D. Salinger. I devoured those books and those authors.

I even took notes. That really sealed my love of reading, which would stick with me for the rest of my life.

Reading took me to all kinds of places I had never been before, even though I'd now been to Europe. Each book was a whole new world to explore. *Cry, the Beloved Country* by Alan Paton made me feel like I was *in* apartheid South Africa. In her mystery novel *We Have Always Lived in the Castle,* Shirley Jackson writes in the voice of an eighteen-year-old girl who lives with her agoraphobic sister and her despondent uncle in an estate with many secrets. It was amazing. Reading, I decided, was the next best thing to being there, and my grades even started reflecting that.

Also, it probably didn't hurt that my mom invited Mr. Quinn to dinner once or twice at the house.

CHAPTER 9

RACE CARD

Donald was pissed. Boy, was he pissed.

I was at my grandparents' house, kicking a soccer ball in the backyard before taking a break for a Coke with Gam. Just a normal afternoon for preteen me. Yet I remember it like it was yesterday because of what happened next.

Donald came stomping in.

"You wanna see something?" he barked to me.

Donald had a cotillion white Cadillac Eldorado convertible. I knew he loved that car. It had a titanic, 500-cubic-inch V8 engine and a three-speed, automatic transmission that made it go zero to sixty in just shy of eleven seconds. With its leather interior, power seats, steel-belted radials, and AM/FM radio, there was a lot to love about that car, even if it only got fourteen miles a gallon. It had a canvas top that went up and folded into itself at the push of a button.

"Look at that," he said when we got to the Eldorado, which was now parked in the driveway.

There was a giant gash, at least two feet long, in the canvas roof of his convertible. There was another, shorter gash next to it.

"Niggers," I recall him saying disgustedly. "Look what the niggers did."

I knew that was a bad word.

Had I heard it from some of my friends in Goose Pond Park? Of course I had. In the streets of Queens? There too. But neither of my parents had a racist bone between them, and I never heard that word around our home. Even when my father was drinking. If someone is a raging racist, it'll almost always come to the surface once the booze starts flowing and the inhibitions are drowned. You notice these things. Drunk or sober, my father never used the N-word, not that I ever heard.

And neither had I.

Donald hadn't seen whoever had done this. The car had been parked on Hillside Avenue. The slasher or slashers got away clean. He returned to where he'd left his beloved Eldorado, saw the damage, then went straight to the place where people's minds sometimes go when they face a fresh affront.

Across the racial divide.

Living amid the towering oaks in lovely Jamaica Estates, it was easy to find refuge in "us-versus-them." And that was part of it, I believe. The affluent enclave was near some far tougher neighborhoods, along with many middle-class developments like the ones Fred Trump was famous for. When police shot and killed an alleged school-bus thief and looting erupted in South Jamaica, I could see the flames out of my bedroom window. We could smell the smoke in the living room.

Then as now, Queens was one of the most diverse places on the planet. More than a hundred languages were spoken there. People came, literally, from everywhere and mostly got along. But with its five hundred hilly acres and proud collection of Tudors, Victorians, and Colonials, Jamaica Estates was also the borough's original gated community. Though anyone could come and go through there, that 1908 gatehouse still stood at Hillside Avenue and the Midland Parkway Mall, a stone-and-granite reminder of some longstanding presumptions that still held firm.

If something bad happened, *they* were the ones who did it. Almost certainly, it was *them.*

So, was Donald a racist? People have been asking that question for decades. And I will try to answer it.

I hate racist language and the impulses that make people use it. But on a topic like this one, nothing is ever as simple as "yes" or "no." I haven't offered any easy answers here, and I'm not about to start now, certainly not on a topic as complex as race.

Some context, please.

This was Queens in the early 1970s—Archie Bunker, the aftermath of the riots, the war on drugs, and a thousand ethnic punch lines. "Brown Sugar" and "Everyday People" were on the radio. Hiphop was busting out of the Bronx from pioneers like DJ Kool Herc and Grandmaster Flash. The Ramones hadn't officially assembled yet, but Joey, Johnny, Dee Dee, and Tommy had all graduated (or not) from Forest Hills High. Things were more out in the open then. More raw. Less PC. Back then, people said all kinds of crude, thoughtless, prejudiced things. I don't need to list them here. In one way or another, maybe everyone in Queens was a racist then. Like many things in life, it was partly a matter of situation and degree. I never heard my grandfather use the N-word. Then again, he did sometimes say *schvartze,* the Yiddish slur for Black people, and his tenants were uniformly white.

That had to mean something, didn't it?

This was a big company. My grandfather did not review every rental application. But the message filtered down clearly from above, starting at the central office on Avenue Z and landing with the building managers and rental agents in the field: These apartments were for white people.

By the light of today, it's impossible to defend any of that, and really, why would anyone want to try? But if we are truly going to understand these family members and their attitudes, they need to be evaluated in the context of changing times. Whatever you want to say about the Trumps who came before me, you also have to say about many others around them—their city, their nation, and their world. Those are the limitations of being from *anywhere*.

Is that an excuse? No, it isn't. But it also can't be ignored. No matter what else was happening, the explosive subject of race was never far behind. So instead of making sweeping generalizations or tossing labels around, let me tell you what I know and what I saw.

When I was growing up, I never heard that my grandfather had attended an anti-Black rally as a young man. That never came up at the family dinner table. He never mentioned it, and no one else in the family did, if they were aware of it at all. But if you google "Fred Trump" and "race," which I have done, you can read all about Memorial Day 1927 and a violent demonstration in Queens.

"KLANSMEN RIOT IN QUEENS," declares a report in *The New York Times*. "KLAN ASSAILS POLICEMEN," a second *Times* headline reads. "Fist Fights in Jamaica."

"SCENE AS POLICE AND KLAN CLASH IN QUEENS PARADE," *The Brooklyn Daily Eagle* announces above a dramatic photo of white-robed Klansmen with an American flag on Queens Boulevard. "Officer at left is about to swing his nightstick over the head of white-sheeted knight, whose friends rushed to assist, causing a free-for-all with two auto loads of policemen," the caption says.

According to the *Times*, among those who were arrested that day was one Fred C. Trump of 175-24 Devonshire Road, which the 1930 U.S. Census pinpointed as my grandfather's home address. He'd have been twenty-one at the time. But all these years later, some important details are impossible to pin down. The *Times* doesn't say if my grandfather was a member or supporter of the racist Ku Klux Klan. The *Times* doesn't say if he was just a bystander or someone who was swept up in the crowd. It doesn't say exactly what he was accused of, only that he "was discharged." And the city police records from the incident can't be found. Another article, in the long-forgotten *Daily Star*, says Fred Trump was detained "on a charge of refusing to disperse from a parade when ordered to do so," so that might have been it.

I can say that I never saw Klan robes in my grandfather's bedroom or racist literature in the drawers . . . and believe me, I climbed through every inch of that house as a kid. I poked through all the closets, looked under all the beds, and explored every dusty corner of the attic, just like any nosy child would. But still. It's hard to imagine that *The New York Times* made up that story in 1927. That doesn't make any sense at all.

What most surprised some people in our family when that story was dredged up again? It wasn't the disturbing suggestions about my grandfather's racial attitudes. It wasn't that he might already have developed the reflex of us-versus-them. It was that a young Fred Trump, who was work-work-work-all-the-time, would ever make the effort to attend a political rally as a twenty-one-year-old. Something must have motivated him to slip away from one of his construction sites. Normally, he wasn't public-spirited enough to bother.

And then there was this: I was nine and had just gotten a new bicycle. I was riding between our apartment building and Jamaica High, the largest public high school in New York City, which would eventually be closed because of poor performance and rampant violence. Three teenagers confronted me. They were tough-looking Black kids, bigger than me. I was a skinny white boy with white-blond hair, and none of my friends were around.

"Gimme your bike," one of the kids demanded.

It was a Signature blue Schwinn Sting-Ray. Awesome banana seat, the kind where my sister or one of my pals could hop on right behind me. It had the high sissy bar to the middle of the back. It had a long, cool front fork. You sat back like you were riding a Harley.

No wonder they wanted to steal it.

I gripped the handlebars one last time. I did not want to give up that bike. But in the moment, that's what I did.

I knew if my dad had been there, he'd have said that was the right approach. Since he wasn't, I had to improvise.

I said, "Oh-kay . . ."

What was I supposed to do? It was a great bike. Just not that important. I didn't need to fight for it. Three of them and one of me. Not very good odds. Two of the boys had already grabbed me hard and weren't letting go.

I wasn't hurt. Rattled? Sure. And they had taken my bike.

I went home and told my mother. She called the 107th Precinct, which covered our part of Queens. She also called Uncle Donald.

I don't know how they did it. But a few hours later, the police called to say they had one of the young robbers in custody. They also said they'd recovered my bike. Donald drove me to the police station on Parsons Boulevard.

I can still remember how vehement Donald was. "You have to charge him," he told the desk sergeant. "Don't just let him go. He needs to be punished. You gotta lock him up."

"Yeah, I hear ya," the desk sergeant said noncommittally.

I didn't feel strongly about that one way or another, and I never heard what the police decided to do. I was grateful I wasn't hurt and grateful the cops had found my bicycle. I just wanted the boy to get home safe and me to start riding again and call it a day. But I never forgot Donald's heated words.

I couldn't say I was surprised almost two decades later when Donald took out full-page ads in the New York City newspapers, demanding harsh punishment for the Central Park Five, Black and Latino teenagers accused—wrongly, it turned out—of brutally assaulting a young white female jogger.

"BRING BACK THE DEATH PENALTY," the headline said. "BRING BACK OUR POLICE!"

Suddenly, I was right back at that precinct in Queens.

Uncle Donald, meanwhile, was busy assuming control of what I'd always thought of as "my grandfather's company." Clearly, that wasn't how Donald saw it anymore. At twenty-six, he had his own ideas about where the future was, and my grandfather had seemingly signed on to all of it.

"Donald is the smartest person I know," he told *The New York Times* in 1975, a comment I'd heard in various forms at my grandparents' dinner table. "Everything he touches turns to gold."

The point of that article was to describe how a renowned family-owned real-estate company that had helped define Brooklyn and Queens was now launching an exciting push into Manhattan. Or as I heard Donald put it: "Come on, that's where the real money is." My father was still working there, but he wasn't even mentioned in the *Times* piece. His next younger brother had his hands on the wheel now, and everything in the family was revolving around him.

"The big change in Mr. Trump's operations in recent years is the advent of his son, Donald," the *Times* said. "Born in 1946, Donald is the second youngest of five children . . . and the only one of them to display an interest in real estate."

Well, that last point was kinda true.

In the accompanying photo, Donald is standing beside his mustachioed father, who is wearing a polka-dot tie, a topcoat, and a German-style homburg. In those days, Grandpa often stood on his tiptoes in photos to match Donald's height. Behind them is the Brooklyn skyline, dominated by Trump Village, just the kind of outer-boroughs development the family company was famous for and was now said to be moving away from.

Here was Donald's trajectory as my father gradually flamed out: He first started working in the company's Brooklyn headquarters while he was still in college, then came on full-time when he graduated in June of 1968. It was a meteoric rise from there, especially once the military draft was no longer a threat. In 1972, he was handed the title of company president as my grandfather kicked himself upstairs to chairman of the board. It was right around then that Donald suggested a new name to reflect his grander ambitions, the Trump Organization. And Donald was fast becoming the Donald the world would get to know.

Brash. Opinionated. Unapologetically bullish on *Donald*. And now he was gazing across the East River at the bright lights of the future, otherwise known as Midtown Manhattan. By contrast, my father had gone from reluctant heir apparent to disillusioned scion to TWA trainee to family-business returnee. There was no doubt who held the future in his hands.

But wait.

The company's outer-boroughs history couldn't be turned off overnight. There were still some lingering—let's call them *issues*. The National Urban League had sent Black and white "testers" out to rent Trump-owned apartments. A clear pattern emerged. The white applicants were offered leases. The Black applicants were not. It didn't take long for the Civil Rights Division of the United States Justice Department to sue the company for violating the 1968 Fair Housing Act by refusing to rent to Black people.

My own mind went back to The Highlander. There had not been too many Black folks in those elevators.

There was a burst of bad media, something our family wasn't used to, not after all those Horatio Alger–type of stories about my grandfather's rise. All the New York papers covered the latest uproar. *The Village Voice* was especially relentless. "Racially discriminatory conduct by Trump agents has occurred with such frequency that it has created a substantial impediment to the full enjoyment of equal opportunity," one Justice Department official said, hitting all the legal buzzwords.

As the negotiations got rolling, Donald's new vision had to be temporarily sidelined. Manhattan would have to wait.

This was a painful period for the company and therefore for Donald, as the negotiations ground on. All the publicity was bad publicity. The "r" word—"racist"—was thrown around.

No one really contested the basic allegations. But cases like this one all tend to settle out of court, and that is what happened here. By 1975, the lawyers for the company and the Justice Department were able to negotiate what they called a "consent decree," which basically added up to: "We don't admit any guilt here, but we won't do it anymore."

And life could go on.

Once the case was over, Donald could really chase his dreams across the East River. He had his father's blessing. He had his father's funds. He had his father's credit rating. His older brother had been fully neutralized.

It was full speed ahead.

PART II

BREAKING US

CHAPTER 10

FREDDIE'S DEAD

One day in the future, my uncle Donald would shock the world by winning an important election. But let me point out that he wasn't the first member of the Trump family to confound the experts with a stunning victory at the polls.

That would be me.

And I have to give at least some of the credit to my restroom hand towels.

The paper kind.

The ones that roll out of a boxy metal dispenser on the lavatory wall.

I knew all my opponents in the race for Student Council president. They were friends of mine. That's what happens at a small school like Kew-Forest, where I'd been with some of my classmates for the full twelve years. But that didn't mean our race for Student Council president wasn't highly competitive. To have a chance, I knew I'd need to reach my fellow students in unexpected ways.

Something more than colorful posters in the hallway. Something more than a promise of less homework or improved lunchroom cuisine.

Brand-savvy me took a low-tech approach. After school, I unlocked the big rolls of paper towels in the student bathrooms. I took the rolls home and handwrote over and over on each of them, "FRED FOR PREZ . . . FRED FOR PREZ . . . FRED FOR PREZ." I must have written that slogan a few hundred times. Such dedication.

Early in the morning, I put the rolls back in before anyone noticed they were missing. All day long, my campaign rolled out . . . literally. To lock in the brand for the rest of the school, I got a couple of giant poster boards and placed them on the sixteen-by-sixteen-foot wall at the entryway, right where everyone came through the door. You couldn't miss them.

FRED

FOR

PREZ

No exclamation points. Just clean, clear, very accessible.

Okay, maybe my slogan lacked the universality of Donald's "MAKE AMERICA GREAT AGAIN," a phrase that, by the way, had also been used by Ronald Reagan, Bill Clinton, and Hillary Clinton over the years.

In any case, mine worked.

When all the votes were counted, I came out on top. These people knew who I really was. They'd been with me for years. They'd seen me up close and personal, going through all kinds of stuff, good and bad.

Kew-Forest hadn't been able to tame my uncle Donald. But the people there gave me room to fly.

Not too many people can say this, I know. But high school was a great time for me. It really was the culmination of all I'd been through so far, emphasizing the good parts and getting past some of the bad. Learning to navigate such a rambunctious extended family. Surviving my parents' divorce. Being there for my mother and sister. Focusing on my father's many good traits even as he had trouble taming his demons.

It's surprising, isn't it? Even people who are struggling, as my father was, can have a positive effect on those around them. My father certainly did on me. With a deep reservoir of patience, he taught me how to drive. I always felt welcome to stay with him, wherever he was living at the time. Though his pilot's career failed to take off the way he dreamed it would, he shared his love of flying with me and delighted in watching me embrace the airborne thrills that he had.

It started when we had that place out in Montauk, a long-ago casualty of the divorce. Back then, he had a Cessna 172. He taught me all about that plane. By the time I was fifteen, he was picking me up early in the morning at our apartment in Jamaica and driving me out to the airfield in Islip, Long Island, for lessons with a flight instructor he knew. The instructor put me through all my drills. He recorded everything I did in a leather-bound training log, carefully initialing each new milestone. One day, the instructor said to me: "Let's fly out to Brookhaven."

Brookhaven was a decommissioned Navy base with long, broad runways.

We took off. We landed. As usual, I handled some of it, and my flight instructor handled the rest. It was all going smoothly, when he said to me after the third or fourth landing: "Pull over there." And he started to hop out.

"Where are you going?" I asked him.

"You're going to solo," he announced.

That's when it hit me. "Wait a second. Do you know I'm fifteen?"

"What?" he said, incredulous. I guess he didn't. "You're fifteen? How did you get your medical clearance?"

Actually, I knew exactly how that had happened. My dad *knew a guy*—the chief medical officer at the FAA, who also happened to own a horse ranch in Montauk. The FAA doctor signed something that put me in the cockpit, no more questions asked.

My instructor didn't like the sound of any of that.

"Kid," he said to me, suddenly sounding all serious and official, "let's go back to Islip. We can't do this now."

I was so disappointed. With those jumbo runways, Brookhaven would have been an ideal spot to solo for the first time, like learning to drive in a Walmart parking lot before the store opened for the day. And I certainly *felt* old enough. I'd done my drills. My father had taught me a lot. But I knew it would be only a few more months. I just needed to be patient, still not one of my greatest skills.

I knew I'd be back. And I was.

After years of prodding from the family and his friends—and maybe some soul-searching of his own—my father decided to give rehab a try. Maryanne drove him out to the Carrier Clinic in Belle Mead, New Jersey, a supportive gesture she would find many occasions to mention in the future. The place sounded nice enough, "a safe, compassionate, respectful environment, set on a beautiful, 100+ acre country setting, in the foothills of the Sourland Mountains." I got a postcard my dad sent the day he arrived, saying he was doing great, was enjoying the countryside and was ready to take a break from the booze. The very next day, he left the residential rehab facility and never went back.

They say you have to be ready. My dad would never be ready.

It was heartbreaking. It was like he had just given up.

There weren't many secrets in the Trump family. Who in our family had the self-control to keep a secret? Whatever people were thinking—about each other, about anything—it just came right out in the open.

"Your dad couldn't do it," Donald said the next time I saw him.

That was true, though I'm still not sure why his younger brother felt the need to rub it in like that.

Not long after that, my father and I were in the car together. I was driving him back to my grandparents' house, where he was staying at the time. We were just talking about stuff, nothing important enough that I can even remember. But I can recall exactly where we were—on Highland Avenue and 168th Street, a short walk from the F Train station—and as long as I live, I will never forget what my father said to me that day.

"You know," he said, "you have inherited a bad gene."

A bad gene? What was he getting at? He didn't wait for me to ask.

"You have to be very careful about drinking," he said. "Never forget that."

I was still seventeen, but I knew everything he had gone through with alcohol. How it had drowned his dreams and narrowed his horizons and how hard it had been to shake. I never thought that drinking was my father's main problem. His issues went deeper than that. There was all that stuff with his father and his middle brother and all the expectations inside the family. There was the way he was pushed into and then out of the family business. The fact that he'd never quite been able to find his own way. The drinking, I was convinced, started out as a way to suppress all that and to ease his fear and anxiety. But if you drink enough—and you're inclined in that direction—the drinking can also become *the* problem all on its own.

I still marvel at the courage it must have taken for him to say that to me, after the price he had already paid.

"Thanks," I told him simply.

I would take his warning to heart. In the years to come, we'd have to see if I could also put it into action.

• • •

There was no doubt what I'd be doing after high school. My parents expected it. My grandparents expected it. All my teachers expected it. In our senior class of twenty-nine at the Kew-Forest School, *everyone* was going to college. Harvard, Dartmouth, Johns Hopkins—the fat envelopes came from all kinds of fancy places. My cousin David was already off at the University of Chicago. My great buddy Michael Siegel, who'd been in my class since first grade, was bound for Amherst. As I've mentioned, I certainly wasn't the scholar in my immediate family—Mary had that all sewn up—or in my 1980 graduating class. But I was definitely going to college.

I applied to a bunch of schools, and Rollins College was one of the ones that accepted me. Rollins had a beautiful campus amid the palm trees and red-brick walkways of Winter Park, Florida. Olympic swimming pool. High-dive platform. A campus where you could enjoy every imaginable sport under a blazing Florida sun. To me, Rollins was the Harvard of the South. Ah, there's nothing quite like slalom runs around alligators or hitting the wake on trick skis on Lake Virginia.

I had some really good professors there, who continued to encourage my love of reading and history, watering the seeds planted so painstakingly by my great teachers at Kew-Forest. I was thrilled to be on my own in Florida and thrilled to be at Rollins. In a way, it was like going to camp on Cape Cod, except that I spent time in the library and my stay could conceivably last for years. When I didn't make the varsity soccer team my freshman year, my dad tried to soothe my disappointment. "You're going from a small pond to a big pond," he told me. Even though Rollins wasn't *that* big a pond, it was a whole lot larger than Kew-Forest.

Once I was away at college, my dad really began to deteriorate. The alcohol wasn't only sabotaging his life plans now—it was also robbing his health. He was sick a lot, in and out of the hospital, and not feeling so hot even when he was back at his apartment. When he felt a little better, he did small maintenance chores at some of the family apartment buildings, but as the year rolled on, that became even more sporadic. I visited him whenever I was back in Queens for a long weekend or a holiday, and my dad always seemed excited to see me. Though his energy level was just above lethargic and his face was pale, he rallied whenever I appeared.

We talked about all kinds of things. What I was studying in college. How I liked Florida. Any news about my grandparents. How the weather had been. As usual, we didn't talk a lot of sports. He certainly had no interest in sports other than fishing and boating. Every way and every day, he remained his own person. The black sheep of the family. The adamant free speaker. Not a member of anyone's tribe.

At the same time, he certainly didn't seem inclined to change the behavior that was so obviously destructive to him. Really, what incentive did he have? His marriage was over. His children were growing into adults. What exactly did he have to get straight for? His pilot dreams were ancient history. He'd already made clear how he felt about being part of the Trump family business. A lot of this was in his mind. But in his mind, he was truly trapped with no way out.

He got occasional calls from his Lehigh fraternity brothers, but when I was there, I never saw anyone from the family stopping by. I got the strong impression that their visits were few and far between. He did mention Rob, which made perfect sense to me. Donald or Maryanne must have assigned that task to him. "You go visit Freddie." That way, the other siblings could feel like they had discharged any duty and didn't have to feel guilty about leaving their ailing brother alone. He asked about Mary, but I don't think they were in much contact by then. She never said to me, "I'm going to see Dad," and he never said, "I saw Mary."

They both missed out, but I didn't press either one of them.

By the start of that summer between my first and second years at Rollins, his hospital stays were getting more frequent. I visited him at Jamaica Hospital, the well-endowed medical center that for decades had been a favorite charity of my grandparents. That's where Donald and several other family members were born. That's where my grandmother went whenever she needed to. Jamaica Hospital even had a Trump Pavilion for Nursing and Rehabilitation. I'd driven past it hundreds of times when I was on the Van Wyck. Now it felt different. My father was there in a battle for his life.

But that didn't mean my father had lost his spirit. He never did. Even at the lowest point, some part of that spirit still shone.

When he wasn't in the hospital, he was often staying at my grandparents' house. Not in his childhood bedroom. In the attic. Where Mary and I used to stay sometimes as kids when we spent the night. There were a couple of twin beds up there that looked like army cots. To me, this felt like the low point. I visited him several times, but I'm not sure how many of my relatives climbed the stairs to look in on him. As far as I knew, the only other person who stayed in the attic was the housekeeper.

Until my dad.

He didn't complain about it. Not to me, at least. But here he was, a grown man, living on and off in his parents' house—and he didn't even get one of the bedrooms. It was a big, fancy mansion, but these were not fancy accommodations, though later on as he deteriorated, he did move for a little while into Rob's old room. To me, the scene did not feel right.

And soon, he was back in the hospital.

That's where he was the next time I went to see him, which was January 1981. After we caught up, he handed me a bank withdrawal slip, already filled out. "Go to Chase," he said. "Get this amount of money. I want you to buy a Polaroid camera."

I was thinking, *Great, a camera . . . I could sure use one of those during the three weeks I'll spend overseas as part of my second semester.* I went to the bank like he asked me to. I found a store that sold Polaroid cameras. I chose one of the nicer models and brought it back to the hospital. My father seemed like he'd been waiting for me.

"Okay," he said, "there's a young girl down the hall. She has cancer. I don't think she's going to last much longer. And she wants a camera. The nurse will show you her room. Give the camera to the girl."

Wow.

Here I was, thinking, *Oh, boy, I'll be taking this camera with me to Europe.* But my father's gesture was so moving, I didn't mind that he had a different plan. This was even better. Beneath all the pain and torment, yes, that indomitable spirit still shone.

That told you everything you needed to know about Fred Trump Jr. The life was slipping out of him. His biggest dreams had crashed and burned. He had every reason to feel bitter and disappointed and mad. And yet . . . and yet . . . he still had the deep-down instinct to care for someone else—*the underdog,* as he would say. There was no point at which he couldn't take the time to be kind to another person.

There was so much love and passion inside him. Despite it all, he was just a good, good guy.

September 27, 1981. A couple of weeks into my sophomore year at Rollins. The phone rang in the common room of my dorm. It was 6:15 in the morning.

"Trump!" a bleary voice called out. "It's for you."

Mena Bonnewitz was my mom's first cousin and my "surrogate mother" while I was at Rollins. She and her husband, Van, lived in Orlando, about twenty minutes from campus. I had known them and their kids all my life. They were a great Catholic family. When I came down to Florida for college, they kept a friendly eye on me. They often had me to their house for Sunday dinner. They tried to stay in touch. Still, this was unusual. They didn't normally call at 6:15 a.m.

"Hi, Fred. It's Mena. There's an art exhibition going on at Rollins this morning. Sheila and I are going to go over there. Can we stop by?"

"Okay," I said. "Sure."

Something was strange about all this. I hit the shower, took an aspirin, and drowned my eyes with eye drops. I didn't overthink what was going on. I'd long since learned not to go looking for trouble. If trouble had my name on it, it would surely find me soon enough.

Standing in the door of my dorm room, that's where Mena and her daughter broke the news. "Fred," Mena said right away, "your dad passed away last night."

Instead of telling me over the telephone, I guess my mom had asked her cousin to do it in person. If I needed an embrace or a shoulder or anything in that moment, Mom had made sure I'd be taken care of.

I heard her words without really processing them. I just kind of let the message sink in. I took a hard breath and gritted my teeth. I wasn't rattled exactly. I was numb. *Okay,* I thought, *at least I won't have to go to an art exhibit.*

After the time I'd spent with my father that year, I can't say the news was a big surprise. Standing there in the door of my dorm room, all I really knew was that I had lost my father and my life would never be quite the same again.

"We have a reservation on a flight for you. I know you'll want to get up there."

I did. I wasn't looking forward to anything that was about to happen, but I couldn't imagine not being there.

And then there was this: The flight from Orlando to JFK was on a

TWA Boeing 707, the exact aircraft my dad had trained on. He loved the 707 and knew every inch of it, from its swept-wing design to its Pratt & Whitney JT3C turbojet engines to its six-abreast seating in economy. I spent the whole two hours and forty minutes thinking how sad it was that my father wasn't in the cockpit.

What might have been.

CHAPTER 11

SO LONG

It's surprising all the places your mind can go while it's wrestling with something difficult. I wasn't only thinking about myself as I tried to come to grips with the news about my father. I was also thinking about my little sister, Mary. Neither of us was at home when we heard.

Mary had just started the eleventh grade at the Ethel Walker School, a private all-girls boarding school on the former Phelps-Dodge estate in Simsbury, Connecticut. Founded in 1911, Ethel Walker was one of America's first college-prep schools for girls. The alumnae include the daughters and granddaughters of some of the most prominent families in the world, last names like Rockefeller and du Pont. The actress Sigourney Weaver went to Ethel Walker, as did Farahnaz Pahlavi, the daughter of the Shah of Iran.

Mary had transferred from Kew-Forest, and it was turning out to be a wonderful place for her. Of course, she was doing well there. I had no doubt she would.

I joked with her about her wanting to go to boarding school. "You'll be the only one there with just three names, Mary Lea Trump," I told her, the way only a brother can talk to a sister. "All the other students will be like Constance Biddle Smith Barrow. They'll have four names, maybe five."

Mary responded with a knowing laugh.

Thanks to my grandfather and now my uncle Donald, the Trumps were becoming a brand-name family well beyond New York. But all that prominent-family stuff was taking a little getting used to. Mary and I still felt most of the time like a couple of kids from Queens.

Mom met me at JFK. We drove to the Port Authority Terminal on the West Side of Manhattan to meet Mary's bus from Connecticut. Then, we headed back to my grandparents' house in Queens. My aunt Maryanne and my cousin David were there. So were Robert and his wife, Blaine. So were Donald and Ivana. She was nine months pregnant with her daughter, Ivanka. Son Donnie, who was three, was playing on the floor.

From what I could piece together, my father was at his parents' house on Saturday afternoon, which would have been the twenty-sixth of September, when my grandfather called for an ambulance. The ambulance didn't take my father to Booth Memorial, where my mother and my grandmother had been such dedicated volunteers, or Jamaica Hospital with its Trump Pavilion. The ambulance crew drove him to Queens Hospital, a sprawling public institution in Jamaica. I'm sure the doctors there work miracles every day, but it wasn't the kind of place most people from wealthy families ended up. He went alone. My grandfather called Donald, who called my mother. "It doesn't look good," Donald said. Not wanting to be alone, my mother went to my grandparents' house. That's where she was when they got the call from the hospital. He'd been pronounced dead at 9:20 p.m.

Frederick Crist Trump Jr. was forty-two.

The date was September 29, 1981. The official cause of death was a heart attack, as a result of alcoholism. By the time I'd flown up from Florida and Mary had come down from Connecticut, the fight about my father's remains had already begun.

Actually, the fight was pretty much over.

My father had been clear: He wanted to be cremated and have his ashes spread across the water. Did he put that in a will or another official document? I don't believe he did. My father wasn't tidy in ways like that. But he'd told everyone in the family, including his siblings, his wife before she was his ex-wife, his children, and, I have to assume, his parents too. There couldn't have been any doubt in anyone's mind. My father wanted to be cremated and have his ashes spread across the water. More than anything, he did not want to be buried in the ground. Had anyone noticed that my father loved planes and boats? Did he seem like someone who'd want to spend eternity six feet under?

My grandparents, for reasons I couldn't fathom, were opposed to his wishes. There was no way they were going to allow it. They simply told my mother, "No."

They weren't strong environmentalists. That couldn't have been it. I really don't know what the issue was, but they were firmly against it. No was no, and that was that.

I hated the symbolism of that. Even in death, my free-spirited dad was being bossed around by his controlling father, and none of his siblings were speaking up.

Everything that happened next was just as sad as I expected it to be.

There was a low-key wake at the R. Stutzmann & Son Funeral Home on Jamaica Avenue in Queens Village, followed by cold cuts at my grandparents' house. Donald and Ivana stopped at the supermarket and brought some platters back. Even though it was Rosh Hashanah, the beginning of the Jewish New Year, several of my father's Sigma Alpha Mu fraternity brothers made the trip to Queens. That was nice to see. They all loved my father—and they *got* him.

To me, so much of this is still a blur. But I know we all stood around and accepted condolences. I'd been to funerals before, but I was always the one saying, "I'm so sorry." This time, I was standing there with my relatives and answering, "Thank you for coming. Thank you very much."

Mary, the aunts, the uncles—everyone was quiet, and not a lot of tears. I kept looking over at my mother. Though she and my dad had been divorced for a decade, there was no denying the connection that remained between them, all the way till the end. And I had to think it was far more than just the fact that both of them were loving parents to Mary and me.

I didn't have to imagine the challenges of being married to my father. I didn't have to imagine because I'd witnessed so much firsthand. But deep inside her, there was no denying that my mother still felt something for my father. She couldn't live with him. He was impossible to live with, given the self-destructive path he had chosen for himself. But that didn't mean the feelings were gone. Partly, it was the memories of all the good times, meeting in the Bahamas, slowly becoming a couple, their exciting young-married years, hosting their friends in Marblehead, bringing two precious children into the world. That's a lot to share, and they shared all of it. It didn't come for free. My mother had to navigate my father's cruelly judgmental family. That certainly took a toll. In their eyes, no matter what she did, my mother never quite measured up. That was painful in ways she could hardly express and had every right to feel. But through it all, she never stopped caring for my dad.

She'd felt the pull of his charisma. She appreciated what a natural dad he was. She was there when he needed her support, like Kansas City with TWA, as long as he would let her provide it. And she was truly saddened, I was certain, that he had to struggle so much to be the person he wanted to be.

My mother could never walk away from him entirely, and, no, she never tried to.

This was her loss too.

• • •

My dad, Fred.
Thanks, Dad, for teaching me to fish
and for the great adventures.

TWA acceptance letter
for Dad

Me and Dad, North Hills Country Club, 1963

Me and Dad, my first flight

Dad, me, and Mom at Gam and Grandpa's house

Mary, Mom, Dad, and me at The Highlander

Mary, Mom, me, and Dad at my grandparents the Clapps' house in Florida

Dad, Mary, and me in the Bahamas

Me, Dad, and Mary, Easter

Mary, me, and Dad in the Bahamas

Dad with members of the Deep Sea Club in Montauk, when he caught the second-largest swordfish, 1968

Mom and Dad with friends at Dolphin Cottage in Montauk

Me at Cape Cod Sea Camps with a
baseball mitt from Aunt Elizabeth

Me fishing on Cape Cod Bay

The Kew-Forest School Class of 1980

Geraldine Ferraro and me
during my 1983 internship
in Washington

Me on honeymoon in
Lake Como, 1989

Lisa and me, 1989

Lisa and me on honeymoon in the Seychelles, 1989

Lisa and me on honeymoon in Florence, 1989

Ivanka, me, and
Donnie at a
family event

Mom and me

Lisa, me, and Mary at an
event for our grandfather

Trump family photo at
Trump Tower

Me and Lisa

Andrea, me,
William, Lisa,
and Cristopher
in Avalon, New
Jersey

Me, Andrea, and
Lisa at Mar-a-Lago

My grandfather and Andrea. Grandpa Mike was thrilled to meet her. My nonnie died too soon.

Gam, Andrea, and Grandpa (great-grandparents to Andrea)

Grandpa, Lisa, Cristopher, Andrea, me, and Gam in "the breakfast room"

Andrea and Cristopher, our second winter in Connecticut

Mary, Gam, Cristopher, and Andrea, lunch in Connecticut

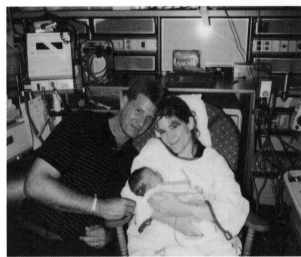

Me, William, and Lisa in the NICU

Andrea, Cristopher, and William in the NICU

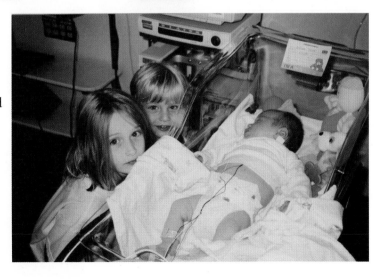

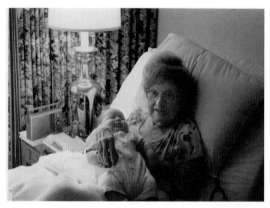

Gam with William

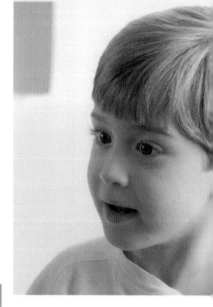

William, 2003

Cristopher and me at
Marine Air Terminal on
our way to Mar-a-Lago

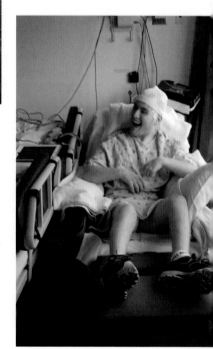

William during a five-day
EEG at NYU just before
COVID

Me in the Oval Office in 2017. Oh, the comments I got.

Me and Donald in the Oval Office, 2018

Lisa, Donald, and me at a birthday dinner for my aunt, 2017

Lisa, William, and me at William's formal at
The Center for Discovery

Our son William.
Thanks, buddy, for teaching us what matters most
and for the great adventures ahead.

No Marble Collegiate Church this time. The service, which was held right in the funeral home in Queens, was nicely attended. I wouldn't call it a large crowd but a nice one. In many ways, my father had faded into himself in the final years of his life. But he'd also touched a lot of people along the way, and those who were assembling all seemed to understand what a tragic loss this was.

I was standing in the back with Donald and Robert as the people streamed in. That's when Donald glanced toward the front of the room and said to me: "Why don't you say something, pal? People would like that."

I was taken aback by the last-minute suggestion. Who else was going to be speaking? The answer to that became quickly apparent. No one. To me, that showed how little thought his siblings had given to the details of the service.

"None of you are going to say *anything?*" I wanted to be sure I understood correctly. "You're leaving it all up to me?"

I got two nods in return.

"Fine," I said. "I will. Of course I will. But am I really going to be the only one to eulogize him? Nobody else is going to say a word?"

What I thought but didn't say was . . . *and you don't have the fuckin' balls to get up there? Or are you just embarrassed that your brother is dead at forty-two?*

I didn't say that, but I can't deny the anger.

And that's what happened. Other than the minister and me, nobody else said a word. Not Donald. Not Robert. Not Elizabeth. Not Maryanne, who had often proclaimed how much she loved my father and how concerned she was about his well-being—and I still think she felt all of it. Neither of my father's parents spoke. Just me and a minister who had never met my father and didn't seem to have made any effort to find out about him.

"I didn't know Fred," the clergyman began. "But I know he was one of God's children . . ."

That's about where I tuned him out.

I'm sure he said something about the afterlife and being with the Lord and death equaling freedom from human suffering—whatever he said, I wasn't paying attention. I was thinking about what actually needed to be said.

When the minister finished his rote presentation, which didn't take long, I walked to the front of the chapel and spoke from the heart.

I said how much I loved my father and his free spirit. I said he had paid a price for that, but he was always true to himself. I lamented how he was gone "much too young." I said that despite the challenges he faced in his own life, he was unfailingly decent to others, strangers and loved ones, worthy or not, right up until the end.

A good dad. A great friend. A kind soul wherever he traveled. But mostly, he was his own person in an environment where that was almost impossible to be.

I didn't get specific about why that might be. Eulogies are no place for score settling. I was up there to give my father a proper send-off and tell him so long.

There aren't a lot of criers in the Trump family. But I saw the Trump-family equivalent—stone, sad faces—all across the room. From Gam especially. It was hard not to feel her pain.

Someone I wanted to single out was my sister, Mary. I had a special message for her.

"Mary," I said, "I know you and Dad had your differences, and you may not have been so close at the end. But Mary, Dad really loved you. He loved you so much."

I knew that was true, and I knew it needed saying. I knew Mom would appreciate it and I hoped Mary would too. No one else was going to say it, so I did.

· · ·

My grandparents got their way on the burial, as I knew they would. After the service, we all rode out to the All Faiths Cemetery, a sprawling property on 225 acres, hard against Metropolitan Avenue in the Middle Village section of Queens. All Faiths was already the eternal home of half a million New Yorkers. With its nineteen miles of roadway and never-ending rows of headstones, the cemetery is unimaginably massive for crowded New York City. Now, it was also going to be my father's permanent address.

The Trump family plot: In a family known for large-scale real-estate developments, this might be the smallest property in the entire portfolio.

As the headstone made clear, my German-immigrant great-grandparents were already there, even if their names were Americanized in death.

"FRED TRUMP," the carved stone said. "MAR. 14, 1869 – MAY 30, 1918.

"ELIZABETH TRUMP. OCT. 10, 1880 – JUNE 6, 1966."

Mr. and Mrs. Fred Zero, where the story of the American Trumps began. The amazing fact that jumped out at me? My great-grandmother had outlived her husband by a full forty-eight years. The Spanish Flu felled him during World War I, and she lived all the way until the days of Vietnam.

By all rights, the next place on the headstone belonged to my grandparents, whenever their time might come. But it hadn't come yet. God willing it wouldn't for a while. So that space below my great-grandparents was still blank. And now, with the death of my father, the natural order of things had been turned upside down. The child had died before the parents. His name would need to be carved next.

When we all got to the cemetery, my grandfather explained that the headstone would be sent back to the carver, who would update it appropriately, then return the stone to its rightful spot. By then, my father's ashen remains would be in the ground beneath it forever more.

Not just dead. Dead and buried. Exactly where he didn't want to be.

I didn't know how to cry. I didn't cry when Mena told me my father had died. I didn't cry at the funeral or the cemetery. I think the last time I cried was more than a decade earlier when my mother told me she and my father were getting divorced. So, I didn't have that emotional outlet. Even I could see that couldn't be good.

That night, after we all got back from the cemetery, I said to my aunt Elizabeth: "Liz, you wanna go to a movie?"

Liz was the Trump sibling known by hardly anyone outside the family. She led a purposely quiet life. Where she got that instinct, nobody knows. She lived at home. She would get married eventually, to a movie producer named James Grau. But that was still eight years in the future. For most of her career, she had worked as an administrative assistant at Chase Manhattan Bank, heading back and forth to Chase Plaza in total anonymity.

She adored me, and I adored her. Really, what wasn't to like? Liz was nice. She was supportive. She seemed incapable of causing any kind of fuss. She drove a powder-blue Ford Thunderbird, which was a lot of car for someone as petite and unassuming as she was. As far as I could tell, she was living the life she had chosen. She didn't have to tell me how hard that was in this family. I'd just buried a father who struggled mightily with that.

"Sure," she said to my movie idea. "What do you want to see?"

"How about *Arthur*? It's at the Midway."

The Dudley Moore comedy had been playing for several weeks by then, but neither one of us had seen it. It sounded like perfect counterprogramming, if there was such a thing, to burying a brother and a father. The Midway was one of our local theaters. It was in Forest Hills, right on Queens Boulevard.

On one level, *Arthur* is a dark romantic comedy about a drunken, spoiled Manhattan millionaire who is about to marry a wealthy heiress when he falls instead for an attractive young shoplifter from Queens. One of the key characters in the movie is Arthur's loyal butler, Hobson, played by John Gielgud. About halfway through the movie, the Gielgud character dies.

"Oh, my God," I whispered to Liz in that darkened theater. "This is what I'm living through." Not exactly, but close enough. My father had just died. And Arthur was left in a family that made absolutely no sense to him.

I headed back to school that next weekend. And do you know how many phone calls I got from my aunts and uncles to see how I was doing? None.

And I still didn't cry.

I spent the rest of the school year at Rollins, letting the Central Florida sunshine bake some of the sadness out of me. But somewhere along the way, an idea got lodged in my mind, and I couldn't seem to shake it.

Maybe I should transfer to Lehigh, my father's university.

I knew how much he loved Lehigh. I'd been hearing Lehigh stories for as long as I could remember. The beauty of the Pennsylvania countryside. The inspiring professors and courses. The camaraderie of the brothers of Sigma Alpha Mu. He'd even picked up some Jewish humor from those guys . . . *Mel Bergstein and Fredzy Trump.* And the Lehigh campus was—what?—two, two and a half hours from Queens? After my father was gone, I felt like I needed to be a little closer to home. Rollins was a fine school, and I was grateful for the time I had spent on campus. But I could also see myself getting into a lot of trouble there.

Academically, Lehigh was ranked higher and therefore harder to get into. But I decided to give it a try. I'd been getting solid grades at Rollins. Who knew? Maybe they'd take me at Lehigh.

I never said out loud that transferring to Lehigh would also be a tribute to my late father. But that element was probably floating in my head somewhere.

Anyway, I completed the application the way you used to, pen on paper. I got a reference letter from the father of my Kew-Forest buddy Michael Siegel, a top Manhattan lawyer, and another one from Sol Magid, one of my father's fraternity brothers at Lehigh. They'd stayed close. My dad and I used to visit Mr. Magid. When I called to thank Mr. Siegel, whom I'd known since I was seven, he joked, "I meant every other word of it, Trump." Mr. Magid sent me a copy of his letter with a note scribbled in the margin: "Let me know when you're accepted."

It didn't take long. When the fat envelope arrived, I thought immediately about my dad. "Dad, we did it!" I couldn't have been more elated.

Then, about a week later, I got another letter on Lehigh stationery. I could hardly believe my eyes.

"Upon further review, we've decided to rescind your acceptance into Lehigh University. We are sorry for this late notice."

The letter was signed, "Sincerely, Godfrey Daniels."

Holy shit . . . I just about fell on the floor. But then it hit me.

Wait a second, I thought. Wasn't "Godfrey Daniels" an expression that W. C. Fields like to use for "God damn"? My father used to say that. "Godfrey Daniels, what were you thinking?"

If I wasn't mistaken, there was also a bar called the Godfrey Daniels in Bethlehem, Pennsylvania, not far from the Lehigh campus.

I knew I'd been pranked.

It turned out that the phony letter had come from a Kew-Forest friend of mine, now a junior at Lehigh, who thought that kind of thing was funny—and had gone to elaborate lengths to give his deceptions multiple levels of meaning. I didn't know whether to admire his crafts-manship or wring his neck. Was it possible to do both? My father prob-ably would have appreciated it, at least in his young days. That was almost a zombie-at-the-gas-pump-Freddie-level prank.

When I looked more closely at the letter, I spotted a couple of typos. But I sure hadn't been focused on that as I saw my Lehigh future evaporating in front of my eyes.

My father knew what he was talking about. I had a terrific experience at Lehigh, where I spent my junior and senior years. The professors were engaged and inspiring. They were there to teach. I studied business, politics, and history, and I kept reading voraciously (a word I'm sure I learned from a book). Ernest Hemingway's *A Farewell to Arms* (thanks to a great professor who actually looked like Hemingway). *The Autobiography of Malcolm X* (with a little help from Alex Haley). Like my father, I also understood: Education isn't only what happens in the classroom. Education is twenty-four hours a day. For me, that also included music, which helped to form me almost as much as books did. How could I not be influenced by seeing The Clash in Times Square or The Ramones in Brooklyn (about twenty times—yes, that probably explains a lot).

I was active in intramural athletics. In a school so large and sports-focused, there was no way I was making any of the varsity teams. I did stuff I had never done before. I wrestled. I boxed. What was I thinking? Did I mention I boxed? I became a major fan of the Engineers, support-ing our teams any way that I could. I loved what everyone at Lehigh called The Rivalry, our annual matchup with Lafayette, the most played college football rivalry in the nation. It goes all the way back to 1884 and has been played ever since.

Every day on campus, I thought about my father and how much he loved his time there. I honored him by doing the same.

CHAPTER 12

TRUE LOVE

L isa and I met at Studio 54.

Wait, I know what you're thinking. Before you start jumping to conclusions about my after-hours credentials, I should probably say that by the winter of 1983, Studio 54 wasn't exactly Studio 54 anymore. Andy Warhol, David Bowie, Bianca Jagger, and all the other 1970s nightlife icons, even Donald Trump—they were long gone by then. I didn't even see any drugs there. But the club had reopened in September 1981, the same month my father died. It was still in the same location on West 54th Street, and they were doing college nights to bring people in. I was twenty, and this was two years before New York State raised the drinking age to twenty-one. So everything that follows was *totally* legal.

My college buddy had asked me that afternoon: "You wanna go to Studio 54? There's no cover charge for Lehigh students."

Sounded good to me, so we drove into the city—about two hours, a little quicker because of how fast we drove.

They had five or six schools that night. We were supposed to meet a friend of mine from summer camp who went to Tufts, but she didn't show. The Michael Jackson music video for "Billie Jean" had just come out, and they were playing that over and over on what must have been a hundred screens. At some point in the evening, I noticed a couple of nice-looking blond women and managed to strike up a conversation.

They were childhood friends, and one of them was named Lisa. She said she'd already graduated and was working in the city at Mount Sinai Hospital.

"That's where I was born," I told her.

I couldn't tell if she thought that was interesting or funny or just an odd thing to say. I was nervous. Studio 54 was not my kind of place. I was self-conscious being there.

I asked her to dance. She agreed. We talked a bit. She seemed really nice and really smart, and did I mention she was attractive? I wore an earring then. She said she liked my earring. She told me she was living with her parents in New Jersey, commuting on the train with her father, but she was hoping to move into the city soon.

It was getting late. I needed to make the long drive back to Pennsylvania. She found a Studio 54 card and wrote "Lisa Lorant" and an address in Princeton, New Jersey.

Hoping she heard me over the music, I promised I'd be in touch.

A few days later, I handwrote a note on wide-lined Lehigh University stationery. "It was very nice (and lucky) meeting you. You're a real nice girl to talk to and sure made my evening at 'Studio' worthwhile."

I told her she was lucky to be out of college and working in the city—at the hospital of my birth, no less—and I had a suggestion for her: "If you are still interested, it would be real great to see you again, perhaps this time in an atmosphere where we don't find each other shouting to get the other to understand what we just said. Anyway, if you would like to get together, please let me know. Anytime is fine—I'll drive 'anywhere, anytime' to see you again.

"Hope to hear from you soon. Take care, Fred."

I guess it must have worked. She called and agreed to go out with me.

She told me later: "When I got a letter from someone named Fred, I called my friend and said, 'Who's this Fred guy who's writing me from Studio 54? I thought I met someone named Craig.'"

What can I say? The music was loud in there.

We went on our first date to the Grand Hyatt on East 42nd Street. Once we settled into the restaurant, I explained that my uncle Donald had renovated the hotel, which was why we didn't have to wait in line. Lisa said she'd never heard of him and didn't seem to have a clue who my family might be.

That was refreshing. It truly was.

She said her father grew up in the city and she'd come many times to visit her grandparents. "I love the city," she said. "I always wanted to live here."

She wasn't the only one who'd approached our date with some confusion about the other person's name. With Lisa's last name and her blond hair and hazel eyes, I thought she might be French. She laughed when I told her that. "No, not at all," she said. "My family's German/Eastern European, and I am Jewish. My mom's maiden name was Schwartz. The reason Lorant might sound French is because of the proximity of the German town my grandfather was from."

Whatever. As Juliet once said, "What's in a name? That which we call a rose by any other name would smell as sweet."

Our chemistry felt natural. She was indeed super-smart, easy to talk to, and she laughed at my jokes. Over the next few weeks, we met up a couple of times and walked all over Manhattan. Eventually, she asked her father, who worked as a business consultant, if he'd ever heard of the Trumps. He told her they were a real-estate family in New York City. He mentioned that a new building called Trump Tower had just opened on Fifth Avenue. But truly, Lisa had no idea what she was getting herself into, hanging around with someone who had so much family baggage, though she would certainly come to grasp it . . . *eventually.*

Our lives didn't sync up right away. I was still finishing college and living in the wilds of eastern Pennsylvania. As the "older woman" in our relationship (by two years), Lisa moved into the city as she had said she would. She was making her way in the work world, shifting from the business side of the hospital to an insurance company. We definitely enjoyed each other's company, but neither one of us was eager to get too serious. After I'd been in the city a little while and before I started working, we flew down to Ocho Rios in Jamaica. We had a wonderful trip, basking in the Jamaican sunshine, spending more time together than we ever had, and still comfortable being ourselves. We went scuba diving, walked on the beach, and squinted at the sunsets. I think Jamaica is where I decided I was in love.

It took a while for me to meet her family and for her to meet mine, which was okay by me. No one had to tell me how complicated families could be.

We invited Lisa's parents and sisters, along with my mom, to all meet each other. The Lorants were very welcoming and very different from the Trumps—and the Jewish-Christian thing was the least of it. Her father, Reginald (he insisted my mother call him Reg), was born in London. By the time we met he had long been a U.S. citizen and was a VP at the consulting firm Towers Perrin. We talked a little bit about colleges and when I would graduate. That's when I learned he was an alumnus of the Wharton School—just like Uncle Donald, but ten years earlier. Her mother, Suzanne, was a social worker in the Princeton area and seemed to like me.

I couldn't help but notice how the Lorants all hugged each other and openly expressed their warmth. By contrast, even the Trumps who loved each other didn't do a lot of hugging. At our family gatherings, you were expected to show up. That was the main thing. All the better if you made some friendly conversation and lighthearted banter. But that was pretty much it. Outside of Thanksgiving and Christmas, you could usually get away with "hi . . . how ya doin'? . . . see ya later."

I guess the way the Lorants expressed themselves is what other families do. I know my Trump uncles rarely spoke to me like that. Occasionally Robert. And when he did, it was memorable.

Lisa and I didn't push anything. We dated on and off for the next four or five years. We just let things unfold. Given where both of us were at the time, that felt like the way to go. I'd finally graduated and was starting my career as a commercial real-estate broker . . . but not at the Trump Organization. I never wanted to do that. There was never any discussion of my joining the family business. No one ever asked me to, and I never assumed I would. I got my own apartment.

In many ways, I was figuring out who I was and what it meant to be an adult. Put it like this: Two steps forward, one step back. I was maturing . . . gradually. As Lisa got to know me better, I do think she grew more curious about my family. She certainly wasn't someone who was impressed by my relatives or a name that ended up in the New York gossip columns. She just wasn't wired that way. She met my sister, Mary, and my cousin David, and they were friendly. Not too revealing but friendly enough.

Lisa wasn't quick to insert herself in any of our family drama. Quite the opposite. She always expressed interest, but she had an appreciation for boundaries. I think you'd call that "finesse." She did say to me at one point: "There must have been a lot of stuff between your mom and your father's family."

You think?

After my father died, trusts were set up for Mary and me. The trusts were funded by minority interests that my father had owned in various Trump properties. After my father's death, those interests went to us— but not right away. Since Mary and I were so young, the assets were put in trust for our long-term benefit. We had two co-trustees, Donald and a longtime family lawyer named Irwin Durben, who would keep popping up in my life. Their job was to look after our best interests. It wasn't a huge amount of money, I was told. In fact, I didn't know how much it was, and a lot of the assets were shares of real-estate projects. Who knew what they might be worth? All I knew was that, every now and then, Irwin would ask me to sign some papers or agree to some legal move, and I would do whatever he asked me to. I have many questions now I didn't have then. At the time, I chose to trust my trustees.

You can't call it quick. But as 1988 arrived, I spoke with Donald about engagement rings. I told him I might be needing one. Since he was my trustee, I knew I would need his permission to use some of my trust money to buy a ring.

"Go see Ralph Destino," Donald said. "He's the president of Cartier. He'll help you pick out something."

Using Donald's name, I made an appointment. Lisa and I were ushered into a spacious office above the legendary jewelry store on Fifth Avenue. Yes, Lisa came with me . . . no way was I doing this alone. Mr. Destino was generous with his time, patiently educating us on what to look for in a diamond, how to tell true quality, which ones were a good investment, how diamonds are cut and how they retain their value. This was all interesting and new to me, even if I did feel like some kind of impostor just being in the president's office at Cartier.

I knew Lisa well enough to know her tastes were simple. I knew my budget well enough to know that mine had to be, even with the trust to help me.

Mr. Destino showed us quite a few beautiful stones. They were all very large, nothing that Lisa could see herself wearing (I hoped) and nothing I could possibly afford. Lisa was the one who politely thanked him for his time and attention and explained that she preferred something more modest. We were taken to a different floor and introduced to an accommodating sales rep, who showed us some other possibilities.

"Did Donald not understand we live a modest life?" Lisa asked me as soon as we got out of there. "We do fine with both our salaries, but we're not buying a ten-carat engagement ring—nor do I want one."

We agreed it had been a fun experience to visit Cartier and learn about the jewelry business from the president. And Lisa said she loved the ring we chose when I slipped it on her finger after officially proposing to her a few weeks later at Windows on the World in the World Trade Center.

We wanted a wedding that would reflect the traditions that both of us had grown up with. Neither of us wanted to define ourselves by our families. At the same time, our families were important to us. We'd be merging our lives now. But we were both strong-willed individuals and didn't have any intention of losing that.

We found an old Quaker meetinghouse in Lawrenceville, New Jersey, a simple white church that was now an interfaith house of worship. It seemed like the right place for our wedding. I joked with Lisa: "I guess they put up a Star of David for one service, then swap it out for a cross in time for the next one."

And what would be wrong with that? Nothing I could see.

As far as I was concerned, life was more interesting when independent-minded people came from different backgrounds and found each other. What that meant for the wedding ceremony was that, next to the altar, we'd have a chuppah, the canopy that couples stand beneath at Jewish weddings, and I'd get to stomp hard on a ritual glass when the time in the service came. I always liked that part, even when they used a light bulb. We set a date, September 16, 1989. To officiate, we enlisted Reverend Daphne Hawkes, a Presbyterian minister, and Rabbi Albert Ginsburgh. It turned out the two of them already knew each other. The rabbi's wife was an OB-GYN, and her patients included Reverend Hawkes.

As I told Lisa, "You can't get much more *interfaith* than that."

We planned a nice-sized celebration—about two hundred people—but not a super-fancy one. The reception would be at a hotel in Princeton. My mom asked if she could take care of the flowers and told Lisa several times how happy she was her son had found such a wonderful bride. When we sent out the invitations, Lisa's relatives RSVP'd immediately. All of them said they would be coming, and I had no doubt they would be there. We invited everyone on my side too. My cousins. My aunts and uncles. Pretty much everyone named Trump. As the responses trickled in, I was pleased to see that Grandpa and Gam were coming. Donald and Ivana also said, yes, they'd be there, as would all three of their children, Donald Jr., Ivanka, and Eric, ages eleven, seven, and five. So did my aunt Maryanne and her husband, John, and my aunt Elizabeth and her new husband, Jim, and my uncle Robert and his wife, Blaine, and their son, Christopher.

My cousin David, Maryanne's son, agreed to be one of two best men, along with my Lehigh friend Bob Guth. Lisa's sisters, Gabrielle and Stephanie, were her maids of honor, and my sister, Mary, was one of the bridesmaids. Everything seemed to be coming together nicely, and everyone seemed ready to have a good time, despite whatever sadness and other hard feelings might still be lingering from my father's early death.

We truly had something to celebrate. I was marrying the woman I loved and wanted to share my life with, and I was lucky enough that she felt the same way.

As the date approached, we got word that Donald and Ivana might need to be in Atlantic City that night for the Miss USA Pageant. They still hoped to be with us, they said, but we weren't sure of the timing. Donald had someone call the church to see if there was a spot nearby to land a helicopter. But when the big day arrived, the weather was rainy, not ideal for helicopter landings. Donald and Ivana arrived by limo, slipping into the church just as Lisa was about to walk down the aisle. Lisa waved. They smiled and found an empty pew.

After the ceremony was over, Donald and Ivana stayed for a quick family photo, congratulated Lisa and me, then said they needed to get back in their limo and leave at once for Atlantic City. They wouldn't be staying for the reception. And once we all arrived at the reception, we got a second surprise. Donnie, Ivanka, and Eric hadn't come at all.

Uncle Robert was the one with the practical idea. "Is it okay if we add a chair to our table for Christopher?" he asked Lisa. His son was going to be with Donald's kids at the young cousins' table. Now, there was no such thing.

"Of course," Lisa told him. "Totally fine."

Before everyone sat for dinner, Uncle Rob stood and delivered a gracious toast to the man who was most obviously not there . . . and I don't mean Uncle Donald. Robert and Donald's *other* brother, my father, who'd been dead for ten days shy of eight years. As the day approached, I'd been thinking a lot about him. It was, more than I'd even expected, incredibly sad not having him at my wedding, and clearly, I wasn't the only one who felt that way.

"Fred, your dad would be very proud of you," Uncle Robert said.

Lisa squeezed my hand, knowing better than anyone how hard it really was.

I know people are expected to say nice things at weddings, but I really appreciated my uncle saying that. This family had its issues. That was crystal clear. But it was good to see that, once in a while, some of them could show some grace.

As Lisa and I had our first dance, slides were being projected on the wall opposite the dance floor, special photos from the Trump and Lorant families that Lisa and I had picked out. Her late grandparents. She and her sisters in their backyard. Me in Montauk as a child and on the wing of a plane, probably my dad's. A family photo of my mother, my father, Mary, and me. Lisa and I when we were first dating and through our years together. And one more: a warm, relaxed portrait of just my father and me when I was five or six years old.

One image at a time, they told the stories of our lives.

My Trump relatives were all at one table now. Rob, Blaine, Christopher, Gam, Grandpa, Elizabeth, Jim, Maryanne, and John. Those pictures really seemed to strike a chord with them, especially that shot of my father and me. He'd been gone for almost eight years by then. I still missed him every day. I felt a huge hole in my heart, not having him at my wedding. And clearly, I wasn't the only one who felt that way. Everyone was stuck on their memories of my dad.

What exactly were they feeling? They didn't say anything, but I had a pretty good idea. Loss. Shame. Guilt. Love. Disappointment. Wistfulness about what might have been. And a whole lot more, I'm certain, all rolled into one. All of it in the long shadow of my father not being there. I hoped it was cathartic for them, that it brought some kind of comfort. At least they were experiencing it together.

I caught a glimpse of Gam.

As that father-son photo appeared again, my grandmother sat still as a statue, not moving at all. Her jaw was open. She was staring straight ahead. All that activity around her, and she wasn't noticing anything . . . except for that image from the past.

She had earned that feeling of loss, and she made no effort to hide it. Her pain was visible on her face.

Gam was a tough Scottish lady who'd learned over the decades to keep her emotions on a very short leash. She'd raised five children, three sons and two daughters. And all these years later, four of them were getting on with their lives. They had careers. They had spouses. Two of her sons worked in the family business, the business their father had founded and Donald now ran. There was plenty of money to go around for everyone. Even with the usual ups and downs of the real-estate industry, no one in this family was ever in danger of missing a meal.

And yet . . . talk about a mother's heartbreak: She couldn't say any of that about the child who was missing that night. It just wasn't fair.

He was her first, and in many ways her most promising. And for a pile of complicated reasons—something inside him, pressure from his father, the grip of alcohol, who really knows?—that great abundance of promise had evaporated much too early for him.

At forty-two, her boy was gone.

As my father's son, I'd spent my young-adult life trying to process this and never quite succeeding. It had to have been even harder for Gam. There was no part of me that was burdened with self-criticism or blame.

For nearly eight years—and quite a few years before that—she had learned to bury those feelings and live with that hole in her heart. She had other children and grandchildren to look after. She had other demands on her attention and time. There was no point in wallowing in ancient sadness. Hard as it must have been for her, she had to move on.

Had a picture at my wedding brought it all back? On a night of celebration, she was feeling all that pain.

I thought about going over to her. But I could hardly fathom what she was feeling, and I didn't know what to say.

I had lost my father, and she had lost her son.

Those first few years of our marriage, looking back on them now, were absurdly carefree.

Lisa and I both loved living in the city. Everything felt exciting to us. We were gaining confidence, settling into our careers and delighting in each other's company. I was really enjoying commercial real estate, beginning my steady climb up the industry with a series of rising positions in solid companies, none of them named "Trump." No one ever had to wonder if I was really earning the job, or only riding my family name.

Two professional incomes, a nice Manhattan apartment on the Upper East Side (that had once belonged to my aunt Elizabeth) and no kids yet . . . what was there for Lisa and me to worry about? We had lots of people to hang out with—friends from childhood, friends from college—and no more grades. When Lisa got pregnant in 1993, she decided to stop working and devote herself to being a mom. "I don't want someone else raising my child," she said. "We can live without my salary."

"Fine with me," I told her.

Gam even offered to host a baby shower, a thoroughly generous gesture that did cause an unintended flutter of cross-cultural angst. Traditionally, Jewish moms-to-be don't like to receive baby gifts before the baby is born. It's thought to be bad luck. But when Lisa consulted with her mother and her mom gave the green light, the shower was promptly scheduled and judged a rousing success.

Thanks, Gam.

Five days before Christmas 1993, the same day Donald was set to marry his second wife, Marla Maples, our daughter, Andrea, decided, *This might be a good day to be born.* First thing that morning, we took a taxi to Mount Sinai . . . and waited and waited and waited. Apparently, our baby was in no particular rush now. "Walk the halls," the doctor suggested. "That can loosen the levers of the birth canal." Lisa and I paced the hospital hallways for hours, nudging our baby out.

Andrea Karen Trump got the middle names of Lisa's two sisters. Holding her for the first time was just as emotional an experience as I imagined it would be. Overwhelming. Andrea was an amazingly easy baby, even for a couple of first-time parents like us. Many new dads imagine having a son first. I loved having a daughter.

Right around then, I was thinking we might be ready to find a house and move to the suburbs. Lisa was resistant at first. Very. She loved being in her "little city cocoon," as she called our Upper East Side neighborhood, pushing Andrea in her stroller to Jodi's Gym, the 92nd Street Y, and Central Park. But once another baby was on the way, Lisa agreed the time had probably come. At some point, wouldn't our children want their own bedrooms and a nice backyard? We found a house in Connecticut, an easy commute for me on the Metro-North Railroad and plenty of room for a growing family to spread out. Twenty-three months after his sister joined our family, we had Cristopher Frederick Trump, who got my (and my father's and grandfather's) first name as his middle name and our middle name—minus the "h"—up front. Anything to avoid the *IV.* It was time to stop counting, I thought.

Having a son was the blast I always knew it would be. Cristopher was curious, energetic, and filled with life. He was into everything. He wasn't big on limits. He had one speed—full speed ahead. In no time, we had a wonderful group of friends in Connecticut. The adults were friends. The kids were friends. We found a terrific nursery school around the corner, and we all got close to the director. To this day, she swears we were the best group of families she'd ever had, and I don't think she says that to every class. And in the fall of 1998, Lisa learned she was pregnant again.

Life was sweet. We were all moving forward.

Lisa and I were both thrilled to add one more to our growing family. We had room in our house and room in our hearts. Andrea and Cristopher were just as excited as we were. They couldn't wait to welcome a new baby into the family.

CHAPTER 13

FAMILY VALUES

For me, young adult life was becoming one big multitask. I was almost never doing just one thing.

At the same time I was meeting, courting, and marrying Lisa and starting a family with her, I was also graduating from college (summer of 1984, after making up a few stray credits), starting to make a living, launching a career, juggling the ongoing dramas inside my own family, figuring out who I was . . . and learning to hit a little ball a couple of hundred yards down a grassy fairway into something the size of a Dunkin' Donuts coffee cup.

The small one.

I was always a natural athlete. On the soccer field and the basketball court, I was known for my fluid movements and my hand-eye coordination. But when they say "golf is a lifetime sport," they don't only mean you can play into your seventies and eighties. They also mean it just might take you the rest of your life to learn how to hit the damn ball right. Thankfully, I had a knack for it. Who knew I would meet friends for life on those courses.

For me, the golf seeds had been planted years earlier by my uncle

Donald and, even before that, by Gam's sister's husband. When I was little, I used to visit Aunt Joan and Uncle Vic in Florida. My folks would put me on a plane alone, and I'd stay a week, sometimes two, at their house in Riviera Beach, where I had my own bedroom and endless hours to run around in the sunshine. They had no kids, and they couldn't have been more welcoming to me.

Like the MacLeod sisters, Uncle Vic was from Scotland. He had supposedly worked as a butler to a member of the British royal family, though he was tight with the details and some in the family cast doubt on the entire claim. But no one could possibly doubt Uncle Vic's deep affection for the Scottish invention of golf. When I was visiting, he'd watch hours of golf on television, and he kinda got me addicted to the whispering commentators and the high-anxiety putts. And then a few years later, when I was back in Queens, Uncle Donald started taking me with him—not to actual golf courses but to the public driving range in Douglaston.

"Hey, pal, you wanna go hit some?" he'd ask.

The answer was always yes. Donald was a good golfer, and I picked it up fast.

Now that I was starting to make my own way in the world, I was finding my own courses, learning how the game can also be a personal journey, a social outlet, and a business tool—and embracing the lifelong time-suck that goes by the name of golf.

Give my grandfather credit: He had an uncanny knack for living up to his hype.

Back in the early days of his company, he (and his PR reps) liked to compare his rise to that of the boyish heroes in the nineteenth-century novels of Horatio Alger, young strivers who came from nothing and, against all odds, ended up on top of the world due to their extraordinary grit, cleverness, and hard work.

Well, damned if my grandfather didn't win the 1985 Horatio Alger Award.

It's a legitimate thing. It comes from the Horatio Alger Association of Distinguished Americans. Recipients include Johnny Cash, Tom Selleck, Ronald Reagan, Hank Aaron, Bob Hope, Ray Kroc, assorted captains of industry and finance—it's an eye-popping list. And now, Fred Trump. Lisa and I felt honored to be in the Grand Ballroom of the Waldorf-Astoria Hotel for the Horatio Alger Gala, along with Gam and all my grandfather's living children and their spouses, as television's Art Linkletter, another past recipient, extolled his remarkable climb: "He knew even as a youngster he wanted to work with his hands."

True. To a point.

My grandfather was never a terrific public speaker, which was a little strange given how many Rotary, Lions, and Kiwanis luncheons he must have addressed over the years, not to mention zoning boards and tenants' associations. He read from a piece of paper that night. "This is indeed one of the high points of my life to receive the prestigious Horatio Alger Award," he said.

And then he got to the meat of his remarks.

"Students have come to me and said, 'What is the secret of your success? Tell me so I can make it happen.' I tell them there is no secret. There are just two things. One, you must like what you do. You must pick out the right business or profession. You must learn all about it. Learn everything there is to know about it so you become enthusiastic about it. Nine out of ten people don't like what they do, and in not liking what they do, they lose enthusiasm and go from job to job, and ultimately becoming nothing."

It was a great message. Find what you like and like what you do. And despite the slightly stiff delivery, the people in the room seemed to warm to it. But I couldn't help but wonder: What about my father?

How come *he* couldn't be allowed to do what *he* loved? Why had my grandfather pushed him into the family company? When my grandfather mentioned certain people "ultimately becoming nothing," who was he thinking about?

It's a painful irony: my grandfather grasping the overwhelming importance of pursuing a personal passion, then denying that same opportunity to his own son. "Remember," he said before he finished his remarks and headed back to his seat, "you have to find your spark in life because, in each and every one of us, there is a tank full of gas, and they call it enthusiasm fuel, and only you can ignite it."

My father had felt that for flying. Just not for real estate.

It couldn't have been an accident that I ended up in commercial real estate.

I'd grown up around the business, after all, though watching my father's rocky relationship to the field probably should have sent me running for the emergency exit. The lesson I learned from his bitter experience wasn't that there was something wrong with the industry. I'd seen my grandfather and a couple of uncles make successful careers in real estate. The lesson I learned was, "Don't work for your family." And I vowed that I never would. My father might have had a smoother run if he'd worked for the Dursts or the Silversteins or one of New York's other family building dynasties, although I'm not sure he ever would have loved the field. It's no place for free spirits. But maybe he wouldn't have been judged so harshly and he might have been spared the need to take everything so personally.

Who knows?

My first job out of Lehigh was at Edward S. Gordon, one of the largest real-estate service companies in New York. The company leased office space, ran buildings, and advised clients on all aspects of that world. It was Lisa's dad—no one in my family—who helped connect me with this position (though Donald would later take credit, giving me a fun opportunity to set him straight). I went from there to being an owner's rep at First Winthrop Corporation, which would lead to a four-and-a-half-year run at Shorenstein Realty Services. At every stop, I learned more about the business and learned what I was good at—mainly dealing with people.

In that way, I really *was* my father's son.

Even though office leasing was becoming increasingly tech- and data-driven, the real decisions were still being made by human beings. For me, that meant getting to know our clients, their customers, and everybody's needs. Finding things to like about a lot of different kinds of people. And selling. Plenty of selling. Taking people out to dinner. Meeting for drinks. Organizing golf outings. Making human connections in the business world, often lubricated by alcohol.

I know that's supposed to be an old way of doing business. Well, I can promise you this much: It ain't dead yet, not in this industry, anyway.

One of the great satisfactions for me was knowing that I was being judged on my own. By my performance. By my relationships. By my hard work and reputation in the industry. Not by my DNA.

Did it help that my name was Fred Trump? You know, I've thought a lot about that, and my answer might surprise you: On balance, I think it's hurt more than it's helped. People in the industry had heard of Fred Trump, my grandfather. And when I introduced myself, I would often get the raised eyebrow of recognition. *Yeah, I've heard that name!* But as time went on, as my grandfather got older and less engaged, as my uncle Donald got more famous and increasingly controversial, there would be plenty of people who recoiled at the Trump name.

I had accounts I was pulled from. I had deals where I was told, "Stay in the background, okay? Keep a low profile." There were clients and companies that simply would not deal with someone named

Trump. And eventually, some client at dinner, three drinks in, would be asking me to defend some crazy political position that had nothing to do with my own views and chances are I didn't even agree with. There were a lot of exchanges along the lines of:

"How can you defend that?"

Donald was a showman. Bombastic. And most of his comments that made news were things I disagreed with. I spent a lot of time reiterating, "I don't defend it. I don't even agree with it."

It could be a Trump lover or a Trump hater, either one. There were plenty of both. But the name was increasingly becoming a lightning rod in the real world. And I didn't live in the bubble of the family company. I was out there on my own every day.

I understood. All families have baggage. But some days, it felt like I was hauling around a steamer trunk.

That said, the vast majority of my experiences in the work world were highly positive. I was doing well in my career. I got increasing levels of responsibility. I had great relationships with my bosses and colleagues. My income kept rising. I enjoyed going to work and serving the clients and making deals and doing it my way, on my own. And in the end, no one was going to sign a million-dollar lease just because one of the people on the other side of the table was related to someone. I just hoped it didn't turn them off so quickly they wouldn't hear what I had to say. And usually that worked out fine.

Still, the T-name was always there, and I understood: It always would be. I just didn't know quite how much.

I had a decent job. I was making decent money. But there was still no doubt who my grandfather was and what that meant to him, me, and everyone. I put some money down and got a car loan from Apple Bank to buy a five-speed Saab 900 turbo convertible, black with camel interior. It was a beauty. I drove to my grandparents' house. I'd been seeing signs of my grandfather's advancing dementia, and I was about to see another one. He was standing out on the front steps, looking down on the driveway, when I pulled in.

"Grandpa," I called up to him. "Look at my new car."

And what were the first words out of his mouth? Not "nice wheels." Not "drive safely." Not "can you take me out for a spin?" None of that. Fred Trump's mind drove in an entirely different direction.

"How much did it cost me?" he asked.

What?

"How much did it cost *you?*" I responded. "No, Grandpa, I bought it myself."

And you know what? I'm not sure he believed me.

That was my grandfather's world through his eyes. Everything that was ever done by anyone around him, he always figured he was the one who had really done it, and he was the one who was going to pay.

As if we needed any more proof that New York was becoming rougher: My seventy-nine-year-old grandmother was out shopping in Queens on a quiet Thursday afternoon in October 1991 when she was mugged. A teenage boy—police later identified him as Paul LoCastro, sixteen, of Flushing—shoved her to the sidewalk and grabbed her pocketbook, which contained fourteen dollars. Her face was cut. A couple of ribs were fractured. Her hip was bruised. And a high-adrenaline drama broke out on the block when a Wonder Bread driver, who was sitting in his truck, saw the mugging, chased the suspect into an underground passageway of a nearby apartment building, and recovered my grandmother's pocketbook.

Who says New Yorkers all look the other way?

Why would this happen to my seventy-nine-year-old grandmother?

I was steaming mad. And I was also upset that no one in the family bothered to call and tell me about what had happened to Gam. I had to hear about it from a friend who heard the story on WINS radio. I drove immediately to Booth Memorial. When I walked into the emergency room, Rob looked shocked to see me, like, *What are you doing here? How did you find out?*

I don't think anyone was purposely trying to hide my grandmother's mugging. But it was a mindset. I tell that story because it illustrates how—after my father's death, especially—people in the family were starting to think of our branch of the family as second-tier Trumps.

Yes, we were still related . . . but not quite on the same level as everyone else. As if my father's death—and maybe even his life before that—had broken some kind of chain. That wasn't at all how I saw it. This *was* my family. Gam was my grandmother as much as she was David's, Donnie's, Ivanka's, or Eric's.

"Why didn't someone call?" I asked Rob as the ER docs were stitching Gam.

He just shrugged and mumbled, "I dunno."

Gam seemed thrilled to see me. "Oh, thank you, dear. Thank you so much for coming. You know what I could really go for? One of those butterscotch milkshakes they have at Carvel's. Do you think you could get one of those for me?"

Absolutely.

I told her I'd be happy to, and I kept going back to see her, in the hospital and at home, bringing her milkshakes and holding the straws up to her lips, until she was all healed and fully back on her feet.

Two words defined Donald's personal life in those years.

"Tumultuous" and "public."

And the New York tabloids could not get enough.

He and Ivana had been married since 1977, having met the year before when the Czech-born beauty was visiting New York City with a group of fashion models. She'd been an avid skier back home (though maybe not a member of the Czech Olympic Ski Team as the rumors had it). But Ivana had lots of charisma and tons of energy. After their marriage, she threw herself into Donald's business, logging seven years as a senior player in the Trump Organization, while also becoming a mom to her and Donald's three children, Donald Jr., Ivanka, and Eric. As executive vice president for interior design, she'd guided the inside look of Trump Tower, which emphasized pink marble, and also played major roles at the Trump Castle casino and Plaza Hotel. She was great with the media and was credited with giving her husband his force-of-nature nickname, *The Donald.* But by 1990, when Donald Jr. was thirteen, Ivanka was nine, and Eric was six, the marriage was kaput. What happened next might have been the worst divorce ever—or the best, depending on whether you hate or enjoy that sort of thing. (The papers loved it. Donald promoted a lot of it and then complained about it. The kids were caught in the cross fire.) The media pumped up the contrast between the European Ivana and Donald's new love, the blond-haired beauty queen and fitness model from Cohutta, Georgia, Marla Maples. It was all summed up February 13, 1990, with Marla's headline quote on the front page of the *New York Post:* "Best Sex I've Ever Had."

You can imagine how this went down inside the Trump family.

They all blamed Marla.

She seemed nice enough to me. But when Donald started bringing her around to family gatherings, I couldn't help but notice: Maryanne and the others took one look at his "Georgia peach," as the New York tabloids kept referring to her, and gave her the same cold shoulder they'd given to my mom and to Maryanne's husband, David.

She's not good enough.

As usual (except in the case of her husband, David), Maryanne was the one leading the charge. "They're not *simple*," she huffed after some of Marla's family members arrived for the Christmas week wedding and reception at the Plaza. "They're *simpletons*."

Hearing this made me think of how they had talked about my mother, who thankfully wasn't there. I didn't find it funny at all. Marla looked beautiful. Her family seemed like nice people to me. I had left my wife at Mount Sinai to be at what felt to me like an important family event. I wasn't sure why everyone needed to be so mean. Donald obviously loved her. They had a beautiful two-month-old baby, Tiffany. To me, it all just felt like smug cruelty.

I couldn't stop thinking: Imagine how Tiffany would feel? I could mentally deflect this idiocy. But imagine how painful it would be for their children to deal with it. Their infant daughter would grow up and learn about all of this gossip and hostility. I kept saying to myself: This needs to end.

Donald, of course, didn't back down an inch. The guests included Rosie O'Donnell, O. J. Simpson, Susan Lucci, Adnan Khashoggi, Evander Holyfield, Don King, and *Lifestyles of the Rich and Famous* host Robin Leach, who breathlessly declared: "This is the equivalent of Westminster Abbey tonight. It's Charles and Diana all over again. You know what happened with that."

My eighty-eight-year-old grandfather looked a bit wobbly as he came in to perform his duties as Donald's best man. It was Rob who guided him in the right direction and reminded him what those duties were. "You just have to stand there and hand Donald the ring when he asks you to."

Thankfully, Grandpa kept his balance through the ceremony, even if some of the others in the family seemed to have lost theirs.

The high point of the night for me was meeting Howard Stern, who I had listened to for a long time. The low point had to be missing my wife and new baby girl and watching my grandfather struggle. He had become increasingly isolated, seeing fewer and fewer people and sticking to specific, routine daily tasks. Him being out in public, trying to navigate an unfamiliar environment—that was hard to watch. Later, some of my relatives would claim that his dementia began much later than this. Not true. The night Donald married Marla, Grandpa's decline was on full display. I left the reception and went right back to the hospital to Lisa and our new baby, still in my tux.

I really felt for Donald and Ivana's three kids. I'd been there. I'd had the experience of my parents getting divorced. I remembered how painful that was for Mary and me, and our parents didn't blast their messy bust-up on the front pages of the *Daily News,* the *Post,* and *New York Newsday.* There'd never been a more public divorce than this one. I made a special effort with the boys, taking Donnie to New York Jets games and to private ice-skating lessons with Rod Gilbert. Donnie was just then learning to skate, and both boys loved meeting the Hall of Fame New York Rangers hockey star. As time went on, we could go months—more like years—between our visits. But I still remember a great day going for pizza with Eric and stopping at Woolworth so we could get him some Play-Doh. They were good kids in a tough situation. The same way Robert and even Donald had made an effort with me after my parents' divorce, I wanted to do the same with these kids. It faded over time, but I felt like it was the right thing to do, and they seemed to appreciate it.

Donald stayed in the papers—the business pages and the gossip columns in roughly equal measure. And he was getting more and more opinionated on political issues and events. Not running for anything. Not yet. But clearly whetting his appetite for that part of public life. Living in Connecticut had put another bit of distance between us and my aunts and uncles and cousins, all of whom were either in Queens or Manhattan (when the cousins were home from boarding school). There were no more weekly dinners, not that we were invited to. I was also busy with my own family now.

That last development did seem to cause a note of friction I never would have predicted.

Maryanne was upset.

I guess it was a competitive thing. She was perturbed at me—and this wasn't just my impression, I heard about it from others. She didn't like the fact that I had gotten married and begun a family *before* her son, David, had. He was the oldest grandchild, after all. She thought he should get to go first. The way she reacted, it was like I'd been caught cutting in line in the school cafeteria.

Honestly, it never occurred to me that birth order determined marital order or parenting order or anything like that. (When David got married at the Plaza Hotel in 1992, I would be there as his best man.) But now, I had met someone I loved. We were ready to start a new life together. We hadn't exactly rushed into anything. It wasn't like we were all that young. But Maryanne's lingering irritation was impossible to miss. Like I said, in this family, there's always a lot of stuff floating around.

My grandfather's decline wasn't smooth and steady. Advancing dementia rarely is. He'd seem okay some days. Then, he'd be really out of it. He'd remember some things and not other things. It was often hard to predict which. He still liked going to the office, even as Donald Manhattanized the company, further and further from its outer-boroughs roots. Work had been such a huge part of my grandfather's life and his identity, it was impossible for him to walk away. Work *was* Fred Trump. At the same time, Gam was having her own health issues. Her arthritis was constant and painful. Her osteoporosis made walking an excruciating grind. With her brittle bones, she constantly seemed to be breaking something. I felt bad for her. I stayed in close touch with my grandparents, Gam especially, who still seemed to love my company. Stopping by to visit whenever I went to see my mother. Bringing her favorite treats from Carvel. Gam still loved those butterscotch milkshakes. Though I couldn't ride my bike to Jamaica Estates anymore—that would have been tough from Connecticut—my mother was still in our Highland Avenue apartment. It was easy enough to swing by Midland Parkway.

Friday morning, June 25, 1999. I was driving to the train station on my way to the office. I had a cell phone from work, and it rang. It was my cousin David.

It was one of those calls that felt foreboding from the very first ring. It was early for David to call.

"Grandpa died," he said. "We're all meeting out at the house."

Instead of driving to the train station, I headed straight to Queens, which put me on the Van Wyck Expressway close to the Trump Pavilion sign at Jamaica Hospital. I'd always thought that sign was a tribute to my grandmother's volunteer work and my grandfather's financial generosity, though Donald would later say the family had paid $60,000 to have the family name up there.

"Good advertising," he said.

When we all got to the house, Maryanne turned to me and said, "We'd like you to be one of the family members who eulogizes your grandfather, and we'd like you to focus on your grandfather and your father." Grandpa was dead, and Maryanne was in charge.

I told her I'd be happy to. It was a subject I had plenty to say about.

CHAPTER 14

SPECIAL DELIVERY

I got home from my grandfather's funeral—and the short Trump Tower reception that Donald hosted afterward—and went straight to bed. Lisa's water broke around 1 a.m. She wasn't late. She wasn't early. She was right on time. As the contractions got closer, we made it from our house in Connecticut to Mount Sinai Medical Center on the Upper East Side of Manhattan without even driving fast.

Having been through this twice already, both of us had a pretty good idea of what to expect. The ultrasound, the amniocentesis, and the other prenatal tests—they were all normal. Lisa's energy was remarkable, especially since she'd been spending her days running around after two supercharged little ones. The entire buildup to number three had been just about as smooth as could be, even with the late-breaking funeral.

And now here he was.

William Crist Trump, all eight pounds and six ounces of him, was a big, feisty, healthy-looking baby boy with bright blue eyes, eyes that would only get more expressive over the years. The official time of birth was put at 6:25 a.m. on June 30, 1999, just in time for breakfast. We gave him my middle name. And Lisa and I picked William because of his fierce spirit and potent will.

His first eighteen hours were just as smooth as the previous nine months had been. He cried a lot, but then a lot of babies cry. Andrea and Cristopher were itching to meet their little brother. We were excited to get him home. As far as we knew, the biggest challenge we faced was the immediate prospect of sleep deprivation. With a five-year-old, a three-year-old, and an infant, there'd be no such thing as eight uninterrupted hours, not anytime soon.

That afternoon, I performed my usual Dad inventory. Toes . . . *check*. Fingers . . . *double check*. Baby's mighty heartbeat . . . *triple check*. I *oohed* and *aahed* over our newborn. Maybe I was biased, but this was one beautiful boy, just about ready for the world. Lisa and I laughed and talked and watched the news on the hospital room TV.

I went home to be with Andrea and Cristopher for what I could see was going to be a two-book bedtime. They were so excited about their new little brother, I had to read two books before I could get them to calm down enough to sleep. I picked two of their favorites, *Where the Wild Things Are* and, especially, *Goodnight Moon*. To me, reading *Goodnight Moon* to my young children was one of the great small pleasures of fatherhood, some of the best times I ever had as a dad, capturing that tender moment of bidding goodnight to all the things that surround us. I can't count the nights I watched my kids drift off to sleep by the time we got to Margaret Wise Brown's perfect wrap-up: "Goodnight stars, goodnight air, goodnight noises everywhere."

I stopped back at the hospital first thing in the morning to check in on baby and mom. "I couldn't get him to stop crying," Lisa said, "but everything seems fine. I'm just really ready to go home."

The last thing she wanted was me hanging around the hospital, as she took some quiet time with the baby. I know I can't sit still, and didn't want to be annoying. Paternity leave wasn't a thing in my business yet. So, I left the car in the Mount Sinai garage and took a cab to the office to catch up on work. Things did not stay calm for long.

For Lisa and William, this was bonding time. A nurse came down the hall, pushing a neonatal bassinette. "Here's your son," she said brightly.

He was still a little fussy, and Lisa kept doing what she could to soothe him.

It helped for a minute. But then he started crying again, and soon he was making a gasping, gurgling sound.

What does that mean? Lisa's maternal instinct was already shifting into high alert.

When she asked for the nurse, she was assured there was no cause for worry. "It could be extra fluid from the birth," the nurse said. "That happens. Sometimes, the fluid stays in their lungs or their mouth. We can take him to the nursery. The pediatrician will have a look." And when the nurse rolled William back half an hour later, she said: "Everything's fine. The doctor didn't find anything."

Over the next several hours, as William kept crying, Lisa did what good moms do. She picked him up. She embraced him. She placed him gently back in the bassinette. Her eyes never left her son. At one point, while she was holding him, she felt something she hadn't felt before.

His body suddenly stiffened. His head jerked forward. His muscles tightened up.

What is happening with my baby?

Then, he began to turn blue and desperately gasp for air.

Lisa hit the red bedside alarm and called out for help.

This time, the nurse came bolting down the hallway. She took one look at William and declared: "I'm taking you back to the nursery." With Lisa one step behind her, they made it as far as the locked nursery door. Apparently, hospitals had started locking the doors of their nurseries, a security measure so no one could steal the babies. Good idea. But that extra caution was costing precious seconds now.

"Open the door! Open the door!" the nurse yelled as she also banged on the window.

Maybe the staffer at the nurse's station was on a phone call or trying to sort out an insurance issue. It could have been anything. But someone finally pressed a button. The nursery door popped open, and a moment later, the nurse was calling for a doctor too.

What no one realized that morning—not the nurses, not the doctors, not Lisa, certainly not me—was that our healthy-looking baby boy had just had a special kind of seizure not often seen in newborns. One of many to come. In infants, seizures don't look like seizures, not the wrenching kind with unnatural body movements and facial expressions. When it's a baby, the muscles in the arms and legs tighten while the head bends forward. There isn't much to see this early. It's not violent. It's subtle. It's just there. That little stiffening along with a momentary loss of control. And it can be deeply damaging to the early development of a child.

Even now, I hate the fact that I wasn't at the hospital for these scary early minutes. I don't know what difference it would have made, but I should have been there with Lisa as all the drama began to unfold.

The Insignia real-estate company was at 200 Park Avenue, the north side of Grand Central Terminal. Suddenly, my assistant was running down the hall.

"Fred! Fred! You have to get back to the hospital!"

At that time of the day, early afternoon, I knew the subway would be quicker than hailing a taxi. So, I hopped on the Lexington Avenue train and rode to 96th Street with a full-on sprint for the final blocks to Mount Sinai. As I stepped out of the elevator on Lisa's floor, Lisa was standing there. We locked eyes as I caught my breath. A nurse was with her and so was William. I could immediately tell that Lisa was alarmed. They were all getting into the elevator I had just gotten out of, on their way from the nursery to the Neonatal Intensive Care Unit on the third floor.

I stepped back in with them and down we went.

"Wait here," the nurse said to us when we reached the door of the NICU, leaving us in a little waiting area as she rolled William inside. "We need to get him settled first." Through a double-paned window, I could half see the rows of incubators. Many were empty, and some were being attended to by people in different-colored scrubs. Soon, they had William in one of the incubators and were connecting his tiny body to lines and tubes and monitors and I don't know what else. Every time the door swung open, I could hear the beeping and buzzing. Someone said we needed a "metabolic workup." I saw someone taking blood from William, more blood than a little baby should be able to give. I didn't know half of what was going on. To have William in there and us outside, that was terribly frightening. Something was seriously wrong with our son, and no one seemed to know what it was.

They finally let us in for a short visit.

William looked so tiny in his incubator and so vulnerable. Yet as I looked around, I could see he was also one of the biggest babies in the room. Most of the infants in the NICU were born prematurely. William had had a full nine months of beefing up. And now our little big man was connected to a bird's nest of wires, probes, and monitors. Wristbands. Leg bands. IVs. Lines in and out. Bright lights blazing overhead twenty-four hours a day. Medically, the pediatrician explained, they were working to calm him down. But the seizures, or whatever they were, kept coming. And coming. Whatever was happening to him—the stiffening and gasping for air and all the rest of it—they needed to figure it out. They hoped the right medications might help. Phenobarbital. Dilantin. There would be quite a few doctors in and out over the next few days besides William's pediatrician. A cardiologist, a pulmonologist, a gastroenterologist, a pediatric neurologist, a metabolic specialist, and probably two or three others. They were putting the "intensive" in the Intensive Care Unit, summoning whatever troops they had.

And they still didn't seem to know much.

As someone—I forget who—explained to us later: It's especially risky when seizures happen so soon after birth, before the brain has had a chance to get up and running. The newborn brain needs to boot up and be ready for the world. The doctors said all this with much more medical jargon, but that was the basic point, and I didn't like the sound of any of it. Fluid in the lungs seemed like something that could be drained or might even evaporate. But some unknown kind of seizure, what one of the doctors said could be a serious issue with William's brain, that was in a whole different category.

As Lisa and I tried to grasp what was happening, there was no way to know how much of this William was processing. He looked like a healthy baby . . . when he wasn't gasping for air or turning blue. In our emotional trauma and in his, I couldn't help but wonder, how much of this would he remember? Whatever happened in these early days, I knew, could have a profound effect as long as he lived.

When visiting hours were over, a nurse said to us: "We have a room where you can stay tonight."

That seemed like a good idea. We were both exhausted and emotionally drained. The bed was more of a gurney than a bed, but it would do. Lisa and I lay there and stared at the ceiling. I could feel Lisa crying. Something different was happening to me. *Breathe, man, breathe.* I wanted to say something. I wasn't sure of the words. Now, I was breaking down, too choked to say anything out loud. Then, my eyes started welling up. I hadn't cried up to this point. It was such a shock, and lying in bed, decompressing, I felt an overwhelming rush of fear. *Just keep breathing, man.*

"I'm trying to get my head around all this," Lisa said.

Me too, I told her. "It's a lot to absorb."

In less than twenty-four hours, our son had gone from seemingly healthy to fighting for air and fighting for life. What he was experiencing looked like seizures, but no one in this well-respected hospital was proposing anything like a solution or path forward. If the professionals were worried and confused, then *holy shit,* where did we go from here?

After a few hours of tossing and turning and being mostly awake, I told Lisa, "I think I should go home and be with Andrea and Cristopher." They'd been with various family members since we left for the hospital.

I drove the car out of the parking garage. It was still dark outside. There was no traffic, no life, on the FDR as I headed north toward Connecticut. The road home was a blur while I worked to clear my mind. When we had driven to the hospital, we brought a car seat with us, expecting to put our son in it for the drive back home. But now, a bleak new reality was tugging at me: Our boy was still in the hospital. We didn't know how long he would be there. We didn't know what anyone could do for him. And I was driving back home with an empty car seat.

That empty car seat . . . an awful image that lodged itself in my brain. One I would never forget.

It was just before dawn when I pulled into the driveway. I grabbed the car seat and took it inside with me, dropping it on the floor of the family room. It didn't seem like something we would be needing for a while yet.

• • •

As all this swirled around us, Lisa and I did what we could to keep each other calm. I kept telling her, "It'll be okay . . . We don't know what it means yet, but we'll do what we have to do . . . We're in good hands here . . . We'll figure it out . . . We know people. We have resources . . . We have each other."

That last part was crucial. I couldn't imagine going through something like this without my wife of almost ten years. She was the practical one. She was the tough one. But both of us were heading into unknown territory. And I could see the fear in her eyes, just like I had to assume she could see the fear in mine, though in my case "terror" was probably a better word. But we couldn't afford to start asking a lot of "what if" questions. The future was both inches and miles ahead. We had to take this as it came. We had more than enough to deal with in the here and now.

And to add a practical note, these early events were unfolding just as New York City was emptying out for the Fourth of July. You do not want to be in a hospital at the beginning of July. That's the changing of the guard over to the medical residents, the young doctors-in-training who end up providing a lot of the hands-on care. The senior physicians all seemed to be in the Hamptons or the Hudson Valley or somewhere else they spent their holiday weekends. I knew no one was intentionally hiding anything from us. Despite my rising anxiety, I wasn't paranoid. But there was an awful lot of hurry-up-and-wait, and the doctors sure seemed young.

Whenever a new baby arrives, everyone tries to be upbeat and excited. I understood that. And we didn't want to alarm our families. But it seemed like we should let people know what was going on, the basics anyway. We'd just had a baby. They'd want to know, *How's everything? Fingers, toes, hair or no hair?* People always want to know. I stayed in touch with my mother and my sister, Mary. Lisa did the same with her mom, her dad, and her two younger sisters, Gabrielle and Stephanie. All of them were supportive—and concerned. "Let us know what we can do . . . We're here for anything . . . You want us to come to the hospital? . . . Should we go to the house and be with Andrea and Cristopher? . . . Whatever you need, just let us know."

That's what families do, right? Close, loving families.

And what about the other Trumps? The truth is, not one of them called.

They all knew we were having a baby. They'd just seen Lisa *out to here* at the funeral. But nothing. Not a peep.

Instead of getting pissed about that, which I certainly could have, I decided to reach out to Uncle Robert, give him a rundown, and let him tell my grandmother. Word could filter out from there. I'd seen Rob a few times not so long before. We'd been to a couple of soccer games. But when I called Rob's apartment, his wife, Blaine, answered the phone. We'd met soon after she and Robert started dating. Back then Blaine worked part-time at Christie's, the famous Manhattan auction house, and had a fun personality. We'd agreed to meet for lunch.

"Let's go to Burger King," she had said.

To me, Blaine seemed more like a lady who would power lunch at Le Cirque or Michael's, but her suggestion made me like her even more. We went for Whoppers several times before she and Robert got engaged, though we hadn't seen each other as much since then. Still, she'd always been friendly and nice to me.

But when Blaine answered the phone that day and I asked to speak with Rob, she sounded a little put off.

"Oh," she said flatly, "he's really exhausted with the funeral and everything. He's heartsick about his father."

That seemed a bit much to me, given what I was calling about. Was Rob really so broken up about the death of his ninety-three-year-old father that he couldn't even come to the phone? "Well, let me tell you what's going on," I said to Blaine.

I gave her a quick summary of what we knew about William. All fine at the beginning. Then, the scary stuff. "They are running tests," I said. "We're waiting for the results. It may have something to do with his brain. We don't know how long we're going to be in the hospital. It could be a while."

"I'm sure he'll be okay," Blaine assured me, trying to sound encouraging, I suppose, but not quite seeming to grasp the enormity of what we were up against.

I did mention one other thing. "When our first two kids were born, we took them to visit Gam when they were really little. Blaine, that is not going to happen this time."

For whatever reason, that seemed to get through to her. "Oh," she said. "I see. I really appreciate your call. I'll tell Rob, and we'll let Gam know. I know he'll want to talk to you."

It was hard to know how much of this Andrea and Cristopher were grasping at five and three years old. But they certainly noticed that the baby they'd been hearing about hadn't come home yet and their parents hadn't been around much either. We didn't want to overwhelm them with too much information. At the same time, we didn't want to sneak around. We just tried to keep our explanations brief, follow their lead, and answer whatever questions they had.

"William has something wrong," Lisa said. "We don't know what it is. We're trying our best to help him feel better."

Lisa's explanation seemed to do it for a while. As long as the older kids felt safe and loved, the rest was just another job Mommy and

Daddy had. Thankfully we had lots of family help. My mother, my sister, Mary, and Lisa's mother and Lisa's sisters all pitched in, just like they had promised to. So, Andrea and Cristopher had loving caregivers they were already comfortable with. In a crisis like this one, nothing beats strong support from family. And we also had a terrific young woman who helped with the two older kids, who'd been with us for a year.

When I got back to work after the holiday, our office manager pulled me aside for a quiet conversation. "We have a tradition at Insignia," she said. "Whenever someone has a baby, we send a teddy bear."

"That's nice," I told her, wondering what she was getting at.

"Would you like us to send one?"

Just as I was saying "sure," it hit me. She'd heard our son was having serious issues in the hospital. She had no idea which way this would go. She didn't want to do anything that might add to our upset, like having a stuffed animal arrive if, God forbid, William didn't make it. I caught my breath and said to her, "We'd love a teddy bear." I could feel her relief immediately.

Clearly, I needed to get used to talking about this to other people. It did not come naturally.

It took a few days, but Rob did call back. He asked how our son was doing. I gave him the abbreviated rundown. I told him we might be in for a long ride here with a lot of medical care and that William's future was still a big question mark.

"Listen to me," Rob said reassuringly. "Whatever it takes. Just do it. Get him the help he needs. Don't worry about anything."

That made him the first Trump to reach out after William was born and express any kind of concern, even if was just returning my call. I especially appreciated his message. It had been a little weird, not hearing from my father's side of the family in those early days while my mom and Mary and the Lorants were so engaged and helpful. But the Rob on the phone that day sounded like the Rob I'd known as a kid. Warm. Concerned. Generous. Interested in how I was doing. "You holding up okay?" he asked.

I told him I thought I was . . . considering.

"Whatever it takes," he said again. "Don't worry about anything."

Before saying goodbye, I told Rob how relieved I was to get his call.

For part of the time William was being treated at Mount Sinai, Lisa and I got a hotel room so we'd be closer to the hospital and wouldn't have to drive back home every night. Every time the room phone rang, both of us gasped. It usually meant bracing ourselves for more bad news. But one time, we were pleasantly surprised. It was one of the nurses calling to say William was taking breast milk through a bottle and reacting well to it. That meant Lisa should be able to nurse him just fine.

Doctors had worried that our son might not be able to metabolize Lisa's breast milk. But his physical growth remained strong, one of the bright spots on his medical chart.

Amid so much bad news, it was easy to go overboard when something good happened, and I guess we did just that cheering the breast milk report. At the same time, these successes were rare enough that they *had* to be celebrated, even the small ones.

"And damn it," I vowed to Lisa, "we're gonna celebrate every last one of them."

One day, without warning, my grandmother called. She had heard from Robert, she said. She asked about William and said she was looking forward to meeting him whenever the time was right. I told her how sad

I was about Grandpa's death and asked how she was holding up. I said I was looking forward to introducing her to her new great-grandson.

"That would be lovely, dear."

Warm all around.

But Gam wasn't just calling to check in. She also had a favor to ask. She said she had some relatives visiting New York from Scotland, and she wondered if Lisa and I would be willing to have dinner with them. "It'll be good for you to get away from the hospital," Gam said.

I couldn't argue with that. Gam had a point. Lisa and I had been consumed by all the madness since William was born. I told Gam we'd be happy to see her relatives. We arranged for my mother to come to Mount Sinai and stay with William the night of the dinner.

As Lisa and I walked into the restaurant, who should be eating at another table? Donald and his girlfriend, the Slovenian model Melania Knauss.

He barely looked up from the table as we passed. "Hey," he said, "I hear your kid's pretty sick."

I nodded. "He is."

And that was it. The extent of our exchange.

We had a nice dinner with Gam's relatives.

Even now, it is impossible to fully describe what a shock all this was to Lisa and me, to go from thinking, *ho-hum, our third kid,* to facing the painful realization that number three wouldn't be anything like the first two. And we didn't know the half of it. We didn't know the *tenth* of it. Just to visit our son, we had to walk through a series of heavy, sealed doors. Each time, I didn't know if I had the courage to go inside. We never knew what we might confront on the other side of those doors. To me, it felt like a prison in there. A place they locked our children away, separated from the people who loved them. Sometimes, Lisa and

I were told to stay outside, and we had to stare in through the window. I couldn't help it. I had to squint to see the digital readouts for William's oxygen level and his pulse rate—and would root for improvement like I was sitting in the bleachers at a Lehigh basketball game.

"Come on, come on. Get over ninety. Get over ninety!"

"They'd better not go down," I'd say fervently to myself.

And I kept wondering: Are the nurses paying close enough attention? What happens if the readings drop again? From hour to hour, we just didn't know.

Though the explanations came maddeningly slowly, we picked up little snatches here and there. "This isn't normal," I overheard someone say one morning as Lisa and I were heading in see William in the NICU.

I hated that "normal" word when I first heard it in the hospital. I hate it even more now. I realize millions of families have been through traumas like this one. I suddenly had immense appreciation for all of them. When your kid's the one in the Neonatal Intensive Care Unit, it's hard to keep things in perspective.

For some reason, cerebral palsy came into my mind. I am not sure why. I knew nothing about it except that I remembered they had the CP Telethon, which was hosted by Dennis James and had Burt Reynolds and James Brolin. On that telethon every year, they did local cut-ins for the New York audience, thanking local people who made donations. That part was hosted by Jack Hausman, an Austrian-born textile manufacturer who was a friend of my grandparents. His son Peter had battled cerebral palsy, and the father went on to cofound the organization United Cerebral Palsy. My sister and I had donated one time, and I still remember when Mr. Hausman singled us out: "And thanks to Fred and Mary Trump of Jamaica, Queens, for their five-dollar gift." Truly, I had no idea that my own infant might one day have a profound medical issue or whether the catch-all designation "cerebral palsy" would have anything to do with it. But at times like these, that's the kind of thing that can bounce around your mind.

In fact, it would take another fifteen years—*fifteen!*—before William's medical team could accurately pinpoint the cause of his condition: a KCNQ2 mutation, a genetic misfire that the doctors called a potassium channel deletion. At that point, all we had were questions: What would the future hold for someone like William? How far could he go? How much could he learn? Would he ever have the chance to do the things that other children do?

We just didn't know.

As his hospital stay ground on, things got tense at times. At one point, the Mount Sinai doctors told us William needed an MRI, but it might take a while to schedule it. *What? How could they make us wait?*

I called a friend of mine who I thought might know the right people at Mount Sinai. Maybe he could lean on someone to hurry the test. Then word came back: The reason for the delay wasn't a backup at the hospital. William was considered too young for an MRI. He still needed a few more days. His brain wasn't ready yet. The medical system is a puzzle. Sometimes, you just have to wait for the pieces to fall into place. And when we finally got the MRI, it came back inconclusive.

Shortly before we left Mount Sinai, Lisa and I were walking on Fifth Avenue. I said to Lisa: "What's he gonna be like?"

She shook her head. "I don't know."

"I really hope there's a time in his life he will be able to say, 'I love you.'"

"I hear you," she said. "But I don't know. That's almost kinda selfish. I don't need the words. I just want the feeling. But for you to say that, that's huge."

Already, this child was making me feel things I had never felt before. Fear. What would the future be like? Was William going to be okay? Mainly, I felt helpless.

• • •

William ended up staying three full weeks at Mount Sinai, most of that time in the Neonatal Intensive Care Unit. The NICU was a trying, emotional place—so much vital work going on at once. But the more time we spent there, the more I came to appreciate the tireless talent of the doctors and nurses and all they had to juggle. It's not somewhere anyone goes unless they have to. But let me tell you, if your kid needs it, you sure are glad it's there. They are saving lives in there every day. William was discharged from Mount Sinai on July 20, three weeks after he was born, with "no known diagnosis." His medical chart mentioned a "seizure disorder," but with no indication of what kind, what caused it, or what to do about it other than "follow up for treatment."

Talk about an anticlimax. It didn't give us much to go by. Truly, we had no idea what we were going to do next. All we had was a note saying we should return for a neurological follow-up. It was hard not to feel like we were getting nowhere at all, though we did get some good advice from a friend of mine who said: "This is going to be hard, way harder than you think. You need help."

Thank God we listened. Guided by one of the nursing supervisors at Mount Sinai, we tapped into an informal network of nurses who were willing to work private duty and care for William at our home. They were angels. Over time, they would become like members of our family, instrumental in so many ways—William's care, our mental health, stabilizing our lives, just knowing we had caring and loving professionals who could guide us through this life-changing time. We learned quickly just how desperately we needed these nurses. We did not take a moment of their care for granted. And we had no idea of the cost of any of this. At least we had insurance through my family.

That first night at home, Andrea and Cristopher got to meet their little brother. They behaved just like older siblings usually do: jumping on him, tugging at him, inspecting him like he was a rare creature from somewhere who had just landed in their lives. We got some great video of all that. For this one night, we felt like something close to a typical family—albeit a typical family with a child who needed twenty-four-hour nursing care because of some ailment no one could quite identify. And William did his part. He looked like a baby should look, and he reacted every time his brother and sister nuzzled up to him. Naturally, Andrea and Cristopher were curious about the woman who had come home with us.

"Who is she?"

"She's going to help us with William," Lisa said.

Sometimes with children, even the simplest explanation will do. We went to bed that first night really feeling like a family again. Unfortunately, that happiness wouldn't last through the night.

Just after 3 a.m., after we'd been home for barely twelve hours, William had another seizure, his worst one yet. He wasn't only getting stiff now. His struggle for air seemed even more desperate than before. And Lisa and I were still such amateurs. We had never faced anything like this. At least we weren't totally alone. We had the nurse with us. But it was terrifying. In a flash, our quiet home was in an uproar. We didn't feel like we could wait for an ambulance. This was fly-into-action time, as I piled Lisa, William, and our brand-new home-care nurse into the car. Andrea and Cristopher stayed home with the au pair. We hoped they would keep sleeping. Of course, they didn't.

"Where's my little brother going?" Andrea asked.

All I could tell her was: "We have to go back to the hospital."

I don't think any family has ever raced that fast to the hospital, where William was promptly admitted to the Neonatal Intensive Care Unit, and the testing started all over again, including an electroencephalogram, a brain-wave test that's often referred to by its initials, EEG.

William had had a grand mal seizure, the doctors said. And the horrible details kept coming.

• • •

During the two weeks William was at the hospital, we had an important meeting in the NICU with his two pediatricians and his neonatologist. I'm not sure they shared the full implications of what they saw on the EEG. But when the neonatologist walked us through the test results, he didn't sugarcoat anything. He said the EEG had revealed something called hypsarrhythmia, an abnormal brain rhythm that the doctors said included interictal high-amplitude waves and a background of irregular spikes. Of course, I had no idea what any of that meant, though I knew Lisa would soon be launching a new research project. Then, the doctor put it in terms I could better understand: "This type of pattern can lead to a child not being able to develop, not being able to walk or talk or progress in that way."

And he said this brain pattern needed to be stopped . . . like now.

As the doctor spoke, Lisa and I sat there quietly, trying to absorb the meaning of what we had just heard. It was so overwhelming, it almost didn't seem real to us.

"Well," I finally said, "we're going to do everything we can to try to help our child. What do we do from here?"

Though this hospital was our local, community hospital, it is also part of the Yale New Haven Health System. The doctors had already concluded that William needed more specialized care. On August 5, he was transferred forty miles east to Yale New Haven Hospital. Yale New Haven is eight times larger than our local Connecticut hospital. It is the primary teaching hospital and clinical research center for the Yale School of Medicine, making it one of the top academic medical centers in the country.

Lisa rode with William in the ambulance while I drove the car behind them to what would be my son's third hospital in his first five weeks. "If Yale can't figure this out," I said to Lisa, "no one can."

• • •

At Yale, William was an inpatient at the Comprehensive Epilepsy Center. As part of their investigation, the Yale team had William under twenty-four-hour video surveillance, so they could record everything that happened with him. It was eerie, some of what we saw. Watching one of his seizures on video may have been the most terrifying thing I had ever witnessed in my life. Seeing my young son sleeping peacefully and then jolting into a stiffening pattern and letting out a shrieking cry while I couldn't do anything about it—it was just horrible. It ripped at my heart. Just hearing his screams made me feel like my ears were being gouged at.

At last, the doctors at Yale diagnosed William with infantile spasms.

That was the key phrase. They said William Trump was having infantile spasms, which were being strung together in these body-stiffening, gasping-for-air, brain-rattling seizures. And even more important, that diagnosis came with an actual course of treatment, something we hadn't gotten close to until the pediatric neurologist at Yale did. He prescribed the steroid ACTH, which quieted William's spasms, quickly and dramatically.

This gets a little technical, so skip it if you want to. But the ACTH steroid regulates the glucocorticoid hormone cortisol, which is released by the adrenal gland. It also regulates blood pressure, blood sugar, the immune system, and the body's response to stress. But here's what mattered to Lisa and me: It made his spasms stop.

It didn't get to the bottom of William's problems. But it sure made the problems easier to live with and protected him from the additional and irreversible damage the spasms would otherwise be causing to his brain.

Major, major, major.

There were a lot of other things the ACTH wouldn't do. It wouldn't reverse any of the damage to William's brain. It didn't mean his development would progress any further or any more quickly in the future. But by stopping the spasms, it gave William some protection against further brain damage . . . for now. Some days, before the steroid treatments began, he'd been having as many as a hundred of these seizures, and they'd been growing only more violent over time. Now, he might go days or weeks or even months without any.

"There's always the possibility of new seizures forming," his neurologist cautioned. "The future can't be predicted. Once the brain knows how to have so many seizures, there's a strong possibility it is going to have more. The spasms could return at any time."

We got that, we said. But for now, at least, William and his parents would get some blessed relief.

CHAPTER 15

CUT OFF

One day, I got a call out of the blue from Irwin Durben, one of my grandfather's lawyers and one of Uncle Donald's lawyers too.

Irwin was an old-timer with an office on Long Island, who'd been doing work for the Trump family for decades. He was also one of my trustees, ever since my father had died. Donald was the other one. This was four months after my grandfather was dead and buried, meaning it was four months minus one day since William was born. Lisa and I were still in full, round-the-clock William mode.

Our lives remained a mad dash of doctor visits, test procedures, and specialist hunts . . . and still no clear answers to anything. Coming next: getting connected with a valuable program for children with special needs, a crucial conduit to all kinds of services, and also discovering the high-tech mysteries of the hyperbaric chamber at NewYork-Presbyterian Hospital on the Upper East Side of Manhattan. There was so much fun to come! But William was home with us that day.

When I got the lawyer's call, I was in the family room, which I had converted to a makeshift office so I'd be available for work, family, and assorted emergencies. This was none of the above.

"You're going to receive a letter by certified mail," the family lawyer said.

Already that sounded ominous.

"Essentially," he continued, "the letter says that you are out of your grandfather's will. Instead, you will receive a single payment of two hundred thousand dollars. Do not sign the letter. I repeat, do *not* sign it."

This was all news to me. I had picked up some faint rumblings that something might be amiss involving my grandfather's estate. But I hadn't heard any details, and no one ever mentioned anything like this to me. With all the attention on William's fragile condition, I didn't have the bandwidth to focus on family business in the weeks after my grandfather died. I was busy trying to help save my son's life and get him the help he—and we—so desperately needed.

Whatever it is, I told myself that summer, *I'm sure someone will sort it out. I have other things to worry about.* Clearly, I would need to pay attention now.

"This also applies to your sister," Irwin added. "Both of you."

In my bleary-eyed, sleep-deprived state, I didn't have an easily definable reaction to the news that Irwin called to deliver. Anger? Hurt? Disappointment? I hadn't reached any of those stages yet. For now, I was caught somewhere between dazed and numb.

"Irwin," I said, trying to focus, "I need to come out and talk with you."

"Bring your sister. Both of you should come."

Then I hung up the phone and got back to work.

When Mary and I sat down with Irwin Durben at his office in Garden City, he didn't try to soft-pedal this surprising development or the impact it threatened to have on my sister and me. If anything, he sounded more dire than he had on the phone.

"You're out," he said. No equivocation there. "Your aunts and your uncles say your grandfather's wishes had changed, and you're not part of the will anymore."

Mary and I were both stunned.

How could this be? What did the lawyer mean Grandpa's "wishes had changed"? *When?* Over the past decade, as his dementia worsened, my grandfather was in no condition to be making financial decisions of any kind. He was ninety-three when he died! He could barely pull his socks on! Who was in charge here? Did Gam even know?

As Mary and I tried to grasp all this and figure out what our options might be, Irwin kept answering our many questions with "I don't know . . . I don't know . . . I'm sure that will become clear."

The timing made no sense to me. I had just spoken at my grandfather's funeral, standing in for my late father, addressing the whole family. Donald and his siblings would never have asked me to do that if they knew my grandfather had decided to disinherit me.

Would they? *Would they?*

I had a whole lot of questions and hardly any answers.

For starters, I had no idea how large my grandfather's estate might be. That wasn't the kind of thing that was ever discussed around my grandparents' house, not in the thousands of times that I was there. I knew my grandfather was immensely rich. He was *famous* for being rich. But how rich, I couldn't say. I just knew that he'd worked all his life, that he'd been enormously successful, that he owned a massive portfolio of real estate, and that he always seemed to treasure the family legacy he would one day leave behind. I had always assumed that when he died, his estate would be divided five ways, a share for each of his five children. Since my father was gone, his share would come directly to Mary and me, just as the shares of his other four children would, sooner or later, be passed to *their* children.

Multigenerational wealth, I believe that's called.

So, was one branch of this big family tree being chopped off now? What did that make us? Sawdust?

Before I got too dramatic, I knew I needed to take a deep breath and gather some information. I was angry. I couldn't believe what was happening. My grandfather had certainly never given any indication that anyone in the family should expect to be left out in the cold.

Now Mary and I would need to decide exactly what, if anything, we were going to do about it.

After we had gotten word about my grandfather's estate and before Mary and I had mapped out our next steps, a thought was really nagging at me. Gam needed to meet William, and William needed to meet Gam. I had such warm memories of our first Gam visits with Andrea and Cristopher. Each time, the love had poured both ways. I understood how different things were now. But Gam was William's great-grandmother, and he was her great-grandson.

Amazing! That fact should not be forgotten with everything else that was going on.

William wasn't making many field trips in those tense early weeks, unless you counted hospitals and doctor's offices. At this point, he hadn't laid eyes on a single one of my Trump relatives. Wasn't it time? None of them had come to visit. Other than Robert returning my phone call, none of them had even bothered to call and ask how he was doing. To them, he really was the invisible Trump. "They must really be broken up about Grandpa's death," I grumbled to Lisa, not bothering to hide my irritation.

If anyone should have been despondent over Grandpa's passing, it would be Gam. After all, she was the one who'd just lost her husband. And that wasn't all. She was also dealing with an array of her own painful ailments, including her serious arthritis and brittle bones that kept breaking, landing her in her two homes-away-from-home, Jamaica Hospital and the Hospital for Special Surgery. But at eighty-seven, Gam could still be a force for good in the family, even though she'd lost a step or two. I couldn't believe she knew anything about the details of the will. I hoped not, anyway. And if we could get to see her, I certainly wasn't planning to get into it with her. Given all the weirdness floating around, a nice, simple sit-down would be fine.

So, I gave my grandmother a call and asked if she'd be up for visit. "Of course, dear," she said. "Come by."

I can't tell you how excited I was.

That Saturday, I slipped an oxygen tank into William's diaper bag. He didn't need the extra oxygen all the time. But it had to be nearby in case something scary happened—and that was a chance we didn't need to take. We loaded Andrea and Cristopher into the car. No reason they shouldn't come. Our nurse also piled in. With Lisa, William, and me, that made six of us, a full family affair, as we made the forty-minute drive to Gam's house in Queens.

When we pulled into the driveway and carried William inside, Gam seemed positively thrilled to meet and hold her latest great-grandson. She clearly understood that William was struggling. She asked about the doctor visits and the latest prognosis. We told her what a brave little boy he had been, how his parents were doing every-thing they could to get him all the help he needed, and how all of us were hoping for the best. She brought out a big bag of gummy bears for Andrea and Cristopher, who each gobbled several fistfuls. The adults also indulged. It was almost like a little party, and Gam couldn't seem to get enough of William. Seeing my grandmother hold our son, I felt like I was witnessing a bridge across the 1900s: an old woman who had come from rural Scotland when the century was still young and a little boy born in New York City as that same century was coming to a close.

What a distance she had traveled; what a distance he had to go.

At one point I looked over at Gam. She wasn't saying anything. She just had a giant smile on her face, beaming down at this baby with soft, worried eyes. To me, that rush of emotion, tugging in two directions at once, summed up exactly how Lisa and I felt. Inside that envelope of warmth for her precious great-grandson, Gam seemed genuinely shaken and concerned.

"Oh, William," she said before handing him back to Lisa and then turning to me. "What a precious little boy he is. Don't worry, dear. As long as he lives, he will never want for anything."

Over the years, Uncle Robert had become the Fredo of the Trump family. You know Fredo, the dim little brother in *The Godfather* movies who was constantly being handed the least pleasant tasks. It was . . . *Robert, run this errand. . . . Robert, take this schmuck to the airport. . . . Robert, tell some vendor we aren't renewing his contract.* And all through the 1980s . . . *Robert, you be in charge of the Atlantic City casinos.* That one would really turn out to be a curse.

I still remembered Rob as my father's cooler younger brother, not to mention a college soccer phenom. But now, I guess even I had fallen into the habit of looking at him like the others did. Hadn't I just called him with the news about William, expecting him to be the delivery boy?

Let Robert do it.

So, as the legalities around my grandfather's estate began to unfold, of course Uncle Robert was sent our way.

"Are you ready to sign the papers?" he called to ask me.

"No," I told him in no uncertain terms. "I'm not ready to sign anything."

"You really should sign."

"Tell whoever you need to tell. I'm not signing."

There was an underlying message that didn't need to be spoken. This wasn't only coming from Rob.

I don't believe Robert really expected my signature, not if he thought about it at all. He was just being Fredo Trump and delivering the message. And who was that message *from*? I was beginning to have my suspicions, but the truth is I really didn't know.

Meanwhile, Lisa and I were in the throes of the care of our infant son. The efforts at Yale had eased the seizures, which was wonderful, and we were deeply thankful for the relief the ACTH seemed to be providing. But all our son's developmental issues were right where they'd been. As each week passed, he seemed to be missing another milestone, and that was becoming more obvious. Would he be stuck with the brain of an infant forever, even as he got bigger and bigger and looked more and more like a growing boy? That possibility was dawning on Lisa and me. As usual, she was the one carrying the heaviest part of the William load, caring for our son, dealing with the doctors, pursuing new courses of treatment, seeking out experts around the globe, while both of us also looked after Andrea and Cristopher and I did my best to work for a living and deal with the occasional incoming blow from my family. Truly, I couldn't imagine how Lisa was able to handle so much.

There was no way we ever could have done this alone.

With William at home with us for the foreseeable future, we really came to appreciate the nurses and all the care they were helping with. Lisa still needed to heal from giving birth. She was still pumping breast milk to get William the best nutrition possible. His seizure-suppressing ACTH was administered by injection, and he needed to be watched carefully for the steroid's many possible side effects. It lifted a big load of stress off Lisa and me, just knowing those wonderful nurses were there. Meanwhile, we were trying to bring a regular routine back to Andrea and Cristopher.

The nurses helped with all of that, juggling the drug administration, medical issues, side effects, growth-and-development monitoring, upcoming doctor appointments, and everything else we were supposed to pay attention to all at once. We needed their help and so much more. While William was in the hospital, one of the nurses had mentioned the local branch of an organization called ARC.

"You really need to tap into those people," she urged. "They can be very helpful."

Lisa and I were both so overwhelmed at the time, honestly, neither one of us paid much attention. Our reaction was pretty much, "Yeah, thanks, we'll get to that when we can." But once we were home and establishing a basic rhythm, Lisa kept saying she wanted to be "proactive." Spending so much time in the hospital, it was like we had no control over anything. Clearly, we needed a new normal, whatever that might be. It was probably time, we decided, to follow up on that group we had heard about.

Funny, I used to drive by a sign for ARC on my way home from the train station, though I can't say I ever paid much attention. But when I discovered what the letters stood for, it almost knocked the wind out of me.

"Association for Retarded Citizens."

First of all, ever since I was a kid, I hated that word, "retarded." It sounded so cruel. When I first started working at the Insignia office on Long Island, a colleague of mine got mad at someone and erupted angrily: *"What a ree-tard!"* When I heard him say that, I pulled him aside. "Please don't ever use that word again," I said. "Not in front of me." To me, it was as awful as a bad racial slur.

And now that label was being applied to my son?

In a way, I'd been kidding myself, clinging to the notion that whatever was wrong with William might somehow get better, once the doctors figured out what it was and how to treat it. But retarded? I couldn't believe that people were still using that word. What did this place have to do with my son? How was our life going to work from here?

Lisa didn't want to bring extra people into the house while William was taking the ACTH since the medication could compromise his immune system. That was one of the possible side effects. But once he was weaned off the steroid, she made the call. When the woman from ARC came to our house, she couldn't have been kinder. She sensed immediately just how frazzled Lisa felt. "It will not always be this way," she said reassuringly. "You will get the help you need. Things will get better."

Just hearing that seemed to lift a load from Lisa. From William's first rush down the hospital hallway, no one had ever quite said that. Though our fears would never entirely disappear, some kind of normalcy was gradually settling in.

ARC staffers were all about early intervention and customized therapies and helped us figure out what William needed, what we were entitled to, and who might be able to deliver it. They had a state-supported program called Birth to Three that connected us with a physical therapist, an occupational therapist, and a feeding therapist, all of whom made house calls to work with William. They also offered to introduce us to other families dealing with similar issues.

None of this was a magic potion, but all of it made us feel less alone. Someone within ARC back then must have agreed with my aversion to the R-word. Over the years, the organization would rebrand as Abilis, whose name reflects its focus on ability instead of disability. The nurse at the local Connecticut hospital was right. Those people were beyond helpful, and they would remain in our lives at every turn.

I can see now how this began the genesis of our drive to get involved with organizations like these that can help families like ours. Through Abilis, the community of inclusion grew stronger.

• • •

Though our grief and fear were always with us, they were also being swallowed by love: the love we had for our little man and our fierce determination to make things better for him. We might fail at this or that, but it wasn't going to be from lack of trying. Those few decades ago, the information we needed was harder to gather. The Internet was dial-up. Google was web crawler. No one was nearly as tech-savvy back then. But Lisa was unusually resourceful and driven, and what we needed did eventually trickle in.

Soon, we had so many doctors, it was hard to keep up with all of them. Pediatricians in Manhattan and Connecticut. "If one is good," Lisa said, "wouldn't two be better?" We had two neurologists, one in our local hospital and one at Yale, and an ophthalmologist since William had cortical visual impairment, which is common in children with developmental delays. At one point, I counted twelve different specialists. I might have forgotten a couple. And Lisa was the air-traffic controller, getting the planes safely up and down.

And what was all this costing? I could only imagine. I say that because we really didn't know. Unlike most families, we were well insured.

My entire life, I had received medical insurance through a Trump family policy that my grandfather provided to all of us. My aunts and uncles. My cousins. Everyone. It all went through the family company. We got a special Trump family policy card. I'd had this insurance since I was born, just like all my relatives did. Once I got married, I put Lisa on the policy, then added the kids one by one as they arrived. It was a great family perk.

However expensive William's care was, I said to Lisa when we finally managed to catch our breath, "at least we don't have to worry about the medical cost."

"Thank God," she agreed.

I assumed that's what Robert had been referring to when he told me on the phone that day that we should get William all the help he needed and not "worry about anything."

Now, things were about to get complicated . . . for all of us.

I trusted Irwin Durben. I'd known Irwin since I was a kid. When my father died in 1981, Mary and I inherited minority interests in some Trump-family properties, ownership slices that had been in my father's name for years. Since Mary was sixteen and I was eighteen and we knew next to nothing about finance or real-estate investing, Irwin was appointed our trustee, along with Donald, to advise us, look after our interests, and make sure we got everything we were due. While Donald was off being Donald, I had the sense that Irwin took his responsibility seriously. He always seemed happy to answer my questions and explain things to me. He certainly knew a lot about the Trumps. He hadn't served the earlier generations only as a lawyer, he'd also been a senior executive for several Trump-related companies and a fiduciary to other family trusts.

The only way we could get what we were expecting from the estate, Irwin assured Mary and me, was to hire competent counsel, go into court, and challenge the legality of my grandfather's will. And Irwin seemed to think we ought to try.

"These cases are never easy," he said. "But what's happened to you and Mary isn't right."

I didn't need any convincing there.

It wasn't a case he could handle, Irwin said. Representing so many Trumps over the years, he had conflicts in all directions. But he took us to meet Jack Barnosky, a partner at a large Long Island firm called Farrell Fritz. Irwin assured us Jack was experienced in the ins and outs of trusts and estates. Jack seemed like the real deal, a big, blustery guy who didn't appear intimidated by anyone. We met with him and the firm's managing partner, Charles Strain, a brainier type with college-professor glasses, who played golf at the WASPy Garden City Men's Club, one of the most elite golf clubs from Palm Beach to Kennebunkport.

They made a striking pair and agreed to take our case. Mary and I agreed to hire them.

My sister and I understood what a major step we would be taking, going into court against our own relatives. It wasn't something either of us *wanted* to do. Our aunts and uncles certainly wouldn't like it, even if our cause was just. But it didn't seem right to do nothing at all when tens of millions of dollars—*tens of millions,* Jack had estimated—had been secretly and bafflingly taken from us. And as Mary kept saying to me, "Really, what choice do we have?"

Before we filed anything in court, while we were still weighing all this, I got another call from Uncle Robert, asking if Mary and I would meet him at the Drake Hotel, a favorite Park Avenue hangout for the Midtown business elite. When Rob said he wanted to "sit down and try to work this out," both Mary and I were ready to listen.

"Who knows?" I said to my sister as we headed to the hotel that morning. "Maybe he has something to propose."

I couldn't have been more mistaken. What Robert had for us was a lecture and a barrage of threats. This time, it seemed, little brother's assignment wasn't just, *Deliver a message, Fredo.* It was, *Tighten the screws.*

"We love both of you," he said as soon as we all sat down in the Drake's understated lobby. And that, right there, was the end of the sweet talk. My uncle's tone stiffened fast. "You really have no choice," he said. "You can't fight this. You *have* to sign. If you don't accept your grandfather's wishes, you'll get nothing, and you'll be paying taxes for the rest of your lives, taxes on properties you have no control over.

It'll be a total disaster for you. It could be devastating." And then our concerned uncle, just looking out for his brother's children, added, "Couldn't you use two hundred thousand dollars?"

Rob's hard sell got very emotional. The way he put it, it would almost be a personal insult to him if we didn't surrender immediately and give up all our rights, whatever they might be. He didn't seem interested in how all this felt from our perspective. He never even asked about that. We just had to agree—and we had to do it *now.*

"I don't understand what the big rush is," I said to him. "I think we'd like to figure out what our options are. I have a very hard time believing these were really my grandfather's wishes, to cut Mary and me out and leave us with crumbs." In fact, I told him, "this seems more like something Donald would do if he needed cash."

Robert didn't react to that. Still, I was pleased with myself for putting it out there.

Mary was even more adamant than I was. "You are stealing from us," she said with conviction. "Why should we agree to that?" And the truth was, Mary had studied the situation a lot more closely than I had. As all this was unfolding, I'd been in and out, focused part of the time but AWOL a lot, dealing with all of William's crises and needs and also juggling work.

Rob's pitch fell flat. He kept insisting he was looking out for our interests and well-being, but nothing he said made us believe him. After discussing everything with Lisa and Jack and Irwin and thinking about it some more, I decided Mary was right: Really, what choice did we have?

On March 23, 2000, after conducting their own careful research and analysis, Jack Barnosky and his Farrell Fritz team went into Queens County Surrogate's Court and filed our formal objection to the probate of Fred C. Trump.

This was family, so the formality of that felt *off.* But you can't just go into court and shout, "It's unfair!" You need a legal basis. And our lawyers were ready with ours. Our core argument: That Donald and two of his siblings, Maryanne and Robert, had unduly pressured their frail and aged father, who was already deep into mental decline, to shut us out, corruptly manipulating him to enrich themselves at the expense of Mary and me.

We didn't know all the details of how they did it. Not at first. As our lawyers explained to us, that's what the legal discovery process would be for. Finding out everything. All I knew at this point was that we were headed into unknown territory, and I needed to prepare myself for a war with my family, a war I did not expect or want, especially given my son's medical challenges.

It was just a few days later that I got another call I didn't expect.

The call was from Donald. We hadn't heard from him since William was born.

"Pal," he said brightly. "You should have called me. You and I, we could have worked this out."

Donald, always the dealmaker. At least pretending to be.

From his words and his tone on the call, Donald left the strong impression that he didn't know anything about the bitter back-and-forth that had already been under way for months. That he had no idea Robert had met with us. That Robert hadn't reported back to him. That Donald hadn't played any role in excluding his late brother's branch of the family from their fair share of the estate. That he hadn't done anything to promote the feeling that Mary and I were somehow lesser grandchildren because his older brother was our father.

That all seemed preposterous to me.

That last implication was especially galling. I had spent my entire life in the thick of the Trump family. Showing up for every holiday meal and family function. Bonding with my grandparents. Always making time for my aunts and uncles and cousins. Being there whenever this one or that one was in need.

Now, Donald wanted me to believe that all this stuff had been happening around him, and he didn't have a clue.

I just didn't believe it.

"So, what do you have in mind exactly?" I asked him. "What would you like to do about it?"

"It's too late now," he said. "The moment has passed. I don't think there's anything we can do. I just wish you'd called me."

Of course, at any time, Donald could have called *me*. He was my uncle . . . and my trustee, who was supposedly protecting Mary and my interests along with Irwin Durben. Supposedly. He was the one who ran what had been my grandfather's company. He was the one with his hands around the family fortune. If someone should have called someone, wasn't it him calling me? But Donald-the-dealmaker had become Donald-the-bystander, almost overnight.

There must have been a reason for his phone call, but I've never been able to figure out what it was. He didn't sound especially sincere. It was almost like he wanted to be able to say later that he had "tried."

Nothing good ever comes by certified mail. That was one lesson I was learning the hard way.

On March 30, seven days after we filed the probate lawsuit, another certified letter arrived at our house in Connecticut. The letter was from Louis Laurino, the attorney representing Uncle Donald, Aunt Maryanne, and Uncle Rob. I knew the name sounded familiar. Laurino, it turned out, had his own rich history in the court system of Queens. In 1971, Governor Nelson Rockefeller appointed him Queens County surrogate, the judge who would handle cases just like this one. Those surrogate judgeships are powerful, allowing the judges to assign big-dollar/interesting/high-profile trials to attorneys of their choosing. Laurino remained on the bench for two decades, amassing huge influence throughout the Queens court system. But his time on the bench was not without controversy. He was censured by the state Commission on Judicial Conduct for ethical misconduct and conflicts of interest. He had resigned in 1991.

Among the allegations against him: that he had pressured a lawyer to hire his son and a nephew, that he had rented office space to three lawyers he'd appointed to lucrative posts, and that he had made an improper political contribution to the Queens borough president, Donald Manes. Laurino's political games continued up until he left the bench. He put in his resignation just after the filing deadline for that fall's primary election, which allowed the Queens Democratic bosses to install his successor without the voters having a say. That lucky successor, Robert Nahman, was now the judge who'd be overseeing our case. And Laurino, instead of wearing black robes, was now a private-practice estate lawyer with an office in Garden City, Long Island. He would now be defending my relatives, who had been so generously enriched at the expense of my sister and me. Of all the lawyers my aunt and uncle could have hired, this was the character they had chosen. Clearly, we were in for a fight.

In that first letter of his, Louis Laurino wasn't writing just to say hi. He had a message to deliver . . . *to me*. It felt more like a shot across the bow. Or a punch in the face.

His message was that our medical insurance, the coverage my grandfather had provided to all his family members, the one I'd had since birth, the insurance that was now paying for my son William's life-or-death care, was being cut off abruptly.

What?

Of all the cruel, low-down, vicious, heartless things my own relatives could do to me, my wife, and my children, this was worse than anything else I could possibly imagine. Which, I suppose, was the point.

I had an infant son, desperately in need of medical care as he fought for his life. That care was his lifeblood, his only hope of finding his way out of an unimaginably horrific situation, and my very closest relatives had decided to kick him—and us—to the curb.

Maybe I shouldn't have been surprised. Wasn't that how it had always been with the Trumps? If you ever challenge the family, even if you are *part* of the family, you'd better be ready for war. That had become almost a Donald mantra over the years—somewhere between "shtick" and a "mantra": Come at me with a knife, I'll come at you with a gun. Come at me with a gun, I'll come at you with a bazooka. Come at me with . . . well, you get the idea.

How could anyone do something so cruel to someone they were related to? What could I have possibly done to cause something like this? If this wasn't evil, I really couldn't say what might qualify.

I knew we had to take action, and act we did.

On May 10, Lisa and I, with Mary and my mom joining us, filed another suit in Nassau County Supreme Court, as our lawyers laid out the history of the family insurance policy and the devastating consequences of cutting off the coverage. William's medical care had already topped $300,000, our lawyers explained to the court, a lowball estimate. It would be far more than that when all the bills came in. We described the reality of William's condition and how urgently he needed round-the-clock nursing care. "These nurses are critical," we said in the suit. In a recent medical emergency, "Had a nurse not been with him, he would not have survived."

I didn't mince words as I explained to the court exactly what was motivating my wealthy relatives: anger over our lawsuit seeking our fair share of our grandfather's estate. As I stated in the court papers, "My aunt and uncles thought nothing about taking away my critically ill son's coverage in an attempt to browbeat me into abandoning my claim in the probate contest."

The media picked up on the lawsuit, especially the New York *Daily News,* whose front-page headline on May 11 read: "TRUMP TAKING LUMPS FROM KIN."

Up until then, Lisa and I hadn't done any interviews or spoken publicly about the estate fight. We preferred to try our case in the courtroom, not the media. We hoped that once we had gone into court and laid the facts out, Donald and the others might see how unfair the situation was. Who knew? They might even try to make things right again.

Talk about wishful thinking! Once they yanked the insurance, they killed all hope of an amicable settlement. They took the fight right to the gutter, delivering the lowest of low blows.

By December, a Nassau County judge ruled that the Trump family must continue paying for the health insurance until the matter was resolved. The *Daily News* coverage was written by a relentless reporter named Heidi Evans, who did an excellent job nailing down all the details and giving both sides a chance to say their piece. I wasn't eager to talk. I had no desire for the limelight. But Jack pushed hard. He said the time had come to let people know what Donald was doing to his own relatives. Not only squeezing us out of our inheritance, but also *cutting off our disabled son's medical insurance.* Jack had a point. I didn't think Donald should be allowed to do that under the cover of darkness. It was time to let some light shine in. And Lisa and Mary agreed.

"This was so shocking, so disappointing, and so vindictive," Lisa told the reporter in December, a comment any parent could relate to, especially the parent of a sick child.

Mary summed it up perfectly. "William is my father's grandson," she said. "He is as much a part of that family as anybody else. He desperately needs extra care." Then, my sister gave the knife an extra twist. "My aunts and uncles should be ashamed of themselves. I'm sure they are not."

When I spoke with the reporter, I told her exactly how I felt and how I thought my relatives were behaving. "I just think it was wrong," I said. "These are not warm and fuzzy people. They never even came to see William in the hospital. Our family puts the 'fun' in dysfunctional."

Yes, that last comment was dripping in Trump-family sarcasm. I knew that was a language that Donald understood. "You have to be tough in this family," I said. "I guess I have what my father didn't have. I will stick to my guns."

My father had let his father pressure him all his life. But I wasn't going to bend.

We really didn't feel like we had much choice, I told the reporter in May. "If it was just me, I wouldn't care," I said. "But my son has serious problems. When William was first born, Robert told me not to worry about the medical care. 'Whatever it takes,' he told me."

For their part, Donald and his side came out with guns blazing. If they felt any chagrin about their cruelty to William, they did not let on. "Why should we give him medical coverage?" Donald scoffed.

When the reporter asked if he thought he might be coming across as just a little coldhearted, given our son's medical condition, my uncle shot back: "I can't help that. It's cold when someone sues my father. Had he come to see me, things could very possibly have been much different for them."

Yes, *that* again. Yesterday, today, and tomorrow, it was always about Donald.

Years later, when Donald had time to reflect and was asked about all this by *The New York Times,* he didn't even try to hide his motives: "I was angry because they sued."

One of their lawyers also jumped into the fray, telling the *Daily News* reporter in May that the case was about "pure greed," making us sound like spoiled children on Christmas morning at Gam and Grandpa's house, pitching a fit over toys. "The Trumps providing of medical benefits was a gift freely given and like any gift, it can be freely taken away," said Trump attorney Dennis Hasher. "The family decided that when these two individuals decided to sue the people giving them the gift, they'd be jerks to continue giving it."

So there.

"These two individuals": What a way to describe your relatives.

Robert even piped in, claiming that William didn't actually need twenty-four-hour care. He compared our dedicated team of nurses in court documents to "high-priced babysitters," despite William's need for oxygen, despite the seizures and the seizure-rescue meds, despite all the other emergencies the nurses had been dealing with. Instead of hiring a nurse, Robert alleged in court documents, Lisa and I should consider taking a CPR course from the American Red Cross so we could resuscitate William.

That was so awful, it wasn't worthy of a response. It seemed Robert was so caught up in the fight that he had lost his sense of humanity.

How far we had come from my grandmother's words: "Don't worry, dear. As long as he lives, he will never want for anything."

CHAPTER 16

FAMILY FEUD

Appearances can be deceiving.

From the sidewalk, the Sutphin Boulevard courthouse looks like a grand, neoclassical edifice with its Corinthian colonnade and Alabama limestone façade. But once we climbed the broad front steps and moved through the heavy revolving door, Mary and I might as well have been inside a South Jamaica crack house. Dim lighting. Dingy hallways. Restrooms you'd only visit in a dire emergency. And a stiff, eye-watering aroma that landed somewhere between urine and cleaning fluid.

For us, this was where justice was going to be done.

I half expected the elegant Mr. Strain to lay a starched white napkin between his nicely pressed suit pants and the grimy wooden chair. As for the air inside the high-ceilinged courtroom, it had the smell of backroom deals, decades and decades of them. This might be a temple of modern justice, but it sure felt like a repository of broken dreams, especially in the Queens County surrogate's part, where wounded people come to fight over the leavings of the dead.

"You ready?" Mary whispered to me.

"Ready as I'll ever be."

Mary and I were in this together, a united front.

Our lawyers were there, Jack Barnosky and Charles Strain. Uncle Rob was there with the family's ex-judge of a lawyer, Lou Laurino. Irwin Durben and his partner Vinny Tosti were there, representing— I'm not quite sure who they were representing. Everybody? Nobody? Maybe a little of both.

Once everyone was seated, the judge came onto the bench. But he didn't want to hear anything about our claim or our case or our issues. What he wanted, it seemed, was for the two sides to go off somewhere and settle the damn thing. Instead of taking any testimony or hearing any arguments, the judge sent us into a windowless conference room. I could only imagine the kinds of deals that had been hammered out in there.

And if I didn't have enough to be concerned about that morning, just as we were about to get started, I got a call from Lisa. It wasn't about William this time. It was about Andrea, who'd had some kind of emergency at school. Now even our easiest kid was in the mix! Was it something Lisa could handle? Or was there something I could do to help?

Rob noticed the look on my face. "What is it?" he asked in a flash of family concern. Like the old Rob might have.

"Something's wrong with Andrea."

He nodded without asking what.

Lisa said she was able to manage the situation, but it definitely gave me a moment of . . . *and what else now?!* I really hated being there.

Once we got down to business, Jack began laying out our argument to the other side. That Mary and I had been unfairly denied our inheritance because my father's siblings had pressured their out-of-it father to change his will. "All my clients want," he said, "is what they are entitled to."

I got the impression that the main thing Rob wanted was for the case to settle as quickly as possible, avoiding any more publicity about any Trump family squabbles. No need to drag all these ancient family secrets further into the light of day. Pretty soon, the media would be printing stories about Grandpa at the Nazi rally, or Great-grandpa's Alaska brothels. "Can't we just work this out?" the family lawyer asked about five different ways. We didn't want a public fight either, but we also felt like we needed to get to the bottom of what had happened here and, at the very least, sort out the facts. And the lawyer's version of "work this out" sounded a whole lot like Rob's version, meaning Mary and I should fold immediately, go away practically empty-handed, and give up any and all claims.

I could understand why *they* might feel that way, but I couldn't for the life of me understand why we should agree.

It seemed to me that, at the very least, we needed to figure out what had happened here. How was it that Grandpa's will had gotten changed? What shape was he in at the time? Who might have influenced him to take what was rightfully ours? The only way to make any progress, Jack made clear to the other side, was to begin the depositions.

In a family feud like this one, time is no one's friend.

Once the case was up and running, it was like a curtain slammed down on all our Trump family relationships. No more hi-how-ya-doin' calls from Robert. No check-ins with Maryanne. No more bumping into Donald on the golf course. Blaine didn't suggest another Whopper run. No more contacts with my younger cousins. Things even seemed tense with my older cousin David, Maryanne's son, the one we were closest to. Lisa, William, and a nurse were in Manhattan, on their way to a doctor's appointment, when they looked up and saw David walking toward them on the sidewalk. But instead of stopping to say hello, he abruptly looped across the street and avoided them. David had been the best man at our wedding, and I was at his. But somehow, he couldn't even stop to speak with them.

My relationship with David ended that day.

I wasn't sure exactly what David knew, but I'm sure he was told that Mary and I had turned on the family. I could probably even put quotes around that: "turned on the family." That's how generations of Trumps had learned to think. Blood or no blood, Mary and I were now the enemy, and you could add Lisa and our kids to the list. Trump family loyalty, as I well knew, was always a one-way street. It was fine to screw a niece and nephew; not fine for them to utter a peep of complaint. The extended-family equivalent of orphans, we were immediately consigned to the deep freeze.

It sure made me appreciate my mom and sister and the Lorants. They all had their own lives, but they stayed by our side as we dealt with the daily challenges of caring for William and I scrambled to replace the family medical insurance that had been so abruptly snatched away. The total cost of William's care was daunting, far more than even a well-off family could possibly afford. And I say that having seen only *some* of the numbers. I really can't hazard a guess what it was all adding up to. Thankfully, I managed to shift most of our basic medical expenses onto an insurance policy I had through my office, though that still left quite a few expenses uncovered.

The biggest and most crucial one: the critical nurses we had become so dependent on after we came home from the hospital—I mean, *hospitals*. There was no way Lisa and I could do this alone. It was a full-press operation just feeding him, bathing him, and moving him from room to room. Whatever anyone else might think, this wasn't regular child-rearing. This was on a whole different scale. William required 24/7 medical monitoring, medications, and the extra intuition that comes with love and care. There was no doubt in my mind the nurses were worth every penny of whatever they were being paid. But the amount of care William needed was really adding up. And it probably won't surprise you to hear that the insurance company's idea of what was appropriate and our idea of what was appropriate didn't always mesh. Lisa and I took the only approach we could imagine taking under the circumstances: We'll get William the care he needs and then we'll figure out how to pay for it.

Hadn't that been the Rob Option, before Rob had gone to the other side? *Do what you have to. Don't worry about it. Get him the help he needs.*

How dramatically things could change!

That summer, as the case rumbled on, I got another call from Gam. I always loved hearing from my grandmother. I can still remember where I was when she called. Lying on my back on the floor of the family room. Lisa was reading. Andrea and Cristopher were playing over in the corner. William was sprawled on my chest. It had been a long day. The TV was on in the background. We were all just relaxing at home.

We hadn't spoken since Mary and I filed the lawsuit. Our regular check-ins had already become a casualty of that. So I was thrilled to hear her voice on the phone. It hadn't been that long, but I had missed her. And I really didn't know how she felt about any of this. I had to assume she wasn't thrilled to have her children and grandchildren in litigation against each other. What matriarch would be? Then again, I also had to think she must have *some* sympathy for Mary and me and the position that her late husband or her children or some combination of them had put us in. I'd always felt a special affinity with Gam, and I knew she felt the same for me. We'd invested a lot in each other. Whether I was riding my bike to her house as a ten-year-old or bringing treats to her at-home hospital bed in the "library"—

Gam and I *got* each other, and I knew that went both ways. She'd taken an extra interest in me after my father died. We'd sipped a lot of Cokes together over the years. God knows she had responded with extraordinary warmth and understanding the last time I saw her, that emotional day when Lisa, William, and I went by for a visit. I was so touched by what she told me, that my son would "never want for anything." She remained the one Trump family member who had spent any time at all with our son.

I don't know if my grandfather's death accelerated her decline. But I have to say that, at eighty-eight, Gam sounded much weaker and more hesitant on the phone. After an exchange of pleasantries, there was a long pause. I heard another voice in the background.

Then my grandmother spoke again. She didn't sound like herself at all.

"Why are you doing this to me?" she asked.

I had to wonder whether she was speaking to me or to the voice in the background. I took a shot and assumed she meant the lawsuit.

"Gam," I answered calmly. "We're not doing anything to *you*. This is all about what was done to *us*. You know Grandpa would never have done this. Not if he was thinking straight. Not if he was the one making the decisions. You know that, Gam."

The next words she said to me, I will never forget as long as I live. They cut me like a jagged knife.

"I hope you die penniless just like your father did."

I was too stunned to answer. Catching my breath, I could hear the voice in the background again. I couldn't make it out word-for-word, but the tone was familiar. It sounded to me like Aunt Maryanne.

What had just happened?

I looked at William, sprawled on my chest. All I could think was, *I hope my kids will never hear anything like that in their lives.*

And that was the last time I spoke with my grandmother. On

August 7, a few months later, Gam died. *The New York Times* gave her a four-paragraph obituary:

"Mary MacLeod Trump, a philanthropist who supported charities near her home in Jamaica, Queens, and elsewhere, died on Monday at 88 at Long Island Jewish Medical Center, her family said."

The obit explained that she was born Mary MacLeod on the Isle of Lewis in Scotland on May 10, 1912. The writer went on to say that, on a visit to New York City in the 1930s, she met Fred C. Trump, that they married in 1936, that they settled in Jamaica Estates and he went on to become "one of the city's biggest developers."

These were the basic facts that made up her life, though they left so much unsaid. I hated the way things ended with Gam.

It seemed so pointless. It was so sad . . . and unfair.

Given our tense, final phone call, I didn't know whether I should attend my own grandmother's funeral. A year earlier, such a question would have been unthinkable. I discussed it with Mary. She was no more certain than I was. I thought about it. I thought about it some more. Then, I decided to call Rob.

"I just want to say I loved her very much," I told my uncle.

Rob's only response was, "You killed her."

"Sorry for your loss, Rob." I quickly ended the call.

The funeral was being held at Marble Collegiate Church on Fifth Avenue, the same church as my grandfather's funeral thirteen months earlier. In the end, Mary and I decided we should attend. I wouldn't feel right not being there. I wanted to remember my loving grandmother the way I had known her for all but our final phone call.

Mary and I had no interest in running into anyone in the family or even being seen. We certainly didn't want to cause any kind of fuss. So we waited outside the church until everyone else was inside, then quietly slipped in the back.

We were standing there—discreetly, I thought—when one of

Donald's security men spotted us. I could see him whispering to Donald. Then, the bodyguard walked over to Mary and me, obviously delivering a message from our uncle.

"You can sit in the back . . . ," he said, hesitating a second before he finished the sentence, ". . . just don't sit with the family."

Point made.

"Maybe it'll help. No guarantees, but it might."

That's what the doctors said about the hyperbaric chamber at New York Hospital, but that was all we needed to hear. As soon as the paperwork was done, Lisa and I were getting up at five in the morning and driving with William and a nurse to the Upper East Side of Manhattan for regular sessions in the hospital's hyperbaric chamber. It was in a brightly lit room with super-high pressure and a super-high oxygen level.

Very close quarters. It was very intense being in there.

We would suit William up in his protective gear, which was like an early space suit with a big helmet connected to a tube. Lisa or I would go into the cramped chamber with him, holding him all the way through the session, which lasted for an hour or an hour and a half. To help pass the time, a small TV was on. But who could possibly pay attention? Two children and two adults were usually in the chamber at the same time, including infants like William. Crying. Shaking. Peeing. Pooping. Anything could go wrong at any point. My ears popped every time I was in there. My nose often bled. Every time, it was a tense, trying experience, but we had done our research, and this was a therapeutic intervention that could potentially help William and his development.

Enough said.

Altogether, we would do more than a hundred of these hyperbaric treatments.

Were they helping? I don't know. They could have been. They didn't hurt, and we dared not stop them.

Almost every time, as we drove back home to Connecticut, we stopped at a bagel shop. That was our morning treat. Living with the constant stress as we were, it was amazing what relief even a short break like that could provide. Anything to get our minds off the somber business at hand. I'd drop everyone back home, then hop on a train to Manhattan and go to work—or do it from my work corner of the family room . . . or should I call it my war room? This was still the easiest part of my day, while Lisa dealt with our new reality.

I wish we'd gotten an early heads-up.

But my grandfather never said anything to me about changing his will. He never said anything to Mary. Neither did Gam before we were in court, if she knew anything about it back then. And now there was no way to ask either of them. But as the case revved up and the hard feelings kept intensifying, I kept racking my brain. Had anyone said anything at all? Clearly, some of them had to know. Then, it hit me. I remembered a conversation I'd had with Uncle Rob. It seemed innocuous at the time. But given what I had learned since then, now I could see that maybe there was more to it than I realized. Maybe there was a warning in there.

Too bad I'd missed it.

This was a few years before my grandfather died and William was born. I went out to the Trump Management office in Brooklyn to meet Rob for lunch. My grandfather was still puttering around the executive suite, though he was already pretty out of it by then. He moved slowly. He was more hesitant. He didn't recognize people he'd known for years, including the crowd at Gargiulo's, an old-school Italian joint near the Coney Island boardwalk where he had lunched for decades.

I was sitting in Robert's office before we headed out to eat.

"How's it going at work?" Rob had asked me.

"Actually, it's going well," I said. "I'm working on a couple of good deals."

"Well, you'd better be," he said. "You may need it."

It struck me at the time as a strange thing to say, though I didn't think too much of it. I'd given a small, uncomfortable chuckle. I did wonder briefly, *Why would he say that? What does that mean?* Then, I promptly forgot about the comment as we headed out to Gargiulo's without Grandpa.

But that was ancient history. It didn't really matter whether Rob intended to tip me off or not. We needed facts now, not murky messages or gauzy recollections. Our lawyers had already begun the gargantuan task of trying to get to the bottom of things. Gathering documents. Hiring experts. Reviewing my grandfather's medical records—and anything else they could get their hands on—while they began trying to schedule depositions with the three defendants in the case.

It turned out there was quite a lot of paper around. When you operate at the level my grandfather and his children did, with a successful family company and lawyers and accountants with their fingers in everything, you can leave quite a paper trail. And my grandfather did. Jack was eager to quiz Donald, Maryanne, and Robert. It seemed clear to me they had played some role in getting my grandfather to change his will. According to our lawyers, our whole case could hang on our ability to pin that down, and the depositions could very well make or break it. My aunt and uncles didn't seem eager to answer our questions or explain themselves. They were all very busy—at least they said they were as the lawyers went back and forth trying to nail down some dates. But no one could delay forever, and the dates eventually came.

Depositions aren't like open-court testimony. Mary and I weren't allowed in the conference room while the others were being deposed.

We would get Q-and-A transcripts eventually, Jack said, though that could take a while. In the meantime, all Mary and I could do was to sit in the hallway outside the conference room, while our relatives went behind closed doors to be questioned by Jack and his team. More tense waiting.

When Donald went in, he had a grim look on his face. He breezed past Mary and me without saying a word. We were sitting right there—he had to see us. But it was almost like he had blinders on. He was behind closed doors with the lawyers for a couple of hours. I couldn't wait to hear what they were quizzing him about. But when he was done, I guess he felt a need to register something before he headed back out to his car. Or maybe he just felt relieved that the deposition was over and felt chattier than he did on the way in. It was never easy for Donald to walk past an audience. He stopped and said hello.

"You know," he said to Mary and me without a bit of prompting, "your mother is the reason your father started drinking."

Really?

First of all, no one can blame their drinking on someone else. And I can promise you, my father never would have tried to, even when he was drunk.

Why did he feel the need to say such a cruel thing in that moment? It was classic Donald: feeling frustrated and lashing out by trying to put the onus somewhere else, then reveling in the pain he hoped he had caused—in this case, to his own brother's children. And for what? His brother, after all, had been dead for more than two decades. There were no scores left to settle. My father had lost the ultimate battle, his life. Donald had long since gained total control over the family empire. And now with my grandfather's death, there wasn't anyone else on the scene. Why open these old wounds? To punish Mary and me for daring to question him? To punish us for our choice of a father? To put a wedge between us and our mother?

Donald didn't hang around long enough for us to answer his nasty declaration. As quickly as he stopped in front of us, he was gone.

Donald and Maryanne each had some nasty crack as soon as they left their depositions. A sharp, demeaning comment designed to—what?—twist the knife a little further? Make us feel worse? Cause pain? (See the knife-gun-bazooka tactic.) Personally, I think they just lacked control and couldn't help themselves—amped-up hostility being the only reaction they knew in the face of any kind of question or challenge.

Aunt Maryanne was up next. When she left her depo, she snapped at Mary and me in just about the same tone that Donald had. Except she brought up her ailing husband, John.

"How dare you do this while my husband is dying," she snapped.

I liked John Barry. But Maryanne's hostility made no sense. Mary and I hadn't told Grandpa when to die or told his children when his will should be filed in Queens Surrogate's Court, any more than we had told Grandpa to cut us out. John was indeed battling late-stage lung cancer. I felt terrible for him. He was a great addition to the family, a warm, friendly, down-to-earth Irishman who was a reliable source of sanity in Trump World. I learned later that he had even played a role in beating back an early attempt by Donald to hijack my grandfather's estate. I wished his wife and her siblings had listened *more* to John. He could have saved us all a lot of trouble.

As for his health: John was the last person in the world who would have blamed anyone else. He spoke openly about the lifestyle choices he had made. He was always the first to say with a smile: "Decades of smoking and drinking! What did I expect?"

I could have said: "How dare you do this while my son is fighting for his life?"

Given the post-deposition greetings we'd gotten from Donald and

Maryanne, I could hardly wait for Robert's parting words as he exited the closed-door conference room. But unfortunately, I had to miss that shining moment. I realized I had already agreed to take Andrea and Cristopher on a short trip to Jamaica.

The island, not the Queens neighborhood.

I said to Mary: "Do you mind being there by yourself?"

She told me, "Go."

Jamaica had become a family tradition for us. Lisa and I had taken the older kids there a couple of times already, and they loved it. The island would eventually become a favorite of William's too. The older kids didn't know the details of the lawsuit. They were still too young. But they certainly noticed how disrupted their routines had been and how stressed their parents seemed. Just the parade of aides and nurses, that certainly wasn't normal for them. And watching their little brother fly into seizures while the adults panicked around him, that was anything but.

There was no way that William could leave the country. And there was no way that Lisa was going to leave him at home. But she strongly urged me to make the trip with Andrea and Cristopher. And that's what we decided to do.

CHAPTER 17

MONEY GRAB

It was amazing what our lawyers were able to discover . . . and what our relatives ultimately admitted to under oath. The more I learned as the case unfolded, the more I was certain that Mary and I had made the right decision to sue. We *had* to get to the bottom of what had happened with my grandfather's estate, and the only way to do that was in the push-and-shove of Queens County Surrogate's Court.

And there it was, the Trumpiest story ever: how my uncle Donald—at first with Maryanne's resistance and then with her, along with Robert's, support—apparently managed to manipulate my aging grandfather into disinheriting two of his grandchildren. As we discovered in shocking detail as the case rolled on, Donald did this with cunning and persistence. He methodically manipulated his vulnerable father by exploiting some ancient prejudices and disappointments deep in the history of our family, most of it involving my late father.

Mary and I hadn't done anything to deserve this. We'd been loving grandchildren, always engaged in the life of the family. In a way, it wasn't even personal, Donald's self-interested decision to target us. He needed money. His creditors were coming after him. He thought they might grab his share of his father's estate. We were collateral damage of his selfish but typical scheme to skip out on his mounting debts. And after initially raising objections, two of his siblings went along with Donald's divisive plan . . . once it became clear that they too would get more money if Mary and I were squeezed out.

It's a wild and maddening inside-the-family story that came to light gradually, fact by fact by fact, as the irrefutable evidence piled up.

Some of it came from court records. Some came from other parts of the legal discovery process, where the two sides in the case turn over certain documents and other information. And a whole lot came from the depositions of our aunt and two uncles, Donald, Maryanne, and Robert. It can be jaw-dropping what your relatives will reveal when experienced attorneys like our Jack Barnosky frame the questions right. Jack and his team deserve big credit here. In our legal challenge to my grandfather's will, the facts dribbled out slowly . . . but dribble they did. Along the way, we got deep into Grandpa's cloudy head and into the relentless maneuvering of three of his four living children, Donald especially.

It was all right there in black-and-white in hundreds of pages of deposition transcript, the point-by-point Q-and-A, as three of my closest relatives explained in their very own words how they took tens of millions of dollars away from my sister and me and our families and our future.

As usual, middle-child Aunt Elizabeth stayed out of the fray.

The best place to start this story is in 1984. That year, my grandfather wrote a will, exactly what responsible people do in looking out for their families. He left the bulk of his large estate to his wife and then equal shares to his five children. If any of his sons or daughters predeceased him, as his oldest son already had, that share would go to that child's children. Standard stuff for someone who was creating generational wealth, passing the assets down, helping to keep the peace, and investing in the generations to come.

By the time my grandfather put his signature on that 1984 document, my father had been dead for three years. So, there was no confusion about who stood where. At seventy-nine, Grandpa was still hanging around the office as chairman of the Trump Organization, but Donald had been in charge for thirteen years. Donald had already moved the company's focus away from middle-income apartment houses in Brooklyn and Queens like the ones Mary and I and our cousin David had grown up in. (Donald's kids had very different upbringings.) The outer-boroughs cash flow was strong, but Donald had no interest in those dowdy developments. He was all about the luxury sector in Midtown Manhattan, along with the glamour, glory, and profits he was certain were right across the East River, just waiting for him. In fact, these were rock-and-rolling years at the high end of the New York market. In that era, it was hard *not* to make money in luxury Manhattan real estate.

And the hits kept coming.

In partnership with the Hyatt hotel people, Donald had already turned the old Commodore Hotel next to Grand Central Terminal into the Grand Hyatt, which got things rolling for him in 1980. Donald and The Equitable insurance company then built the iconic Trump Tower, opening the black-and-golden-hued mixed-use condo building on Fifth Avenue in 1983. It was either fifty-eight (regular math) or sixty-eight (Donald math) stories tall, depending on who was doing the counting. Trump Plaza came next. The thirty-six-floor co-op apartment building with retail below topped out on East 61st Street in 1984, by which point Donald had already decided to try his luck in Atlantic City. The Trump Plaza casino hotel started taking bets and renting rooms in 1984. The Trump Castle casino hotel followed in 1985. Both projects were heavily indebted, but the rosy income projections made them sound like a total lock. Donald put his younger brother, Robert, in charge of the company's casino division, a move he would soon come to regret. But so far, so good. The constantly rising tide was lifting all of Donald's boats.

It's true that Wall Street had a bad crash in 1987, but that didn't kill the housing-and-hotel boom. Not immediately. All those reach-for-the-sky projects had momentum of their own. *Some* momentum. The first real bump came in 1989, when New York City officials, citing "unusual" and "unheard of" accounting methods approved by Donald, ordered the Grand Hyatt to pay the city nearly $3 million in back rent. It was a little embarrassing when the New York City auditors started wagging their fingers, but no big deal in the scheme of things.

The real problems were on the way.

Trump-sized problems.

And soon.

The banks were getting itchy. Donald was getting squeezed. The money wasn't coming in like Donald had promised it would and the bankers had expected it to.

The trickle-down from the Wall Street crash was depressing Manhattan apartment prices. Business travel and office rents were also off. And Donald was rolling nothing but snake eyes in Atlantic City. Despite an avalanche of media hype, the Trump Plaza and Trump Castle properties were groaning beneath high debt and low occupancy. His newest casino hotel, the over-the-top Trump Taj Mahal, was going to be his Atlantic City lifeline. *Oops.* All the Taj did was cadge customers from its two sister properties and raise the debt collectors' blood pressure another notch or two.

Things were getting tense in the office too. One day when I went to see my grandfather, I heard a lot of yelling as I walked in. My grandfather was somewhere else in the building, wandering the halls. And

Donald was yelling at Robert about some issue at one of the casinos. Or as it sounded to me, Sonny Corleone was berating Fredo again.

"You're an idiot," Donald thundered at his younger brother.

"It wasn't my fault," Robert sputtered back. "It was the contractor and the subs."

"And why weren't you watching them?"

It was painful to listen to. I had no idea who was right, whether Rob had been incompetent or Donald was being unreasonable. Either seemed possible. But I did know there was major tension about the way things were going in Atlantic City, and there was no way that Donald was ever going to blame himself.

He might have to deal with it, but it was never going to be his fault. Poor Robert. And it was crisis time.

Donald's entire gambling empire was in "severe financial distress," in the ominous words of New Jersey casino regulators, leading to swift bankruptcy filings at all three Trump casinos. (I had to assume that, somehow or another, Robert was already being blamed for that.) At the same time, the Trump Shuttle and its frequent Boston–New York–Washington flights were bleeding cash and also adding to the debt load. And Donald claimed his first wife, Ivana, was bragging that she expected "a billion dollars" in their upcoming divorce settlement.

Forget about that last one for a minute. Ivana was always the queen of hyperbole. The hard numbers were daunting enough. By 1990, the company owed a total of $4 billion to seventy-two different financial institutions. Especially scary for Donald: He had personally guaranteed $800 million of that debt load. These were truly rattling times for the former Boy Wonder of New York Real Estate, who had been so confident that the future was paved with gold . . . which turned out to be just a shiny gold-colored veneer.

He hired the Trump Organization's first chief finance officer, Stephen Bollenbach, to show the bankers he was doing something. He leaned on veteran comptroller Allen Weisselberg. But what could those two do? Both men had sharp pencils. They were good with figures, and Allen certainly knew the Trumps. But neither of them was a miracle worker. They couldn't fire up the Trump Tower Xerox machine and start printing hundred-dollar bills.

So where could Donald find a big pile of money? And how could he protect it from his hungry creditors? He couldn't plead for patience forever. He couldn't continue telling the bankers he was too big to fail. There had to be a pile of green sitting somewhere, didn't there?

Didn't there?

It turned out there was one. Hidden in plain sight.

So how wealthy was my grandfather?

Assessing the true value of a real-estate portfolio is not an exact science. How much is this building or that building really worth? Well, it depends on how much you think you can raise the rents and how much you're planning to spend on new kitchen appliances and whether you believe you can bust the doorman's union or not. There's a lot of wiggle room in there.

Given that reality, it was hard for Donald or anyone else to pin a dollar sign on my grandfather's net worth and therefore the likely size of his estate. But by the late 1980s, as Donald's need for cash grew more intense, the number was well into nine figures, even if New York rents totally collapsed tomorrow—which had almost never happened since 1626 when Peter Minuit of the Dutch East India Company traded $24 in beads and trinkets for the entire island of Manhattan. Rents in New York City *always* seem to go up!

Enter Donald, just as the bankers were really tightening the screws, threatening to push him into personal bankruptcy. He was a man with a plan. According to his deposition in our case and the depositions

of other family members, which were quoted extensively in the *Washington Post*'s coverage of our inheritance case in 2000, it was then that Donald had asked a lawyer, Peter Valente, to draft a sweeping document for his father to sign, a codicil to the will, as it's known in the law. The immediate purpose of the codicil? To put Donald's inheritance beyond the reach of his creditors and his soon-to-be ex-wife. Valente was never accused of any wrongdoing. He was just the lawyer who drafted the codicil.

But who should show the document to Grandpa? Clearly, Donald put some thought into that. His father didn't know or have any reason to trust Peter Valente. So, he didn't seem like a good candidate. And Donald didn't want to deliver the document himself. That might highlight his own urgent needs. Instead, in December 1990, he dispatched two of his father's most trusted advisers, an accountant and a lawyer. The accountant was Jack Mitnick, who had worked on Trump family matters for many years. The lawyer was our own friend Irwin Durben . . . who seemed to have his hands in *everything*.

The pair of them told my grandfather he needed to sign immediately.

Grandpa was eighty-five at the time. He hadn't been formally diagnosed with cognitive impairment, but family members had already noticed he was already having trouble remembering things.

In a moment of lucidity, my grandfather must have had some concerns about the document that Donald sent to him. My grandmother certainly did. She took one look and told her husband, "You're not signing anything." Instead, he asked his daughter Maryanne to take a look. And for good reason. After graduating from Mount Holyoke, getting married, and spending thirteen years at home raising her son, David, Maryanne had graduated from Hofstra Law and—no surprise—had begun a fast-track career as an attorney. She was among the highest-ranking women in the United States Attorney's Office in Newark and,

as of 1983, a U.S. district judge in New Jersey, nominated by President Ronald Reagan and confirmed by the U.S. Senate. She knew the law.

"I first became aware of this document when my father called me and said he had been given this document by Irwin Durben and Jack Mitnick and asked to sign it, and he said he didn't like what he saw in there and he wanted me to take a look at it," Maryanne recalled in her deposition.

"I have a distinct recollection of him bringing the document to me when we were down at my brother Donald's house in Florida for a weekend that early '91," she said. "He called me on it and brought it to me because he was disturbed by what he read." Her father was also put off by the high-pressure tactics, "sign it immediately," Maryanne said in her deposition. (Neither Mitnick nor Durben was ever formally accused of any wrongdoing.)

Before expressing her opinion to her father, Maryanne turned to a real expert, her second husband, John Barry, who was a prominent lawyer in New York and New Jersey with experience handling trusts and estates. She had him take a look. The document did a whole lot more than protect Donald's inheritance from his debt collectors and his ex-wife, John warned. As Maryanne put it in her deposition: "Donald has sole control of everything as the executor/trustee, can sell, do anything he wants, you know, with the properties."

Maryanne laid all this out in blistering detail, including her strong suspicions about Donald's motives, in her deposition: "Dad was concerned because although he always had the highest respect for Donald and admiration for him, this was a time when Donald was in precarious financial straits by his own admission and Dad was very concerned as a man who worked hard for his money and never wanted any of it to leave the family."

Aunt Maryanne recalled her father telling her: "This doesn't pass the smell test."

"Here's his attorney giving him something that he reads [that] could potentially denude his estate and he was annoyed that should happen that way . . . behind his back," Maryanne said in her deposition. "He had not authorized it, didn't know they were going to give it to him for signature."

Maryanne confirmed her parents' suspicions. She sent word back to her father. Do not sign. And he didn't.

Looking back at this sordid episode, the question has to be asked: Was my grandfather already losing it? Though he was savvy enough to seek the advice of his wife and daughter, was his senility already kicking in? And was Donald trying to take advantage of his father's weakness, just as the old man was slipping into the early stages of dementia? When Donald was asked about this during his deposition, he emphatically denied it, insisting that his father was in tip-top mental shape.

> Q. Do you recall your father suffering from any memory lapses in 1991?
> A. No.
> Q. Do you recall him being diagnosed as having senile dementia in 1991?
> A. No, I don't.
> Q. Do you recall him exhibiting any confusion in 1991?
> A. No.

Really?

I'm no gerontologist. But I still had strong reason to doubt that, and not just because Grandpa seemed increasingly doddering in those days when I went by to visit. Less than a year after Donald dispatched the lawyer and the accountant, my grandfather *was* formally diagnosed. Doctor's notes from my grandfather's medical exam on October 3, 1991, documented "significant memory impairment" and "early signs of dementia." A follow-up appointment with a neurologist several months later revealed my grandfather could not recall his own birth-date or simple facts he'd been told half an hour earlier, according to the *Washington Post*, which quoted the medical records our lawyers were given as part of the discovery process. And personally, I think his decline started way before any of that.

There was no denying Donald was feeling badly squeezed at that point and was looking at his father's estate as a bulging piggy bank and a shield against his creditors. He conceded as much during his deposi-tion. "It was a very bad period of time," Donald said under question-ing, "and if for any reason I was not able to come out of this well, then this would be giving me a trust to protect the money."

Donald couldn't hide from the fact that his first attempt to influence his father had fallen flat.

So live and learn and try again.

"He [my father] wasn't happy about it," he said in his deposition. "In the end, he just didn't like maybe the concept of the document or didn't like the way it was presented or he just wanted to review the whole situation." In a rare flash of self-reflection, Donald added: "I blame myself for that because I think the presentation was probably, in retrospect, not done right, but I had a lot of things on my mind at that point, and this is not the biggest thing at all."

So . . . the issue in his eyes wasn't selfishness or desperation. It was presentation and bigger demands.

Very Donald J. Trump.

Still, if Uncle Donald was anything, it was persistent. And he was not about to abandon his efforts to reshape his father's will to his per-sonal advantage just because his sister and her husband, or even his mother, threw cold water on his first attempt. Still fearing that his substantial inheritance could be seized by the creditors (or, God forbid, his ex), he tried a different tack: enlisting his siblings in the effort to revise the 1984 will.

Now, instead of Donald trying to become the sole executor, he would share that duty with Maryanne and Robert, bringing both of them inside the tent. And there was one other important change in language that could mean a large financial sweetener for Donald, Maryanne, Elizabeth, and Robert—with devastating consequences for my sister, Mary, and me.

It was just a short phrase, but it was planted like a powerful time bomb in the new draft, set to explode on my sister and me. The new phrase said that when my grandfather died, the vast majority of his fortune would go to his wife and then, in equal shares, to "my children who survive me."

"My children who survive me": Read those five words closely. There was a lot of meaning packed in there, especially if you were sitting where Mary and I were. Simply put: If my grandfather signed the revised will, the estate would be divided among his *living* children—four shares, not five. What had been my father's share would be divided among Maryanne, Donald, Elizabeth, and Robert while my father's survivors, Mary and me, would get nothing (except for a single payment of $200,000, the same token set aside for each of the Trump grandchildren).

How dramatic a change was this? So dramatic that one of my grandfather's lawyers attached a memo to the final draft, warning that Mary and I were about to be badly disadvantaged compared to the other Trump grandchildren. Under Donald's plan, we would never get any portion of our deceased father's share of the estate.

Zero.

To drill the point home, the lawyer added an emphatic note to my grandfather: "Given the size of your estate, this is tantamount to disinheriting them. You may wish to increase their participation in your estate to avoid ill will in the future."

That was *my grandfather's* lawyer!

With that sage advice, he could have written *our* brief!

Asked about this change during his deposition, Donald claimed that he discussed the concern with his father and that his father wasn't bothered by it at all. Instead of changing anything, Donald said his father blamed my mother, recalling his father's "tremendous dislike" of our mother and concern that if more of our father's inheritance went to Mary and me, our mother would somehow get her hands on all or part of it, the New York *Daily News* reported.

Our mother. Our dad's ex-wife. Grandpa's onetime daughter-in-law.

Who'd been nothing but nice and accommodating to her in-laws, even as some of them treated her like a low-class, gold-digging stewardess.

The minute I read that, I understood exactly where Donald's post-deposition outburst had come from. He was trying to shift the blame from himself to my mother. He wanted everyone to believe that it wasn't his greed or his need that propelled all this. It was something about his late brother's ex-wife, who had always tried hard to get along with the family even as they kept talking down to her and dismissing her as somehow beneath them.

My mother was the victim here, not a villain. To me, it sounded like a lame Donald excuse.

In her deposition, according to the New York *Daily News,* Mary-anne testified that she too had discussed the lawyer's concern about dis-inheriting Mary and me. "Forget about it," she claimed her father said.

And that's just about how everything went.

Talk about an inside-the-family money grab. Yes, we were to receive the same amount as the other grandchildren, but the others would also eventually inherit their parents' share of the estate. Our father was gone, and Mary and I were left with a tiny fraction of what we were set to receive before Donald set his sights on his father's will. It took two tries, but he got it done. And it all happened as my grandfather's grip on reality was at the very least loosening. It meant an extra helping for my aunts and uncles—and a real gut punch for Mary and me.

And it landed—I cannot emphasize this enough—at the absolute worst imaginable time in our lives.

All thanks to my uncle Donald, the same Donald who, as our co-trustee, had supposedly been looking out for Mary and me since we were teenagers. He was willing to squeeze his own niece and nephew and manipulate his father's wishes, all to try and stop his own creditors from collecting the money he legally owed them. If that meant screwing his late brother—well, so be it. If it meant raiding the inheritance of his brother's two children—well, okay.

Blood went only so far in this family . . . as far as the dollar signs.

In fact, my father was a Trump every bit as much as Donald was. My father's children were Trumps as much as Donald's children were. But cutting off our share of the family fortune didn't seem to cause Donald a second of anxiety or guilt.

For me, the questions kept coming.

How had Mary and I become less worthy? Why didn't our branch of the family deserve the same advantages all the others got? Why were we second-string Trumps? Just because our father had made his own choices, suffered his own failings, and died far too young?

I do believe that my grandfather's disappointment with my father—his drinking, his rejection of the family business, his passion for flying, his choice of a wife, his lifelong free-spiritedness in everything—made my grandfather susceptible to Donald's pressure. It was an emotional button Donald knew he could push, and he pushed it hard. Would my grandfather have ever done this on his own? I highly doubt it. Years had passed since my father's death, and my grandfather never did anything like it until Donald turned the pressure up.

Mary and I loved our grandparents as much as any of our cousins did. We cared for them and spent a lot of time at their house. And I always felt the affection was mutual, delivered in each of their own ways. Isn't that how families are?

That's how this one was . . . until it wasn't anymore.

Donald felt squeezed, so he looked for someone else he could squeeze. Mainly, I think he did it because he could.

On September 18, 1991, my grandfather signed the new version of the will that listed Maryann, Donald, and Robert as co-executors, and no one ever said anything to Mary or me about the dramatic changes it included—or how they would affect our futures. Not Donald. Not Maryanne. Not my grandfather, if he even remembered. No one.

We wouldn't learn about any of this until eight years later, after my grandfather's death, after William was born, when I got that disturbing phone call one day from my grandfather's longtime lawyer (and my co-trustee) Irwin Durben.

What a life changer.

If all this had been as honorable as Donald and his siblings insisted in court, how come none of them ever mentioned it to us outside of Robert's vague hint that day before lunch in Brooklyn? If nothing sleazy had happened, why was it all such a deep, dark secret?

We were kept in blissful ignorance all the way through my grandfather's funeral and my eulogy for him. It was only with that call from the lawyer that the truth began to come out.

PART III

PUTTING US BACK TOGETHER

CHAPTER 18

PALS AGAIN

Our case could easily have dragged on forever.

After negotiating many commercial lease deals, I knew how weeks could turn into months, which could turn into years, which could turn into God-only-knows-how-long. I didn't want that to happen in our family feud over my grandfather's estate. Frankly, I couldn't *afford* for it to happen, and I don't just mean financially, but emotionally too. With all I had going on in my life at that point, being an eternal litigant was never part of the plan.

As I believe I have made clear, this was the busiest I had ever been. I'd never lived with any more pressure. Besides my full-time job, besides being a father to Andrea and Cristopher and a husband to Lisa—and doing all the other things it takes to keep a life afloat—I never forgot for a second that I was also William's father, and believe me, that was no afterthought. Every newborn is a big, life-changing moment. Our third child was the next level of life-changing, that and something more. Our son's needs remained a never-ending responsibility. Emotionally draining too.

I had so many things tugging at me, I had zero time for myself. My

friendships certainly suffered. I'm not complaining. I had responsibilities. That's just the way it was. They were full on. As the court case sputtered on, Lisa and I continued with William's hyperbaric treatments.
Getting him to the hospital. Suiting him up. Hoping these in-the-
chamber treatments would encourage his development. The sessions
were long and often. In small ways at least, they did seem to be helping.
William was more alert. He was a bit more engaged as time went on. It
was hard to know how much to credit the hyperbaric chamber and how
much of it was the physical and occupational therapy and all the other
stuff we were doing. We kept consulting new experts, and Lisa kept
saying, "If we can only figure out what the problem is, we may have a
chance of solving it."

William's progress was frustratingly slow. We truly had no idea how
far he would ever get, except for his physical growth, which remained
formidable. This kid was an eater. He was still packing on the pounds.
But the other milestones that parents typically look for, he just wasn't
meeting. Not even close. No turning over. No first crawls. No standing.
Nowhere near walking. William's sounds were certainly a language of
their own, one we worked mightily to decode. He recognized all of us
in the family, always looking forward to seeing his brother and sister
whenever they'd been out for a while. And he really worked that smile,
not only for us but also for his caregivers, therapists, and anyone who
chose to spend time with him.

We held him and hugged him and felt tremendous love for him,
love he was an expert at returning our way. We had a son who was
missing every developmental stage that the pediatric manuals laid out
for him, but he was an off-the-charts dispenser of love. How did he do
that? He smiled when he played with his siblings. He smiled when he
got hugs and kisses from us. We'd felt such fear after his birth. Now,
love was the easiest and simplest emotion both to give and receive, and
it was always constant.

Through the Birth to Three program and some informal friend-to-friend networks, we were getting to know a few other parents who had children with severe developmental challenges, physical and mental and often both. Those new friends were ready and happy to share their advice and experiences, and they were eager to hear about ours. This long journey might be overwhelming, but it was good to know we weren't taking it entirely alone. It turned out there was a huge army of people out there, all on their own challenging journeys, but all willing to lend a helping hand to another family in need. And we were in need.

All of this felt profoundly important. I couldn't imagine not doing everything possible to give my son the best opportunities, and anything I did, Lisa did that-times-ten.

All of which is to say there were days that fighting with my family over money seemed like the least important thing in the world. I recognize that's probably not the attitude to bring to a hard-fought legal battle, especially when the people on the other side had the last name Trump. I'm just describing how I felt.

If I thought real-estate deals took a long time to wrap up, I had no idea what I was in for in the hurry-up-and-wait world of Queens County Surrogate's Court. As the depositions proceeded and the experts shared their insights and the discovery material slowly trickled in, I kept asking Jack and his associates: "Why are we waiting two weeks for the other side to answer the simplest question? Why does everything have to take so long?"

There was always a reason . . . at least an excuse. And another delay, delay, delay tactic.

I came to suspect that Maryanne, Donald, and Robert and their ex-judge of a lawyer were purposely dragging everything out, knowing what pressure I was under in the rest of my life, figuring that each new

delay would give them a fresh negotiating advantage as the two sides
inched toward some kind of resolution.

The vast majority of cases like ours settle before they ever get to
trial, according to Jack and his team. I had no reason to doubt that.
I was open to a settlement if we could come up with a fair result—
even a half-fair result. I hated fighting with my relatives, and I most
definitely didn't need a hobby to fill my time. As soon as Maryanne,
Donald, and Robert had done their depositions, the settlement talks
seemed to heat up. Gam's death might have also played a role. Whenever the court gave its final approval, the money would go straight
to the next generations. Now that she'd passed, however much it was
wouldn't sit in Gam's account at all. By this point, I guess both sides
knew the strengths and weaknesses of their cases, and maybe both
sides were getting tired of all the delays. I'm sure Donald wanted to
get his hands on his piece ASAP.

On our side, I think we did a powerful job of highlighting the nasty
steps that Donald—and two of his siblings—had taken to pressure my
grandfather to change his will, advantaging them and harming Mary
and me. I knew that anyone who saw that evidence—a judge, a jury,
the public at large—would be sympathetic to our case. The fact that
the other side had gone so far as to cut off the insurance policy for our
severely disabled son—I mean, *really.* That made them appear down-
right cruel.

I knew they wouldn't want the outside world to get any more of an
inside look.

As for the questions about my grandfather's mental capacity, that
was a little trickier. There was strong evidence that he was suffering
from the early stages of dementia when he agreed to change his will. I
had seen that with my own eyes . . . for years. He was clearly susceptible to manipulation by his children. He had lingering, hard feelings
about my father that, in his vulnerable state, could be exploited by his

living children. But exactly how senile was he? Did he still have any kind of grasp on what he was doing? And when did the real decline set in? Those issues were all open to interpretation. Given everything I knew about my grandfather, I can't believe he ever would have done something like that on his own. But we still needed to prove that.

Through the lawyers on both sides, we kept going back and forth.

They'd throw out a number. We'd throw out a different number. They would come up a little but not nearly enough. Mary and I had our own conversations about what might make sense for us. She and I had some differences on that.

It wasn't just a matter of Mary being ready to fight on and me being at the point of feeling like I needed to get everything resolved. We were racking up huge legal bills, even though we didn't have to pay until the case was resolved. Our own family's medical bills were gigantic and getting larger. Our insurance situation was still a mess.

"I really need to get this settled," I kept saying to Mary, "and get back to my son and my family."

Mary was understanding. She really was. But she was also in a different position. She was still a couple of years away from being a mom. She certainly didn't have the endless demands of a special-needs child. She seemed to have flexibility and, therefore, more patience. While I respected Mary's feelings, there was also a point where we had to try to move on.

I knew that weakened my negotiating position. I was enough of a Trump to understand: If the other side senses you are itching to end the fight, that's a weakness they can take advantage of. And I was ready to settle.

It never got testy between Mary and me. But our situations were different, and so were our responses to the case. "I have to end this," I finally said.

Thankfully, our lawyers had just about hammered out the terms of a settlement. Not a perfect one. I'm not even sure I would call it a good one. But a settlement that required them to give us *some* of what we were entitled to.

For years, I had heard Donald boast, "I never settle a lawsuit. I fight to the bitter end."

After my dad died and throughout the trial, Donald was supposed to be my trustee—and trusted relative. While I had no vote in the matter, I had placed trust in that assurance, and now that trust had been violated.

We signed the deal on April 10, 2001, nearly two years after my grandfather's death, eight months after my grandmother was gone.

Part of the deal involved a confidentiality agreement, limiting what either side could say publicly. So I won't be throwing around specific numbers. Let me put it like this: It was better than where we started. But it was nowhere near what my grandfather intended as a one-fifth split for all five families.

In more recent times, Mary came to believe that our lawyers hadn't really been fighting for us, that they were conflicted or corrupted or somehow confused. I have never shared that view. I think this is what happens in a hard-fought negotiation. Neither side gets what they want, especially when one of the plaintiffs doesn't want to spend his whole life at war. I take the rap for that. I was fully cognizant of what my relatives had done. I was clear on how wrong it was. But I still didn't want to fight with them for the rest of my life.

If we would have held out longer, maybe we'd have received more of what was due to us. But I was more interested in getting on with my life and getting back to my family. If I had to pay a price for that, I guess I was willing to pay it.

Mary would continue the battle for years to come, writing a book about her own experiences and going back into court, arguing that new evidence proved we had been defrauded by the relatives and that our lawyers were weakened by conflicts of interest. I get all that. I love my sister. It was time to move on.

I knew I needed to be a different kind of Trump than the brand name had projected for so long.

"Donald would like you to be an honorary member at Briarcliff."

It was a year after the lawsuit was settled. That was the phone message I got from Donald's assistant. My uncle was just then developing an old, bankrupt golf course in Briarcliff Manor, New York, into the Trump National Golf Club Westchester. He had big plans, I knew. The course was in a beautiful spot just a thirty-minute drive from our house in Connecticut. I understood "honorary" to mean free.

So *now* he wants to make nice?

That was the first thought that jumped into my head as soon as I listened to the message.

I hadn't asked for the invitation. I had gotten the call out of nowhere. And I wasn't exactly sure how I should respond. I didn't know what the annual dues were going to be when Donald had the place up and running—but a lot, on top of an initiation fee that was sure to run well into five figures. It was clearly a gesture on his part. Was it a payout from his side of the win? Did he really want to be pals again? I was leaning toward the latter. But with Donald, it was hard to assume there were no other agendas.

The more I thought about it, the less I knew what I thought. Clearly, I still had some lingering resentment despite the legal settlement. But another part of me was also thinking, *Do you really want to be at war forever with your father's family?* If Donald was genuinely reaching out now, maybe I should just accept the olive branch and move on. For the sake of my family and my cousins, I wanted to play through this course, move on, and move forward.

I knew myself. I'd always been the mediator, the go-between, the one who could see things from different points of view. I leaned toward finding solutions. I always wanted things to end amicably. I know this might seem unusual given how hostile things had gotten with my father's siblings. But could I really drag this out longer than it had already gone? Was I ready to forgive?

I gave it twenty-four hours. Then, I returned the call to Donald's assistant. "Tell him I'll do it—but only if I can play a round of golf with him first."

If I was going to try and get things back to normal, I didn't want any bullshit between us. Better for Donald and me to spend some time together on the golf course and air out whatever discomfort remained. Hadn't he just invited me to join the Trump golf club? Then let's spend eighteen holes together and see how that goes.

She called me back with a tee time. Our golf date was on.

I was nervous as hell as I drove the Sprain Brook Parkway to the Taconic State Parkway to Briarcliff Manor that day. My nervousness showed on the driving range, where I stopped for some warm-up swings before our scheduled time. I was conflicted and unsure. It had been a really long time since Donald and I had had a normal conversation. We hadn't even seen each other except at his deposition, and I wouldn't exactly call that a very cheery encounter. The same with the other defendants, Aunt Maryanne and Uncle Robert. I'd had no contact with them at all. It had been a full-on deep freeze with my father's entire family, and it had swept up Lisa, Andrea, and Cristopher too, though it was more of a chilly side wind for them. As for two-year-old William, the family's counterpunch had threatened his medical treatment, just when he had needed it most. He hadn't asked for any of this.

Could a few holes of golf and my name on some legal documents make all that ugly history evaporate? Of course not. But at some point, we did need to move on. I kept reminding myself of that. I was sick and tired of all the fighting. I'd agreed to the settlement. Mary had too. Our future was loaded with horrendous challenges. Lisa and I understood by now: This journey with William was never going to end. I just kept telling myself, *Peace is worth a try. We need to move on for our family.*

When I got out of the car at the construction site that was gradually becoming the Trump National Golf Club Westchester, the "club" part was more a goal than a reality. The course was there, and it looked nice. But the future clubhouse was just a stack of architect's drawings. Construction equipment was everywhere. There were three GE trailers hitched together. One had a little pro shop. One had the men's locker room. Another had a small ladies' locker room with plastic showers. The major renovation and expansion had barely begun.

Donald greeted me outside the pro shop winding up with his usual "Hey, pal," every bit as boisterous as I remembered it.

"Hi, Donald," I answered, not revealing much in my tone.

Our foursome that day included bestselling author James Patterson and Cary Stephan, who'd already begun as the club's head pro. When you play with Donald, you never know who might show up to fill out your foursome.

Donald's golf games, I knew from past outings, were always a rapid-fire affair, frequently punctuated by phone calls. "I gotta grab this," he kept saying. Patterson had a very slow way of approaching the ball, testing Donald's patience. Eye it. Measure it. Practice a couple of air swings. Donald made clear that he thought the famous author was taking a little too long.

I got off the first tee okay, parring it. I birdied the second hole, which is one of the hardest holes on the course. All of that was calming to me. I don't recall how I played after that. Well enough. And we managed some friendly conversation along the way.

Nothing deep, but not tense either.

It still felt weird being with him, like, *Wait, what am I doing here?*

But not as weird as I feared. We stayed for lunch in the make-do dining area. It was all pleasant enough. Nothing serious. Just friendly banter and routine chitchat about sports and the news and golf.

It was only as I was saying goodbye that we got to what I had to assume was the reason I was there in the first place.

Donald took a short breath, and then he said to me: "We're through, right?"

Through?

I wasn't sure what he meant by that.

"It's over, right? We're through."

I took that to mean the lawsuit is over. No more animosity. Now, we were moving on. Like, that was strictly business. Nothing personal. We're done.

That wasn't really how I saw my life, as just another negotiation, and now the negotiation was done. To me, it had felt personal. Utterly personal. I still felt like my sister and I, and the people who depended on us, were the ones who had gotten screwed. But you can't live in that anger forever. Sometimes, you do have to move on.

"Sure," I told him. "We're through."

"Good, pal," he said.

Then, he stepped forward and gave me a hug.

A hug. From Donald. I'm not sure I'd *ever* gotten one of those before.

Then, as he quickly stepped away, he seemed to catch himself. He turned and looked back at me. Obviously, he had something else on his mind. And this being Donald, there was no way he was going to keep it to himself.

"Your lawyer never should have said that thing about your grandfather's toupee."

Oh, that. I'd heard about that. During Donald's deposition, one of our lawyers had supposedly been making a point about Grandpa's declining mental state. He described how the aging patriarch had so lost his grip on reality, he was going out in public with an almost comical toupee.

I didn't hear that exchange between lawyer and witness. It happened behind the closed doors of the deposition room. But I knew how sensitive Donald was on the subject of men and their hairstyles. Apparently, that even included *his father's* hair, whether the God-given kind or not. And of all the things that might have lingered in my uncle's mind after our long and drawn-out legal battle, the one he couldn't shake entirely was this one.

Your lawyer never should have said that thing about your grandfather's toupee.

CHAPTER 19

MOVING FORWARD

After all the drawn-out drama, it wasn't so easy getting back to being a normal family again.

Wait a second. Who am I kidding? The Trumps were never a *normal* family. We were far too colorful and far too complicated for that. Yes, there was a level of high function in the extended clan, and undeniable worldly success. But my little branch was still pointedly excluded from that, years after we'd all supposedly made peace again. My sister and I were still kept firmly on the outside, never fully invited in. Wouldn't it be great, after so long, if we could end all these divisions for the sake of the next generation? Why should the next generation of children—our children and all their cousins—keep paying a price for these long-ago feelings and disputes? It made no sense. Holidays, weddings, celebrations of any kind—those were the times I most wished things were different.

I didn't know whether Maryanne, Robert, and Elizabeth felt the same way Donald seemed to, ready to put the past behind us and move on. None of the others had made any effort to reach out to me. Mary and I were the ones who had borne the brunt of that past. How hard could it be? I was grateful that my cousins Donnie and Eric had made an effort to reconnect. It was important for our generation to move past the past.

I got the impression that Mary wasn't so eager to mend these broken ties. She had a partner by now, and they had a daughter. Mary was focused on family, education, and her writing career. Mary already had a bachelor's from Tufts and a master's from Columbia, and now she was working on her PhD in clinical psychology at Adelphi University. I had my immediate family too, of course. But I was hoping for something that would be closer to a healthy relationship with all the members of my extended family.

Was that too much to expect?

We would just have to see. It was never easy in a moving-target family like the Trumps, especially with Donald's fame and celebrity just about to really take off.

We may not have been quite breaking bread together, but Donald was always just a TV channel away. In 2004, Donald began starring in *The Apprentice,* which became a runaway hit for him, creator Mark Burnett, and NBC. And it did something that not so many people appreciated at the time. I didn't watch the show. I'm not a big reality-TV game-show fan. But I did pay attention to what was happening *with* the show and *to* Donald. *The Apprentice* took a person who was famous in the New York area and kinda known in other places—and turned him into a full-fledged, A-list, wall-to-wall national celebrity. "You're fired!" became two of the most famous words in America, heard in living rooms coast to coast. Donald was the most famous business executive on earth. Suddenly, he was bigger than big. He had actually earned the "The" that Ivana had planted in front of his first name.

There are few things more intimate than being in someone's living room, even if it's through the magic of a television screen. *The Apprentice,* which was shot in Trump Tower and also sometimes featured my cousins Donnie, Ivanka, and Eric, would run 192 episodes across fifteen seasons and also spin off into *The Celebrity Apprentice.* And by season eight, the episodes wouldn't be one hour. They'd run a full two hours.

That's an awful lot of Trump.

Among the skills that Donald polished on his long TV run: how to heighten the tension in a public standoff, how to create clear heroes and villains, how to position himself as the reasonable man, how to remain calm on camera no matter what else was happening around him. I say "polished" because Donald already knew a lot of that stuff from his years in and out of the media, but he kept getting better and better at it. Those skills weren't only bankable, I thought as the show hit its stride. If properly applied, they really could propel someone into politics, who knows how far, maybe even all the way to the White House.

Donald had always toyed with the *idea* of politics, weighing in on controversial issues, spouting off his pointed opinions, hinting that if some officeholder didn't get with it in a hurry, Donald just might run himself. Was he serious? No one really thought so, including Donald, I suspect. But there was no denying he was building the skills.

You know who else was paying close attention to my uncle? The writers at *Saturday Night Live.* Could there be any more proof that he was something beyond a New York real-estate developer with a TV show? His standing as a national figure might actually be going somewhere. And the *SNL* cast didn't only make fun of him in their sketches and parodies. Remarkably, I thought, he was asked to host—yes, *host—* the show on April 3, 2004, which featured a skit called "Donald Trump's House of Wings," in which he wore an all-yellow suit as the *SNL* cast danced around him in chicken costumes, and again on November 7,

2015. Those appearances certainly weren't a conventional route to the White House. But they were another important step in nationalizing the celebrity of Donald Trump.

We weren't invited to Donald and Melania's wedding at the Bethesda-by-the-Sea church in Palm Beach or the reception at Mar-a-Lago in January 2005. No big deal. We weren't expecting to be there. We weren't at Donnie's wedding to Vanessa in November of that year. Barron was born on March 20, 2006. I didn't meet my newest and youngest cousin until years later. Life had moved on, and so had we. There were other milestones we weren't a part of. In May of 2007, when Donnie and Vanessa had a baby, Kai Madison, making Donald a grandfather, we didn't know until we saw the announcement in the paper. We were living our own lives with our hands full at home.

Around that time, William had begun suffering seizures again. This was terrifying, for him and for us. We'd thought we'd gotten the seizures under control. Now, we couldn't make them stop. We had to figure out what the problem was and what we could do about it. In October 2007, he was admitted to the NYU Langone Comprehensive Epilepsy Center, where he remained for two weeks under the care of the renowned neurologist Dr. Orrin Devinsky. After much testing, Dr. Devinsky and his team put William on two medications, Depakote and Keppra, that stabilized him and finally got the seizures under control. Thank God for them. William would stay on those drugs for years.

In January 2009, Lisa and I went to see Donald at his office. Through the pink marble lobby. Into the shiny elevator. Up to the office floor. Past his longtime assistant. Into the office where all decisions were made. The venue was appropriate. We were there to talk about money. William and money. But before we got started, Donald had a question for us.

"So, what's the problem with him, anyway?" Donald asked. "Like what's *wrong* with him?"

"Well," I said, picking my words carefully. "The doctors don't know exactly, but it's some kind of genetic thing."

"Not in *our* family," Donald shot back. "There's nothing wrong with *our* genes."

In his confident view, any genetic issue didn't come from the Trumps. In fact, I told him, the doctors hadn't figured out exactly what the genetic misfire might be. It might be in *no one's* family. But they were studying it, and they would figure it out eventually.

William was ten years old by then, and the bills for his care were really becoming a burden. The costs definitely weren't letting up. We were there to ask if Donald and his siblings could help to cover some of the expenses of William's care.

"It's becoming a real challenge for us," I said.

I was relieved when Donald didn't rule it out.

"Can you write a letter to Maryanne, laying out exactly what you are talking about?" he asked.

I told him sure.

Lisa and I went home and wrote the letter, detailing William's medical needs and therapeutic expenses and how much we had paid over the years. It took some effort pulling all that together, but I knew how important it was. I hand-delivered the letter to Donald's office. He forwarded it to Maryanne.

Maryanne called me a couple of days later. She had read the letter, she said, and would share it with Robert and Elizabeth. A few days later, she called again, saying that the four of them were setting up a medical fund for William.

"That's great," I said.

"Can you and Lisa come to my apartment and go out to dinner with me?"

"Of course."

This would be the first time I had seen Maryanne since we had crossed paths at her deposition.

Maryanne lived now at 1050 Fifth Avenue, directly across from Central Park between 86th and 87th Streets. It was a luxury doorman building, and her fifteenth-floor apartment was fairly understated given the address. But the place was surprisingly dark and cluttered, like an apartment where someone had lived for decades and never bothered to open the curtains. After all that had been said and done and then all these years of silence, I was a little worried that she might have called for this dinner to unload any anger that might have built up in the interim.

Well, Maryanne was still capable of surprises.

She started crying the minute Lisa and I walked through the door. She didn't only seem glad to see us. She seemed to feel guilt—I almost hate to use the word—about the way it had all gone down. Especially the medical insurance cutoff and how it had affected our younger son.

We explained what life had been like and all the details of William's care. "William is going have a lot of expenses," she said. "This fund is a good idea."

What a relief. With Maryanne you never knew if she was going to be kind and helpful or rip your head off for some random reason. She did ask how we were doing as parents and recognized how much stress we were under. "You should take a vacation," she said, offering us the use of her place in Florida, which was kind, even though we never took her up on it. And most importantly, she sounded serious about the William fund. She wasn't just saying something to placate us or make us think well of her while we were at her apartment. I could tell that she really intended to do this.

She didn't say how much money it would be, or exactly what it would pay for, or how often her brothers and sister might contribute. But the truth was that we did still have a lot of expenses for William, even with the insurance. It had really added up. Anything they were offering was going to help immensely.

I don't know that I'd ever heard anything that touched me as much as those words did. I'm pretty sure I hadn't. After that, she and I started meeting every now and then for lunch in Manhattan. Or I'd stop by her apartment just to say hello. I wanted to rebuild our relationship. She was a connection to my father. She had some of the memories I didn't have. As we started talking again, she seemed to recognize the importance of connecting me back to my father and those times. And before we left her that night, she had a suggestion for me: "You really should get together with Rob."

He and I met for lunch at the Sidecar at P.J. Clarke's on Third Avenue.

We hugged, spent an hour together. I had an iced tea. He had a Bloody Mary and asked about William, Andrea, Cristopher, and Lisa. I thanked him for agreeing to be part of the William fund.

It was a little awkward. The conversation didn't totally flow. But at least we were talking. At least it was a start. Rob was divorced from Blaine by then, and I asked how he was adjusting to that. He told me about his girlfriend, Ann Marie Pallan, and said he was doing pretty well.

It was the first time I'd seen Rob since the lawsuit.

That summer, I also had lunch with Elizabeth and Maryanne. I knew how close Elizabeth and my father had been. I knew how much my father loved his little sister. When I was small and Aunt Elizabeth would give me a big hug, I would jokingly say to her, "Oh, my neck, my neck . . ." So of course, I had to repeat that tradition when I saw her again. It was the first time I'd seen Elizabeth since my grandfather's funeral in 1999. I thanked her for helping with William, and we did some cordial catching up.

Ever so slowly, maybe we were patching this family back together again.

When Maryanne learned that Ivanka was going to convert to Orthodox Judaism to marry Jared Kushner, she was not pleased.

"How can she do that?" Maryanne asked me, sounding almost indignant.

We'd never met Jared. Maryanne said Ivanka had spoken to her about the subject, saying she loved Jared and would convert because it was important to him. It didn't matter to me one way or the other, but Maryanne certainly didn't seem happy about the situation, even after speaking with Ivanka. Maryanne wasn't exactly in the best position to be pointing fingers. After all, she had converted to Catholicism for her first husband and she remained an active Catholic and gave to Catholic charities.

Ivanka completed the conversion process in time for a beautiful tented wedding on October 25, 2009, at the Trump National Golf Club in Bedminster, New Jersey. Lisa and I had been married for twenty years by then, but this was the first Trump-family wedding to take place under a chuppah since our own. All the men in the wedding party wore specially designed yarmulkes. Even Uncle Donald. Unlike our inter-faith wedding, there was only one officiant, Rabbi Haskel Lookstein. This was a *Jewish* wedding. Honestly, given the still-lingering tension inside the family, I was happy that Lisa and I had been invited. And not just us. Mary had gotten an invitation too.

It was a nice day for all of us. Mary, who hadn't seen the family in nearly a decade, told me she was surprised to be invited, and was worried about how she would be received by the various relatives. But in fact, the guest list was so large and the golf club was so packed, I'm not sure Mary ever spoke to any of our close family members.

From what I could tell at the reception, there was tension in the air. Robert and Ann Marie were friendly. But for whatever reason, Maryanne was incredibly grumpy all night. I advised Lisa: "Just give her space." When Maryanne was in a bad mood, there was never any doubt.

We were there to celebrate Ivanka, Jared, and their future, and we were grateful to be there. It was a hopeful night for them as well as us.

"Thanks for inviting us," I told Ivanka before we headed back to Connecticut. "I really appreciate it."

She seemed surprised to hear me say that. "You're *my cousin,*" she said with a smile. "Of course."

"Well, thanks."

Political junkie that I am, I have always loved watching the White House Correspondents' Dinner on TV. That's the annual black-tie gala where a huge throng of reporters hear a comedian roast the president—and then the president gets a chance to answer back.

The 2011 dinner wasn't just a spirited evening. I believe it also changed my family and the world.

That was the night, I am convinced, that pushed Donald into doing more than *talking* about running for president, something he'd been talking about doing for years. That year, he'd been talking again about running, just floating little hints that he might challenge the upcoming reelection of Barack Obama. As usual, no one was taking the talk seriously, not the media and not the family.

"Yeah, right."

That was the general reaction at our house and, I think, at most other people's houses, maybe even Donald's own house, as the Trump-for-president talk was floated again.

As the Correspondents' show began, Donald was sitting at a prime table in the packed Washington Hilton ballroom. Seth Meyers got things rolling with this: "Donald Trump has been saying he'll run for president as a Republican, which is surprising as I just assumed he was running as a joke." That got a few laughs and even more *ughs*. But it was President Obama whose shtick really got the crowd roaring, and also seemed to creep the most under Donald's skin.

You do have to say Donald started it. For months, he'd been poking at Obama, giving voice to the groundless question of whether the president was born in America, and demanding to see his birth certificate. The pounding was so pervasive that the cable-news networks gave it a formal name. Birtherism. After ignoring the demands as long as he could, Obama finally gave in and released a copy of his birth certificate from the state of Hawaii, which seemed to dampen the controversy a bit. And it gave the president's joke-writing team a little pile of gold.

"No one is prouder to put this birth certificate matter to rest than The Donald," Obama told the crowd. "And that's because he can finally get back to focusing on the issues that matter, like, did we fake the moon landing? What really happened in Roswell? And where are Biggie and Tupac?"

The room erupted with laughter. Everyone seemed to be checking out The Donald. The Washington media crowd loved hearing the president roast Trump. But when the camera got a tight shot of Donald's face, he didn't appear to be enjoying the jab at all.

I'm telling you, that is what made him run for president. I was watching when it happened. I could feel it in my bones. Shaking my head, I said to myself: "It's like World War II. You just woke the sleeping giant. Obama just made a big, badass mistake."

I had seen that look in Donald's eyes. I had seen it many, many, many times. It's a look of revenge combined with a firm determination not to lose. It was the same look he had when the New Jersey casino regulators were squeezing him, the same look he had all those years ago when the Justice Department was coming at the company for racial discrimination. He was already calculating in his mind how to get back at him. I have no doubt this was the night he started thinking seriously about running for president.

He didn't run that time.

He thought about it carefully. He hired a pollster. He brought some members of the family into the conversation. Maryanne and I were still putting our relationship back together. Lunches mostly, also some emails and calls. We spent one of our lunches discussing almost nothing but Donald's political dreams.

"You know what?" I said to Maryanne at lunch that day. "Donald's approval rating is, like, thirty-five percent right now. Obama is in the fifties. I'm not sure this is the race for him. Does Donald jump in or does he say, 'I want nothing to do with this thing' and maybe come back later?"

The truth was neither of us really knew. But he came to the same conclusion I was reaching. Wrong year. Maryanne agreed. She did not want Donald to run. She didn't want any part of that.

He decided that challenging the reelection of a relatively popular sitting president just wasn't politically feasible. The 2012 Republican nominee was Mitt Romney, and Obama polished the floor with him. But an idea was planted that night in Washington, and it wasn't going to disappear.

Donald did not like being portrayed as a crazy loser, or a loser of any sort, and that's how he was portrayed in that crowded ballroom. For Donald, loser is the worst thing you could be. He'd had the experience of losing in Atlantic City. He never liked the way that felt. But his payback would just have to wait.

• • •

Lisa, Cristopher, and I were going to fly with Donald and Melania to Mar-a-Lago for a quick weekend visit. This was 2012, before reporters started calling the plane Trump Force One. The flight was leaving from the Marine Air Terminal at LaGuardia. We took a car service down from Connecticut.

It's a stunning aircraft, a custom Boeing 757 with Rolls-Royce engines, Italian leather seats embroidered with the Trump Family crest, and 24-karat gold-plated accents. It has two private guest rooms, three bathrooms, dining and conference areas, and a theater-quality entertainment system. Clearly, Donald loved his plane, and he knew every shiny inch of it. Since I used to fly, I checked out the cockpit and rode up front for a while.

Before takeoff, I'd been drinking a bottle of Coke, which I'd left empty in a cup holder next to my seat. As we were taking off, I heard Donald scream: "Fred! Fuck!"

I didn't realize that as we were accelerating, the Coke went sliding out of the cup holder and tumbling onto one of the leather seats, spilling the last few drops. I swear, it was just a few drops.

"That's a hundred thousand dollars' worth of damage," Donald roared.

Melania didn't say anything. She was just taking it all in. But Donald was seething mad.

I apologized and helped clean things up.

A couple of minutes later, Donald came by and patted me on the shoulder, realizing, I guess, that maybe he'd overreacted just a bit. I don't know if he did that because Lisa and Cristopher had witnessed his eruption or if he just felt bad for screaming at me. I'd heard him dress down people, including his brother Robert, but I'd never been on the receiving end of his outrage, unless you the count the day he and Rob had threatened to send me to military school. I can't say I enjoyed it too much.

• • •

Mar-a-Lago is an undeniably stunning property.

The opulent twenty-acre compound at the center of Palm Beach was built in the 1920s by General Foods heiress Marjorie Merriweather Post. But the 114-room mansion was now a centerpiece of the Donald Trump brand. As soon as he reportedly bought the place for less than $10 million—or whatever he paid in 1985—he was already thinking about how he could turn it from a cost center into a profit center. The first time I visited there, before he'd told almost anyone about his idea for the estate, he and I drove out to a public course for a round of golf. The night before had been rainy. There was mist coming off the back nine, though the sunshine was pouring down now. As we drove in his convertible back to Mar-a-Lago, Donald confided in me about his diminishing relationship with his brother Rob, which had clearly suffered badly from their fights over the Trump casinos. "I don't know if Rob and I are ever going to have a good relationship again," he said.

As we pulled up to a stoplight, he also shared his plans for Mar-a-Lago. "I am turning it into a club," he said. "I can only own things if I make money from them."

Lately, he said, the property had been costing him a fortune. "The taxes are ridiculous. The upkeep is insane because it's right on the water. Salt water. The family comes down, but it's just a money suck."

His answer? Charge people thousands of dollars a year for the right to visit. Then, also charge them for drinks, dinners, and hotel rooms every time they decide to come. Not a bad business model, and it really took off. All these years later, you never know who you'll run into at the pool or on the patio at Mar-a-Lago. That's part of its charm.

It could be a politician, a business executive, a sports star, or just some loudmouth with too much money and a need to impress. It could have been Maryanne and Elizabeth, both of whom bought their own houses in walking distance of their brother's club. One night, as Andrea, Cristopher, and I arrived for dinner on the patio, where did the host seat us? Right next to the table Aunt Maryanne was sharing with Supreme Court Justice Samuel Alito and two friends. They had worked together a long time ago.

She headed the appeals division of the U.S. Attorney's Office in New Jersey when he was hired there in 1977, before she left to become a federal district judge and then a judge on the Third Circuit Court of Appeals, where he had clerked and then became a judge in 1990. Got all that straight? In certain circles it's a very small world. When Alito was nominated to the Supreme Court by George W. Bush, our Maryanne testified on his behalf, telling the Senate Judiciary Committee, "Nobody did it better than Sam Alito," referring to his appellate briefs.

And now here they were, dining at Mar-a-Lago, solid proof for every liberal nightmare about the conservative judiciary . . . if anyone noticed they were there.

She came over to our table near the end of the meal, and, I swear, she teared up *again* as she said hello to the kids. It was like our visit to her apartment all over again.

I was never sure which of Maryanne's moods I was going to get, but she certainly was soft that night, seeing Andrea and Cristopher.

"Why don't you come over to the house tomorrow, and we'll spend a little time together."

I promised I would.

We went over that afternoon, Andrea, Cristopher, and I.

She gave the kids a tour of her oceanfront house, which was lavish in its own right, though certainly no Mar-a-Lago. Maryanne said to me: "Boy, Cristopher's really charming, and Andrea's so beautiful." We stayed for ten or fifteen minutes, and then it felt like it was time to leave.

CHAPTER 20

UNCLE PRESIDENT

There's a shorthand way to tell the story of how Donald went from irritated by a joke to president of the United States. You were there. It goes something like this: Escalator ride. MAGA hats. Hillary emails. *Access Hollywood.* Shocking win on election night.

And those were certainly some of the high points.

However—and this is a big "however"—that little cheat sheet doesn't begin to account for the personalities, the family background, the branding, and the fame, the underlying factors that made such a huge achievement possible, and, oh yeah, the fractious state of the nation, which left the American people open to an unconventional message like Donald's in the fall of 2016.

To me, those are the most interesting parts.

It's always been my belief that there was something deeply ingrained in Donald that uniquely positioned him to pull this off and make him not just president, but the dominant figure in American politics for the past eight or nine years . . . with no end in sight. By now, forty-five other men (those who came before, plus Joe Biden) have gotten themselves elected president. No disrespect to any of them. But not one of them has dominated the American political psyche like Donald has, in and out of office, not in modern times. There is no escaping him on any given day. His impact on our nation is undeniable. For better *and* for worse, our family is the family that helped to make him this way.

I had no vote on the escalator ride of June 16, 2015. No one in the family did. Donald had been talking about the *need* for him to jump into the race for president. But until he did it, I wasn't totally sure that he would.

Once he was in, he was in. He put on his show for America the same way he'd been putting on a show with *The Apprentice* for the viewers of NBC. He chose the timing. Midday on a Tuesday instead of Thursday night. He chose the locale. The lobby of Trump Tower instead of the boardroom. He chose the music. Neil Young's "Rockin' in the Free World" instead of the *Apprentice* theme song, "For the Love of Money" by The O'Jays. (Neil Young would later sue the Trump campaign to stop using his music.) He chose his costars: Melania at his side on the down-flowing escalator. His kids at the bottom, waiting for him.

Oh, and he chose the extras too: loyal staffers, reporters, and some out-of-work actors who were paid fifty bucks to wave Trump signs and make a lot of noise in the lobby, plus some tourists and New Yorkers decked out in MAGA gear. All of them were there for the spectacle. I don't think too many of them thought they were looking at the next president of the United States.

Just because I wasn't asked didn't mean I had no opinion. I'd have told him not to. I think everyone in the family had an opinion. For all our faults, we are not a wishy-washy family (except maybe for Rob).

I would describe Maryanne as highly skeptical of the whole endeavor, questioning not just if Donald *could* win but if he *should* win. With his bombastic personality and his shifting views, Maryanne wondered if her little brother really was "presidential material." And some

of the views he'd been expressing, especially the things he'd been saying about immigrants, she considered almost grotesque. How much of
this was policy and how much was personality, I can't say. But I wasn't
expecting Maryanne to pull on a MAGA hat anytime soon.

Rob's position, as always, was fluid. He and Donald had been at
such odds over work issues, Atlantic City especially, I couldn't imagine
that Rob would be a booster of his big brother's presidential dreams.
But, in fact, the two of them seemed to have patched up their difficul-
ties of late. They'd been working together more harmoniously, especially after Rob had shifted his focus from the casinos to what remained
of the Brooklyn and Queens apartment business. There wasn't so much
to fight about there.

Now, as Donald was jumping in, Rob had become—not exactly
a staunch promoter, but he'd definitely embraced the idea. His post-
Blaine girlfriend, Ann Marie Pallan, was all in, and might have also
bolstered Rob's support.

As for Elizabeth—well, I expected her to hold her usual position,
quiet and off to the side. But she too seemed to have accepted Donald's
march into politics, even if she wasn't leading the parade. As with Rob,
she may have gotten some encouragement in that direction from home.
Her husband, Jim Grau, was full-on MAGA. He seemed to love the idea,
remote as it might be, of being able to say the president was family.

And Donald's older kids were on board.

Donald, Ivanka, Eric—I got no sense of reluctance there. My
first clear indication came when I attended a fundraiser at Trump
National Golf Club Hudson Valley for St. Jude's Hospital. It was
sponsored by Eric's charitable foundation. He and couple of his
friends were saying: "Oh, we're getting all these people on board . . .
It's really catching fire."

• • •

One of the most impactful things a president gets to do is nominate future justices to the U.S. Supreme Court. So of course, the question of judicial nominations was bound to come up on the campaign trail.

And who would Donald name to the highest court in the land? Maybe . . . his sister, Maryanne?

It wasn't totally implausible.

Not too many presidential candidates—like maybe zero—have had a sister who was a veteran federal judge, much less a member of the U.S. Court of Appeals for the Third Circuit, having been nominated by President Bill Clinton and confirmed by the U.S. Senate in 1999. That was Maryanne. Those appellate courts are the AAA ball for elevation to the judicial majors, known officially as the U.S. Supreme Court.

When the subject came up in February, Donald caused some heavy buzz by touting Maryanne to the media, calling her "a highly brilliant woman, known as a great, you know, very brilliant judge." He also suggested that, as a nominee, she would be no puppet of his. "I don't even know what her views are," he said, "and I don't think she'd want to tell me."

Boy, did that last part ever turn out to be true.

The whole time Maryanne's name was being tossed around as a possible Supreme Court justice, she was telling me what a terrible president her brother would make. His bombastic personality, his simpleminded slogans, his lack of knowledge and curiosity about serious issues. "Can you believe this shit he's saying?" she snapped when we were discussing Donald's latest comments about the southern border. "It's abhorrent."

She never said the actual words "I'm not voting for him," but that was absolutely implicit in everything she told me during our lunches from the escalator ride forward. At lunch one day, she said that she and her son, David, were writing an op-ed piece against him. "I *have* to say something," she said. She even showed me a yellow legal pad, where she said she was writing a draft.

I can only assume that Donald had no clue what his sister was saying, because he kept the Supreme Court talk going for months. In late August, he tossed another log on the Maryanne fire by telling Bloomberg Politics. "I think she'd be phenomenal. I think she'd be one of the best," though he also added in that interview that he might "have to rule that out." In the end, he concluded that at seventy-eight, his older sister might not want all the headaches of such a demanding new gig. What did she need that for?

Asked about any lingering possibility of a Justice Trump, Donald told Fox News host Jeanine Pirro on October 11: "I would love to" put Maryanne on the high court. "But I think she would be the one to say, 'No way, no way.'"

There'd be no Aunt Justice Maryanne. And if she got her way: There'd be no President Donald.

Well, the day came at last. Tuesday, November 8, 2016.

America voted, and so did I. But there couldn't have been many Americans who felt as weird about it as I did.

I walked into my polling station, the elementary school near my house. Everything looked like it usually did on Election Day. Rows of folding tables. Election workers signing people in. Flimsy-looking privacy stands where the voters filled out their paper ballots. Optical readers tabulating the results. People coming, going, and milling around.

When I found my way to the right table, I got the usual spiel. *District? Address? Name?*

As soon as I said "Fred Trump," it felt like every pair of eyes in the room was focused my way. No one said anything. But I was pretty sure what people were thinking. *That's a Trump . . . Did he say "Trump"?*

That's sure how it felt, anyway. And all those people kept watching as I signed my name, got my ballot, and walked over to one of the special tables to it fill it out. No one could see what I was writing, but everyone could still see my face. Voting that day was just as surreal as I'd thought it would be.

I didn't go out on the campaign trail or attend any of Donald's rallies, fundraisers, or other events. I followed the campaign closely, just as I had in campaigns past. Every vote matters, I'd always believed.

I had interned in college with Congresswoman Geraldine Ferraro. A lot of my friends told me back then I should follow my passion and think about a career in politics. "You should be the one in the family to be the politician," urged John Barry, Maryanne's husband, saying I knew how to be diplomatic and also understood business. Or as I liked to put it, I knew when supporting the bottom line crossed the line. And would it be fair to mention, I was the one in the family with the natural tan?

This year, just like everyone else, I had no idea where the results were going to land.

I admired Bill Clinton for his ability to connect with people. His natural charisma and common touch. Hillary . . . not so much. She obviously had the résumé—first lady, secretary of state, and U.S. senator from New York. So, why was she so stiff in public? And why had she chosen the lackluster Tim Kaine as her running mate?

Immediately after the Republican and Democratic conventions, I started telling people, "She has no idea of the steamroller that's coming her way." I knew Donald well enough to know that he would never get out-hustled or outworked by Hillary. Never. And those massive rallies of his proved how deeply he connected with his base. He hated to lose—at anything, ever.

In a few different ways, the election had hit home for Lisa and me.

Reporters had often attempted to interview me. *No, thank you.* We woke up one morning to find dead chickens—yes, *dead chickens*—strewn across our lawn. The message would become more apparent with more dead animals and gawkers at the bottom of our driveway.

We decided we needed to hire security, engage with the local police, and add more cameras and alarms. We had our two children living on their own and one child in a residential school. Add security as another cost of carrying the Trump name.

The only gracious moment in the whole campaign, I thought, came with the final question in the second debate, when a voter at Washington University in St. Louis asked the candidates: "Regardless of the current rhetoric, would either of you name one positive thing that you respect in one another?" I liked that. I leaned in for the answers.

Hillary went first.

"Look, I respect his children," she said. "His children are incredibly able and devoted, and I think that says a lot about Donald."

To me, it sounded heartfelt. When Donald's turn came, he thanked Hillary. "I consider her comment about my children a very nice compliment," he said, before adding: "I will say this about Hillary: She doesn't quit, she doesn't give up, I respect that."

In the land of Trump, as I well knew, praise doesn't get much higher than that. I could almost hear my grandfather talking. "She's a fighter," Donald said. "I disagree with much of what she's fighting for. I disagree with her judgment in many cases. But she does fight hard, and she doesn't quit, and she doesn't give up and I consider that to be a very good trait."

Could it be these two vicious enemies were both right? With my diplomatic personality, I liked the thought of it. It was a glimpse of how dialogue needed to start in the real fight of policy over politics. Then, just as quickly as it had arrived, the glimpse was gone. They went right back to destroying each other and also themselves: Hillary's private email server, Donald's *Access Hollywood* video . . . and on and on it went, as the two of them screeched right into Election Day. And so too continued the ripping apart of families and our country. Anyone's kitchen table could turn overheated at the first mention of politics.

As I stood with my ballot and a marker in hand, I filled in the little circle for president. I double-checked to make sure I'd done it right.

I respectfully voted for Hillary Clinton.

I was a Trump voting for a Clinton. Strange. But it was the right thing to do.

For me, policy was thicker than blood.

Yes, Donald was my uncle. Yes, it would be new to have a relative in the White House. But Hillary carried the party with the policy that was important to me and my family. And that's not to say everyone in my family voted the same way. I respected that. At least we could talk about it, civilly. Inserting levity as needed.

I know it's an overused expression, but it really wasn't personal. It wasn't even political, not in the narrow sense of that word. It was policy over politics and personality. Better than most, I knew Donald's strengths and weaknesses, the quirks of his personality, where he came from and how he got that way. I just didn't agree with many of the things he was running on and wanted to do to the country. So, no, I couldn't help put him in the White House. It was as simple—and as complicated—as that. And at that point, I didn't even know yet—no one did—how far the MAGA movement might go.

I thought a lot about this. I asked myself: How were his policies going to help my three children in the future?

Did I want ultrarich guys getting two-million-dollar tax breaks? No.

Did I want the Supreme Court to reverse abortion rights by over-turning *Roe v. Wade*? No.

Did I want to gut environmental regulations, exacerbate climate change, and let big companies harm the earth? No.

Did I want to see Mexicans treated like criminals and rapists, build a wall the full length of the border, and toss Hillary Clinton behind bars? No, no, and no. I didn't want my president doing any of that stuff, and I couldn't imagine advancing those policies with my vote, even if I'd spent my entire life around the guy who was now promising to do it.

"Your vote matters," I said to myself. "Imagine how you'll feel if he won by one vote, and it was yours." I followed my conscience and the policies I believed in, and no one who knew me well would have been surprised.

Donald never asked me how I was voting, any more than he asked Maryanne. Knowing Donald, he likely simply assumed I'd voted for him.

Lisa and I had talked about the election. I watched the campaign coverage on TV from every possible angle, as I typically do: CNBC, ABC, CBS, FOX, MSNBC, and CNN. Checking the sentiments on social media. Listening to local news radio and NPR in the car. Lisa and I discussed the election with Andrea and Cristopher. But I never got into it with anyone in the extended family except for Maryanne.

During the campaign, Hillary made a very important statement that I wish more people had heard clearly, when she stood up for the fifty-six million "invisible voters" with disabilities. That carried significance for the families of veterans, for anyone who might need care one day, and, yes, for families like ours. Unfortunately, those statements were too quiet as Donald outworked, outhustled, and out-steamrolled her. He had a message that connected with millions of Americans, most of them living lives that were very different from the kind of privileged life he had led. And she didn't win the election. He did.

Maryanne's op-ed piece never appeared anywhere.

Election night, Lisa, Andrea, Cristopher, and I all dressed in nice work attire and went into Manhattan for the predetermined "victory party" at the New York Hilton. The music was blaring. The room was packed. There were TV screens everywhere, total sensory overload. The energy shot up and down, cheering when states were won, booing with every defeat. As the night wore on and race stayed close, things got even more intense. As crazy and crowded as it was, we did get to see a few of the relatives, including Robert. That was the first time I'd been with Robert in a long while. Though we were in theory back on good terms, you wouldn't know it by how infrequently we saw each other. He was there with Ann Marie. He hadn't seen my two older children in I don't know how long. Of course, he'd still never seen William.

"Kids," he said to them when he came over to us, "I just have to tell you. What your parents do for William is amazing to me."

It was great of him to say that. I didn't ask why he'd never come to see him, and all we did for him, in person.

The White House transition office contacted me to say we were going to be invited to the inauguration. They said they would coordinate all the details. When the invitations and tickets arrived, Lisa, Andrea, Cristopher, and I were all excited to attend the inaugural festivities in Washington. Mary wasn't invited. I had to assume that was the family's way of saying "all is definitely *not* forgiven," more than a decade after our lawsuit was settled. And if Maryanne was to be believed, we had barely made the cut—and only did because of her strong push.

"I got you invited," Maryanne said to me as the big day neared. "You, Lisa, Andrea, and Cristopher. Robert was vehemently against it. Donald said to Robert, 'He's my brother's son. He's invited.'"

Since I never heard from Robert directly, I can't confirm his "vehement" objection. But it sounded likely enough, and Maryanne was eager to take credit for the invitation. My father's siblings were still convinced that Mary was the driving force behind the lawsuit, which really wasn't true. As I've tried to make clear, that was a decision she and I had made *together.* No one had to push either of us into it. We felt we had no choice. But because Mary attended more of the meetings and depositions while I was dealing with William's care, she got most of the blame.

Which was totally unfair.

That said, it *was* also true that, in the years since, Mary hadn't made much of an effort to get back in touch with anyone. I was the one who checked in with Donald. I was the one who went out to lunch with Maryanne and sat with her in her apartment on Fifth Avenue. To this day, Donnie and Eric would say that Mary made absolutely no effort to get back in touch with them. Of course, they could have reached out to her, and I don't believe they did. I firmly believed that none of this needed to be fought on the cousin level. Still, there was lots of responsibility to go around.

I had no apologies for or regrets about being there. It wouldn't be just my first inauguration ever. It would be the first where *my uncle* was the one being sworn in as president. Could I really miss that? This was part of American history. Whatever we'd all been through together, the good *and* the bad, I was happy I could be there with my wife and two of my children and share that once- or twice-in-a-lifetime special experience.

We drove to D.C. and checked into the Trump International Hotel. It was truly exciting to see how the nation's capital had transformed itself for this once-every-four-years event. We had a driver and escort who said they would take us wherever we wanted to go. The night before the inauguration, we were invited to an incredibly lavish candlelight dinner in the main train hall at Union Station. Lisa, Andrea, Cristopher, and I sat one table over from Donald, Melania, and his children. Some other people we'd met that day were at our table, but I wasn't sure who had made the seating arrangements or how we'd gotten grouped with them.

For most of the meal, we left the soon-to-be first family alone with their steak, potatoes, and vegetables and the steady trickle of power people who were stopping by to offer their good wishes. Then, I said to Lisa and our kids: "You know what, guys. Why don't we go wish him well. I don't know if we're really going to be able to talk with him tomorrow."

The four of us stood for the ten-pace walk to table 1, but we didn't get far. Somewhere between paces three and four, a large Secret Service agent was blocking our path and glaring down at us. He was asking, but not quite asking, "Can I help you?"

"That guy is my uncle," I said. "I just wanted to say hi with my family."

I would describe the agent's expression as "skeptically noncommittal." That's when Melania noticed us, and she tapped Donald on the shoulder, and he did one of those index-finger curls that says, *Come over here.*

"That good enough for you?" I asked the agent.

It was, and we proceeded to the table.

I might've smirked. I couldn't help it. Sometimes, my 718 area code just comes out.

After a fast round of "hey" and "congratulations" and "thank you," Donald leaned in toward me and let his own Queens out. "Can you believe this fuckin' shit?"

"Look," I said, "my mom just wanted me to tell you that today would have been Mom and Dad's fifty-fifth anniversary. The nineteenth of January. They got married in 1962."

"That's great," Donald said with a big smile. "That's really great. Tell her I said hi."

What neither of us had to say out loud was the obvious: that my parents' marriage had ended so much earlier than either of them hoped for, just like my father's life had. And that was too bad. At any Trump event, even this happiest event all these decades later, that part of our family history still hung in the air, the same way it had at my wedding. None of us could ever entirely shake that feeling of *what might have been.*

• • •

For us, January 20 began across Lafayette Square from the White House at St. John's Episcopal Church. That was the pre-inaugural service for the incoming president, vice president, cabinet secretaries, and their families. Then it was off to the Capitol for the big event. It was on our way there that I said to Lisa: "You think we'll be sitting with the family . . . or somewhere in the back?" Honestly, given our just-barely invitation, either seemed possible. But when we presented our tickets, the usher started walking and walking, and we kept getting closer and closer to the front. I kept thinking, *I hope he keeps walking.* And he did. The seats we got were unbelievably close, right with the other members of the Trump family, just a few yards from the podium. *No second-string Trumps today.* Sitting one row behind us was Senator John McCain. This was a day I was sure my children would always remember, a day they'd be telling their future families about.

Donald was sworn in at noon, as is the custom, by the chief justice of the U.S. Supreme Court, John Roberts. "I, Donald John Trump, do solemnly swear . . ." I nodded at Andrea and Cristopher. I smiled at Lisa. This was history. I could barely believe I was sitting there. Just as my uncle began his inaugural address, the slate-gray sky over the Capitol opened up, and a light rain began to fall. As many of the commentators would point out later, it was a fairly dark speech, berating the Washington elites of both parties for ignoring the needs of the American people and allowing the nation's cities to be overrun with "crime and gangs and drugs."

With the arrival of the Trump administration, he promised, a new day was dawning. "The American carnage stops right here and stops right now," he said. "From this day forward, a new vision will govern our land. From this moment on, it's going to be America First."

When the ceremony was over, I knew who I wanted to talk to. John McCain.

I knew what Donald had said about the Arizona senator during the long campaign, calling him a "loser" and saying that McCain, who'd been a prisoner of war in Vietnam, was "not a war hero. He's a war hero because he was captured. I like people that weren't captured." I wasn't sure how the senator would react to me, but I wanted him to know that some members of the Trump family admired him.

"Senator McCain," I said just as he was turning to leave, "I'm Fred Trump."

I waited for a wince when he heard the last name. I didn't see one. "I would like to introduce you to my family."

The senator was extremely gracious, shaking hands with Lisa and me and offering Andrea and Cristopher an especially warm hello.

I turned to the children and said, "Kids, I don't throw this word around lightly, but this man is a hero. What he did for his country is truly worth celebrating. He's a real hero."

"Thank you," the senator said. "That's very kind."

"Thank you, Senator. It's a real honor. Thank you very much."

It was that kind of day. I wished William were able to be with us, but for today, it was all right. He was safe at home with his caregivers.

And the day wasn't close to over. We were all ushered into the Capitol for the post-inaugural luncheon in Statuary Hall.

We sat with Congressman Elijah Cummings and Senators John Barrasso and Trent Lott and their wives. I spoke most with Congressman Cummings.

"Hi, I'm Fred Trump, "I said. "Nice to meet you. I'm sorry Representative Lewis is not here." I knew the two of them were friends. John Lewis, the civil rights pioneer and congressman from Georgia, along with nearly seventy other Democrats from the House of Representatives, had decided not to attend. "Please, if you could express that I think he's an American hero for what he did."

It was the second time I had used that word in a day. I meant it both times.

CHAPTER 21

WHITE HOUSE

I know he was president and all. He had a lot to do and a lot of people who wanted his attention. But honestly, I think Donald missed his previous life and family.

He should have been on top of the world, but the White House can be a lot lonelier than you might think.

Those first few months he was in Washington, Melania and my young cousin Barron stayed back in New York City while Barron finished fifth grade at the Columbia Grammar & Preparatory School on the Upper West Side. They weren't moving down from Trump Tower until Barron could finish out the school year. Ivanka and Jared both had jobs in the West Wing, but Donnie and Eric were mostly in New York looking after the business. The White House ushers and Secret Service agents, efficient as they were, weren't quite the same as having family around.

That April was going to be Maryanne's eightieth birthday and Elizabeth's seventy-fifth.

"I want to throw you guys a party," Donald said. "I'll come up to New York."

To Maryanne, that sounded half-right.

"Don't come up here," she told her brother in no uncertain terms. "I don't want a birthday party turning into tens of millions of dollars of taxpayer money for security and all that stuff. Let's do it in the White House."

Maryanne was right about the high-priced logistics. Anytime a president travels anywhere, it's a vast and expensive production. No president travels light, especially once you consider that the official presidential state car, "the Beast," needs to be sent ahead. The NYPD would have to clear routes and provide security assistance. And along with all the other staff members, my uncle now traveled with a military aide whose job was to carry the nuclear-codes "football." That being said, I think Maryanne might also have *liked* the idea of having her birthday party in the White House.

Donald immediately agreed. And this party brought out almost everyone.

Maryanne. Robert and his girlfriend, Ann Marie. Elizabeth and her husband, Jim. My cousin David and his wife, Lisa. Jared and Ivanka. Eric and Lara, who was pregnant with their first child. Donnie was there. Melania came, but no Barron. He had school.

And Mary. That was big. Mary was invited—reluctantly—and she came. Yes, my sister was still part of this family, even though she continued to take heat for the lawsuit, which had been filed nearly seventeen years earlier. Mary really hadn't made much effort to reconnect, other than with Maryanne. I had to tell Maryanne several times: "Look, this lawsuit wasn't just Mary. It was me too."

Maybe that was finally beginning to sink in. I thought it was time for Mary to attend. And that's what I said to Maryanne. It was the extended family's first chance to celebrate in a while, and also to get a look behind the scenes where the president lived. Even though my children weren't invited, the event felt like a positive gesture. Maybe the ice really was thawing, after all these years . . . though fresh trouble for their dynamic was on the way.

For me, the highlight of the pre-dinner tour was seeing the display of the original Gettysburg Address, which Abraham Lincoln had delivered ninety-nine years before I was born. I couldn't help but notice that the Lincoln Bathroom, next to the honorable Lincoln Bedroom, was outfitted with Trump-branded soap.

We ate in the Family Dining Room in the official residence of the president. The menu was no surprise, the usual meat and potatoes. People traded stories, including quite a few from the old days. Maryanne told the mashed potato story again, and we finally got a chuckle out of Donald on it after all those years. The dinner didn't last all night, but longer than those Sunday visits had when I was young. Before we all left, Donald stood and offered a birthday toast to his two sisters, raising a glass of water in their honor. Then, pretty much everyone but Donald, Melania, Ivanka, and Jared headed back to the Trump International Hotel. Donald had extended a special invitation for Lisa and me to stay at the White House. We politely declined. It was a great night of stories and laughter with the birthday girls. I don't think anyone was ready for the day to end, and we all sat in the lobby bar for a nightcap, as we wrapped our heads around the idea that Uncle Donald was the president.

These were heady days for all of us, and I had a special reason for optimism. One of my bosses at Insignia was moving to Cushman & Wakefield, one of the world's largest real-estate services companies, a real powerhouse in our industry. "I'd love to work with you at Cushman," I said to him. A few days later, I got a call from people over there. A few days after *that*, I was working as an executive director at Cushman & Wakefield. Things sure were happening fast. Two days after I'd started at Cushman, in April of 2017, the New England Patriots were coming to the White House to be honored for defeating the Atlanta Falcons in what had arguably been the most exciting Super Bowl ever. Cristopher was a huge Patriots fan. He and his friend Matty and I went down for the ceremony.

We had spoken to Donald's assistant to get the passes, but I don't think he knew we were coming. Maybe we could have wangled a lunch invitation if he had. It was too bad Tom Brady, the Super Bowl MVP, couldn't make it (he pleaded "family matters"), but Cristopher and his friend still loved standing on the South Lawn with the other team members and hearing Uncle Donald praise their beloved team.

"No team has been this good for this long," he said. Of course, he made a point to mention his own winning campaign. "With your backs against the wall, and the pundits—good old pundits. Boy, they're wrong a lot, aren't they?—saying you couldn't do it, the game was over, you pulled off the greatest Super Bowl comeback of all time."

We did wind up getting to go into the Oval Office a few hours later, where Cristopher and Matty visited with Donald. It was just us and Keith Schiller, one of Donald's longtime bodyguards who'd gone to the White House with him. While Donald was saying hello to the kids, Keith pulled me aside. "Fred," he said, "I just want to let you know. Donald really likes it when you come down here. It makes him think of the days in Queens."

I was happy to be there and feel that connection again too.

These visits were exciting and eye-opening. And I appreciated the view they gave me into a world few people get to see so closely. I didn't abuse the privilege. I didn't pop in constantly. But there were some moments that stuck with me.

One day in April of 2018, I was having lunch in Manhattan with Donald's executive assistant. We usually met in Trump Grill, aka The Cave, which was my name for the dreary restaurant in the basement of Trump Tower. She'd always say, "I can't leave the building because he may need me, and I'll have to rush back upstairs." But now that Donald was in the White House, his New York office staff had a little more flexibility. So, we were a few blocks away at Valbella Midtown, just outside 520 Madison Avenue,which had the same owners as one of my favorite restaurants in Connecticut. This Manhattan location had outdoor seating. It was a beautiful day. I said, "Let's sit outside."

We had a terrific lunch and had just traded our goodbyes when who should come bounding up the sidewalk but Michael Cohen.

I'd met Michael a few times over the years. He was a vice president at the Trump Organization and one of Donald's personal lawyers. I didn't know him well, but he always seemed to have a super-aggressive manner and what seemed to me like a sleazy air about him. But I have to say, on this particular afternoon, he couldn't have been any friendlier. He was certainly complimentary about Donald.

"Hi, Michael," I said.

"Hey, Fred," he said brightly. "How ya doin'?"

We walked together the full block between Madison and Fifth Avenues. He spent the entire walk saying, "Your uncle is such a great guy . . . You're so lucky to have an uncle like Donald Trump . . . He's so impressive."

I didn't quite know how to answer the stream of exuberant praise except to say, "Yeah, fantastic, thank you."

That was a Friday. The following Monday, April 9, the FBI raided Michael's Rockefeller Center office and his room at Loews Regency hotel on Park Avenue, seizing business records, emails, and other documents the agents said were related to several ongoing investigations, including one that involved a payment to the adult film star Stormy Daniels.

That March, Stormy, whose real name is Stephanie Clifford, told

Anderson Cooper on *60 Minutes* that she and Donald had a sexual encounter in the summer of 2006 and that she had been paid $130,000 before the 2016 election to keep her mouth shut. Though Donald had denied the affair and immediately denounced the FBI raid—a "witch hunt," a "disgraceful situation," an "attack on our country"—Michael, his longtime attorney, would soon turn against him. That August, the lawyer would plead guilty to eight counts, including charges of tax evasion, making false statements to a bank, and campaign-finance violations. After striking a plea bargain, Cohen was sentenced to thirteen and a half months in prison (out of a possible forty-five years) and was required to testify against Donald as a prosecution witness in the case over the payment to the porn star.

But Michael sure had seemed to love Donald on the sidewalk that day.

One short follow-up: That same week, Lisa, Cristopher, a friend of Cristopher's, and I flew down to Florda to spend a few days at Mar-a-Lago. Donald would be flying down from Washington in a couple of days to host Japanese Prime Minister Shinzo Abe and his wife. He seemed completely at ease when he got there, as if he didn't have anything unusual to worry about. The wheels in his head seemed to be spinning like they always were. The kids had a great time at the pool and exploring the almost-century-old oceanfront estate, while details of the Michael Cohen raid and the Stormy Daniels case flooded the cable-news channels the entire time.

Just across South Congress Avenue from the Trump Golf Club at West Palm Beach, where I went to play golf, was one of those so-called gentlemen's clubs.

The sign outside read: "Stormy Daniels Making America Horny Again."

• • •

In the summer of 2018, William was in the hospital for almost three weeks with a serious case of life-threatening pneumonia. He was nineteen and very sick. It was incredibly frightening for Lisa and me—and for his brother and sister too. It was always hard to know if moments like these could compromise his health to the point that we would lose him. These are the times that you reach for all the strength you have.

William came home with oxygen and a feeding tube. After more than two weeks on a ventilator, he needed to learn how to eat all over again. We were too often in these setback situations, but you move forward the best you can.

It's times like these when family support is most needed and appreciated. At every opportunity, we let my aunts and uncles know how grateful we were for the medical fund for William's care and recovery. We sent pictures and updates, as we had in the past. And as usual we got no personal responses. It was the dedicated support and genuine love of caregivers that helped us the most.

I was in Washington to meet with some business associates and a few disability advocates when I decided to stop by the White House. Though I'd been in the Oval Office several times before, it was still an out-of-body experience, just being there. I had a great mentor named Jeff Walker. He went to military school with Donald. Among the many wise things Jeff liked to say was, "Always have a pen and paper ready in your pocket."

I was especially thankful for Jeff's advice one day in October 2019 when I was sitting with Donald in the Oval Office and his assistant rushed in. "President Trump," she said, "King Abdullah will be on the phone in ten minutes."

"Should I leave?" I asked.

"No, no," he said, waving off the suggestion. "Stay. Stay."

Soon, Robert O'Brien, the national security advisor, came in. Donald was on the phone by then, being prepped for his call with Abdullah II bin Al-Hussein, the king of Jordan.

"Hey," O'Brien said to me, "do you have a pen I can borrow?"

I wasn't clear yet on what the crisis was. But the national security advisor had just marched into the Oval Office to deal with it, and I was going to play a key supporting role. I lent him my official Fred Trump pen, a black, felt-tip Paper Mate, which was always ready in my pocket. When the call came from Jordan—"Mr. President, ten seconds, four, three, two, tick, tick, *boom*"—Donald put it on speaker.

"Mister President," King Abdullah said, "we just want to thank you. The world is a safer place now."

From the context, I slowly figured out that the king was calling about the ISIS terror leader known as Abu Bakr al-Baghdadi, who had been killed two days earlier, on October 26, 2019, in northwestern Syria in a raid led by U.S. Forces.

"I killed him," Donald said. "I killed him like a dog."

That's exactly what he said. "I killed him. I killed him like a dog."

I recognized what a highly privileged position I was in. I had some access to the White House. And as long as that was true, I wanted to make sure I used that access for something positive. I was eager to champion something Lisa and I were deeply passionate about. Something we lived every day.

The challenges for individuals with intellectual and developmental disabilities and their families.

In our journey with William, Lisa and I had become close to some truly inspiring parents and dedicated advocates who were doing amazing work to improve the day-to-day reality for families like ours. It's a huge lift for everyone, not to mention the constant need to mitigate expenses. There are so many different demands and challenges. But there are things that government can do—some things that can *only* be done by government, both federal and state.

When were we ever going to have the chance again to bring such knowledgeable people to the White House? That's when maternal instinct kicked in. Lisa reached out to Ivanka, who got right back to her and said she'd be happy to help. She provided a contact for Ben Carson, the retired neurosurgeon who was secretary of housing and urban development. We brought several talented advocates with us for the meeting with Dr. Carson and members of his senior staff. "Look," I said as we got started, "I'm the least important person in the room." I wanted the focus to be on the others, who knew a lot more than I did. They immediately started floating ideas, which was exactly why we were there. Our collective voice was being heard. It was a start.

In January 2020, just before COVID hit, Lisa and I and a team of advocates met with Chris Neeley, who headed the President's Committee for People with Intellectual Disabilities, a much-needed federal advisory committee that promotes policies and initiatives that support independent and lifelong inclusion. We discussed the need for all medical schools to include courses that focus on people with intellectual and developmental disabilities. We emphasized how crucial it was for hospitals and other acute-care facilities to help patients transition from pediatric to adult services. We emphasized the importance of collecting sufficient data to explain medically complex disorders. This was not about more government spending. It was about smarter investing and greater efficiency.

We spent the next few months making calls and talking with officials and gathering our own recommendations, giving special attention to the critical need for housing support for people with disabilities. We were back in Washington in May, this time meeting in the White House Cabinet Room—which, incidentally, was much dowdier than I expected. I guess Melania still had some decorating work to do.

By this time, COVID was raging. We were all masked up and COVID tested on the way in. Once we got inside, we sat down with Alex Azar, the administration's secretary of health and human services, and Brett Giroir, the assistant secretary for health, both of whom served on the White House Coronavirus Task Force. The promising agency motto stated: *HHS: Enhancing the Health and Well-Being of All Americans.*

Sharp, direct, and to the point, Azar exhibited my kind of efficiency with no time to waste. His first question was, "Okay, why are you here?"

I made a brief introduction. Our group included a leading doctor and several highly qualified advocates. What followed was a great discussion. Something clicked with Giroir—an idea for a program everyone could agree on that would cut through the bureaucracy and control costs and also yield better and more efficient medical outcomes.

Excellent. We were making progress.

"Really appreciate your coming in," Azar finally said, more warmly than he had sounded at the start. "I know we're going to see the president."

The meeting I had assumed would be a quick handshake hello with Donald had turned into a forty-five-minute meeting in the Oval Office for all of us—Azar, Giroir, the advocates, and me. I never expected to be there so long. Donald seemed engaged, especially when several people in our group spoke about the heart-wrenching and expensive efforts they'd made to care for their profoundly disabled family members, who were constantly in and out of the hospital and living with complex arrays of challenges.

Donald was still Donald, of course. His mind bounced from subject to subject, disability to the stock market and back to disability. Clearly, he had a lot on his mind. *Short Attention Span Theater* was still on, and this one was earning an R-rating. He dropped more f-bombs in forty-five minutes than a Tarantino movie. But promisingly, Donald seemed genuinely curious regarding the depth of medical needs across America and the individual challenges these families faced.

He told the secretary and the assistant secretary to stay in touch with our group and to be supportive. As everyone stood to leave, I waited a minute in the office to thank Donald for the meeting. And I had something else I wanted to ask him.

"Listen," I said, "is there a chance you can give me an introduction to Ken Langone?" Langone was the cofounder of The Home Depot and an old friend of Donald's.

Donald stopped me right there. "I can't do that," he shot back. "It's a fuckin' conflict of interest."

"I get it, I get it," I said. "Don't worry about it. Never mind."

After I left the office, I was standing with the others near the side entrance to the West Wing when Donald's assistant caught up with me. "Your uncle would like to see you," she said.

Alex Azar was still in the Oval Office when I walked back in.

"Hey, pal," Donald said. "How's everything going?"

"Good," I said. "I appreciate your meeting with us."

"Sure, happy to do it."

It was amazing the way my uncle could change his demeanor so quickly. Now he sounded interested and even concerned. I thought he had been touched by what the doctor and advocates in the meeting had just shared about their journey with their patients and their own family members. But I was wrong.

"Those people . . . ," Donald said, trailing off. "The shape they're in, all the expenses, maybe those kinds of people should just die."

I truly did not know what to say. He was talking about expenses. We were talking about human lives. For Donald, I think it really was about the expenses, even though we were there to talk about efficiencies, smarter investments, and human dignity.

I turned and walked away.

CHAPTER 22

GETTING THROUGH

My sister, the author.

In June of 2020, as the primaries were ending and the general election campaign was about to begin, I got a call from my uncle Robert. Actually, it was eight calls before I noticed and finally answered the phone. Rob was obviously eager to reach me.

He sounded furious. Word was out that Simon & Schuster was going to publish a book by my sister, Mary. No one had read the book yet, but the cover had leaked. I know you can't tell a book by its cover, but the title of this one gave some indication: *Too Much and Never Enough: How My Family Created the World's Most Dangerous Man*. This clearly wasn't going to be a puff piece. While I could come up with a list of far more dangerous men, I knew exactly what the reaction was going to be: People would assume that every part of Mary's point of view was also mine.

Which was not true. Mary didn't speak for me any more than anyone else in the family did. I hated that people kept assuming that.

I had not known that Mary was writing a book. Mary did not report her actions to me or speak to me any more than anyone else in the family did. But now, Rob was going into court to block publication, claiming Mary had violated the confidentiality agreement she and I had signed all those years ago when we settled the lawsuit. Rob was adamant that I should put out a statement.

I didn't do anything right away. I thought about it and tried to figure out what I might be comfortable saying, if anything. In July, I got an email from the reporter who broke the book story, and I sent a statement to Eric, saying I had nothing to do with the book, which was true. "My wife, children, and I have a strong relationship with our extended family," I said. "We had no involvement with the preparation of this book, which is a breach of trust and a violation of our privacy. We consider our family matters to be private and will not be commenting further."

Rob's lawsuit ended up going nowhere. A New York appellate court quickly ruled that the publisher wasn't bound by any agreement Mary might have signed, paving the way for the book to be published that July of 2020. The book was Mary's point of view, which she had every right to. It just wasn't mine. Like it or not, moments like those always had a way of pushing our family life into the media and bringing a whole new round of pressure on us, potentially threatening our families, our safety, and William's care.

Reporters started coming to our house again. Our phones and emails filled up with inquiries from media, family, and friends. *Did you know? What do you think?* When Mary went on *The Rachel Maddow Show* on MSNBC, she spoke at the beginning of the interview about our long-settled lawsuit. *Why was this getting dragged out again? What repercussions would it have?* Rachel asked Mary about our son William. *What would this mean for William as he transitioned into a new residential program?* This was horrible timing for us, as support and security for William was already a significant challenge. I would later learn the appearance would give the show its highest ratings ever, multiplying our privacy concerns.

Over the years, Mary had chosen to separate herself from me and my family, limiting the contact between all of us—not all negative, just life-inflicted reasons. We weren't close, but not separated . . . until her book came out. Mary did what she wanted to do in spite of all of us. I knew this would be the last time Mary spoke to the Trump side of the family.

At the same time Rob had been fighting to silence Mary, he was also dying.

That August, a month after Mary's book came out, I was staying in one of the overnight cottages at the Trump golf club in Briarcliff for a couple of days. Rob was really sick. He'd been on blood thinners for a while. He'd had a fall and was in the hospital with brain bleeds. I was tracking his health through his wife, Ann Marie.

"If you have anything you want to say to Rob, now is probably the time," she called to tell me. "Will you speak to him?"

"Yes, I want to."

I could hear the slow beeps of the ventilator as Ann Marie held the phone for Rob.

He didn't say anything, so I just started talking. "I am sorry for all the recent hardships we've all been going through," I said to him. "We had a lot of good times growing up in Queens." I paused. I couldn't hear Rob's voice, but I could still hear the beeping. "I remember those times, Rob," I continued. *Beep, beep, beep* . . . "Rob, I love you. Thank you, God bless you."

Some breathing. More beeps.

Then, Ann Marie was back on the phone. "Thank you so much," she said to me.

"Thank you, Ann Marie."

Rob had tried to play the go-between under pressure. I had picked that up from him. Trying to keep that middle ground, it seemed, was just too trying for him.

Donald was asked about Robert during a White House news conference. "I have a wonderful brother," Donald said. "We've had a great relationship for a long time, from day one." He didn't mention their squabbles in the office or their bitter fights over the Atlantic City casinos. Why would he? He did recall how Robert and Ann Marie had been among his most ardent supporters from the day he jumped fulltime into politics. And what did hearing Donald talk like that make me think? It made me think that if those two could overcome their differences, everyone else in the family should also be able to. After the news conference, Donald flew right to New York, where he visited his brother one last time in the hospital.

The next day, Robert was dead. He was only seventy-one.

The following Friday, Donald held a funeral for Rob in the East Room, the first time a president had held a funeral in the White House for a family member in nearly a hundred years. I sat in the front row. Ann Marie spoke, and she was very moving. Thank you, Ann Marie. It was the music that was especially memorable for me, including a solo by a tenor that really gave me chills.

"He was not just my brother," Donald said. "He was my best friend."

The medical fund for William kept going for a few more years, and it was enormously helpful with our home-care costs and medical expenses. We were always grateful to my father's siblings for contributing. But over the past few years, their interest had seemed to begin waning. Eric, who was the administrator, called me to say the fund was running low. Donald was the only one contributing consistently. Eric said he'd been getting some resistance from Maryanne, Elizabeth, and Ann Marie, Robert's widow.

I really didn't look forward to these calls. In many ways, I felt I was asking for the money I should have originally received from my grandfather. Had Mary and I gotten back then what was due to us, I'd have invested it in ways that would have benefited my family and been easily able to cover William's needs as Lisa and I saw fit.

Now, instead of "how are you doing" and "how about a round of golf sometime," I was talking to Eric about *this*.

"Why don't you call Donald," Eric said. "Talk to him about it."

I thanked Eric for the heads-up and promised I would.

Later that day I was up at Briarcliff. Donald happened to be there. He was talking with a group of people. I didn't want to interrupt. I just said hi on my way through the clubhouse. I called him later that afternoon, and he answered.

I got him up to speed on what Eric had told me. I said I'd heard the fund for William was running low, and unfortunately, the expenses certainly were not easing up as our son got older. In fact, with inflation and other pressures, the needs were greater than they'd been. "We're getting some blowback from Maryanne and Elizabeth and Ann Marie. We may need your help with this. Eric wanted me to give you a call."

Donald took a second as if he was thinking about the whole situation.

"I don't know," he finally said, letting out a sigh. "He doesn't recognize you. Maybe you should just let him die and move down to Florida."

Wait! What did he just say? That my son doesn't recognize me? That I should just let him die?

Did he really just say that? That I should let my son die . . . so I could move down to Florida?

Really?

I'm usually pretty good at getting my head around things that other people say, even when I don't agree with them. But this was a tough one. This was my son.

Maybe I shouldn't have been surprised to hear Donald say that. It wasn't far off from what he'd said that day in the Oval Office after our meeting with the advocates. Only that time, it was other people's children who should die. This time, it was my son.

I didn't want to argue with him. I knew there was no point in that, not at the same time I was calling for his help. I tried to keep my cool.

"No, Donald," I said. "He *does* recognize me."

Donald's comment was appalling. It hurt to hear him say that. But it also explained why Lisa and I felt so strongly about advocating for our son and why we wanted to help other people understand what it was like to raise a child like William. A lot of people just don't know.

People with these disabilities are perceived as *less than* in so many ways. That attitude is everywhere, even at the highest levels of policy and politics.

William deserves a life just like anyone else, and to that end, I knew I had to advocate for him in every way possible. I might never change Donald's mind or change the mind of anyone who lacked love and compassion for those whose voices couldn't be heard and whose lives were fully dependent on others. But I knew what I could do. I could offer my voice, my experience, and my strength to push forward for those who needed it.

The barriers are everywhere, even in communities that are generally supportive, like ours. There are still doorways that can't accommodate wheelchairs. It is still hard to find meaningful day programs that foster independence with learning, socialization, and assistive technology. The whole narrative still needs to change.

I knew that acceptance and tolerance would only come with public education and awareness. Donald might never understand this, but at least he had been open to our advocating through the White House. That was something. If we couldn't change his feelings about William, that was *his* loss. He would never feel the love and connection that William offered us daily.

• • •

The location was different. The procedure was different. COVID had changed so much by the fall of 2020, including where and how I was going to vote on November 3 when Donald ran for reelection as president.

This time, I filled out my ballot at home. Then, I drove to town hall and slipped the sealed envelope into the curbside drop box, which looked like a cross between a panzer tank and a recycling bin in the food court at the Westchester mall.

The nation was sharply divided, even more than it had been when Donald had surprised almost everyone four years earlier with his squeaker of a win over Hillary. For the past four years, he had dominated the national political conversation in every imaginable way. You were either pro-Trump or anti-Trump, with almost nothing and almost no one in between. There was less and less middle ground anywhere—between Republicans and Democrats, between red states and blue states, between conservative families and their liberal next-door neighbors. Everyone seemed to have an unyielding opinion about Donald, and everyone expected another close race this time, as Joe Biden glided to the Democratic nomination. I'd always liked the former vice president. Thirty-six years in the Senate, eight more as vice president, he'd be a much stronger candidate against Donald than Hillary had been. I had no doubt about that. Experienced. Knowledgeable. Temperamentally grounded. He had a genuine decency about him.

I tried to be rational about what issues Donald had championed in the White House. He deserved credit for Operation Warp Speed, the public-private partnership to expedite the development of COVID vaccines and for keeping the economy humming until the pandemic hit. He had a good way of expressing clear principles and projecting

American confidence in the world. For those who felt they needed a "tough guy," my uncle could certainly serve that up. And I appreciated the attention he'd paid to the issues that were most important to me and the community of the intellectually and developmentally disabled, even as I recoiled at the Muslim ban, the praise for Vladimir Putin, the family separation policy at the border, the tax cuts for billionaires, and the campaign to undermine *Roe v. Wade.*

I understood how my unique family circumstance had provided me with incredible access to the highest members of our government. But the truth is, no matter who was president, I would fight for those struggling families and the open dialogue we needed to get the policies that would help them. I was committed to that, no matter what. As always, what Lisa and I were fighting for was smarter, more efficient investments. We needed the leaders in both parties to reasonably communicate. To listen. To take responsible action.

As the moment of decision arrived, I didn't feel quite the same weight I had four years earlier, the novelty and magnitude of having my uncle on the ballot. I'd been through that already. This wasn't theoretical anymore. I had seen what he had done for the past four years. This time, I could just decide. In the end, I did what I had done through my voting history. I voted the Democratic ticket.

I looked in my heart again and knew that's where I belonged.

I voted my experience, which had started with interning for Geraldine Ferraro, the first woman on a major-party ticket for vice president. Kamala Harris was no Geraldine. But to me, she and Joe Biden had more potential to bring the country together and advance the policies I cared about than Donald and Mike Pence did.

And that's how I voted.

Again, it wasn't personal. I still loved my uncle. It wasn't even political. It was about achieving effective policy, about making the world a better place.

The fall of 2020 being so deep into the time of COVID, no one noticed me this time as I simply slipped my ballot into the drop box. I was no longer on display, voting at a flimsy table in a bustling room at the elementary school, laser eyes on me. This was a much more solitary experience. I drove back later in the day to deposit Lisa's ballot. That night, after picking up Chinese takeout, I headed home, checked in with the family, and settled into a marathon of election results. When Florida, Texas, Iowa, and Ohio were all called for Donald, I said to Lisa, "Oh, shit, we're gonna go through all this again."

She reeled me in as usual: "Okay, don't go overboard. It's just getting started."

It was a long, tense night for everyone.

We made it till around midnight. Lisa and I were asleep when Donald stepped before the White House cameras at 2:30 a.m., while the votes were still being counted and many states had not yet been officially called, and said: "We were getting ready to win this election. Frankly, we did win this election. . . . We're winning Pennsylvania by a tremendous amount. . . . We're winning Michigan," he said. "It's also clear that we have won Georgia. . . . They're never gonna catch us."

None of which would turn out to be true.

By the next morning, no one had won. Most of the pundits were predicting that when the final votes were counted, Biden would probably be on top. I had my own mixed feelings, the kind only a member of my family could completely understand. If Donald did lose, I knew he would have a very difficult time accepting that result.

It wasn't until Saturday that the election was called. The former vice president defeated the incumbent president, 306 to 232 electoral votes. Key to Biden's victory: three Rust Belt states—Pennsylvania, Wisconsin, and Michigan—that Donald had won four years earlier. Now, they were firmly in Biden's camp, along with Donald's never-gonna-catch-us Georgia.

But I knew this wasn't over . . . not even close.

I couldn't stop thinking about the fall of 2000 and the post-election fight between Al Gore and George W. Bush. "We're in for another badass time," I said to Lisa. "This is going to be *Bush v. Gore* on steroids."

I didn't realize I would need to add: "times ten."

I'd predicted it.

If I knew one thing about Donald, it was this: He couldn't stand to lose. He couldn't handle being called a loser. To him, "loser" was the worst word there was, and he didn't see any reason he should have to accept it, whatever the official results might say. For him, the whole concept was completely off-brand.

So, no, it didn't surprise me a bit that instead of accepting the results the way Al Gore eventually did in 2000, my uncle denied, deflected, insisted, and fought, pressuring state officials, sending his lawyers into court, assembling teams of fake electors, asserting that he had actually won the election and would be the rightful president of the United States for another four years. That was exactly what I expected from Donald. As judges across America got busy tossing his arguments out of court, he checked in with his merry band of Rudy Giuliani, Steve Bannon, Boris Epshteyn, and a handful of others and quickly came up with a plan.

"Big protest in D.C. on January 6th," the Trump tweet said. "Be there, will be wild!"

There was context. There is always context at times like these. The highly charged election. The adamant claims of voter fraud. The protests and riots the previous summer over Black Lives Matter and the George Floyd case. The burning and looting of stores and the pressure on the police. None of which could fully predict or justify what was about to happen next.

I was home that Wednesday, switching from CNN to Fox to MSNBC and back again, as Vice President Pence made his way to Capitol Hill to certify the election results. At the same time, thousands of ardent Trump fans jammed the Ellipse just south of the White House for a giant Stop the Steal rally. My cousins Donnie and Eric helped to warm up the crowd. Then, Donald really got them going. "We fight," he declared. "We fight like hell, and if you don't fight like hell, you're not going to have a country anymore."

It was all over the media. "And after this," Donald announced from the podium, "we're going to walk down, and I'll be there with you . . . we're going to walk down to the Capitol." Then, as the crowd marched down Pennsylvania Avenue, Donald climbed into the black SUV with his Secret Service agents and returned to the White House, a decision that caught a lot of people by surprise.

Did he have somewhere else to be?

But his U-turn didn't surprise me at all. I knew the history here. Donald doesn't fight physically, he verbally punches. He likes pro boxing and pro wrestling, but that's where his love of physical altercation ceases. In his entire life, I don't know if Donald has been in a single fistfight. The best I can do is repeat a story Robert told me about a memorable day at the Winged Foot Golf Club. That day, Donald was taunting a player he'd just beaten in a golf game when the man slugged him in the face. That was the fight. A lot of tough talk, not too many punches.

So of course, the marchers on January 6 went alone. It was when they got to the Capitol that the right to assemble was rewritten in some perverse way. I watched from home that day as the marchers broke the police lines then barged violently into the halls of Congress, all in the vain hope of stopping the peaceful transfer of power. These were the same halls that I had proudly walked as an intern. Now, look at them.

In the days after the shocking breach of the Capitol, I was especially moved by the story of Brian Sicknick, the Capitol police officer who responded to the mayhem that day, then died the following evening after suffering two strokes. I searched online for hours until I found an email account that belonged to him.

"My name is Fred Trump," I wrote. "I am very sorry about what happened."

Within hours, I got a response. "Please do not contact us again."

Which I completely understood and respected.

To me, Officer Sicknick had made the ultimate sacrifice for his nation. He was defending one of the key tenets of the U.S. Constitution, the peaceful transfer of power after a democratic election. To me, his sacrifice was tragic and profound. As far as I was concerned, he fully deserved to be honored in the Capitol Rotunda and then buried at Arlington National Cemetery.

And the reaction I got from his family, I had to think, was part of what it meant to bear the name Trump. No matter what message I delivered, no matter how I felt or what I said, my last name would continue to precede me. As the uproar over the election continued, I knew the weight of the Trump name would become even heavier.

A lot of commentators were suddenly talking about the Trump brand again. For years, that conversation had hung like wallpaper in the background of our lives, ceiling to floor, every day. There was no avoiding it. What it meant. How much money Donald was making off it. Whether it had been tarnished by the latest controversies, whatever they happened to be. But now, that Trump-branding challenge had grown far more severe and far more personal for me.

It was threatening my career.

It wasn't a new challenge. Out in the business world, the Trump name had always been a double-edged sword for me. As far back as

1995, after I'd been at the same firm for nearly five years, they had to make some cuts when one of their major clients decided to bring a big piece of their real-estate business in-house.

My boss called me in and said: "Since your last name is Trump and you have the financial wherewithal, we're going to let you go."

Gee, thanks. What an honor.

That wasn't news I wanted to hear or bring home to my family. The timing could hardly have been worse, just two months before my first son, Cristopher, was born. It would take months of perseverance before I would land at Insignia, where I spent the next eight years. But after Donald had been in politics for a while, I faced an even bigger challenge with my name. While there were certainly Trump fans everywhere you went, there were also some people—and some companies—that adamantly refused to deal with anyone named Trump.

I was used to my bosses asking me sometimes to downplay my role in a deal, maybe let someone else take the lead in the client contact. I wasn't working for the ego. I wanted to help my employer and serve my clients and get results. So, I tried to accommodate that concern as much as I could. I didn't like it, but what choice did I have? But once Donald got to the White House, clients really started to say, "I don't want to use you because you're Trump." And now, the Stop the Steal uproar was making all that a whole lot worse. Three days before January 6, I was fired from Cushman & Wakefield. Shortly after January 6, Cushman, which had been managing several Trump properties, cut all its ties with the Trump Organization. Cushman was now a Trump-free zone, including no more me.

I could change a lot of things, but I couldn't stop being a Trump. I couldn't remove my name from the top of my résumé and LinkedIn page. The first few calls I made to friends in the industry were highly discouraging, and the issue was clearly Trump.

What was I supposed to do about *that*?

I was hoping that the man in the middle of all this might have some advice for me. So, after things had calmed down a bit and Donald had moved out of the White House, I went to talk to him. "Look," I said, "I'm having trouble making my next move. I think part of the problem is my last name."

He shot me one of his looks like . . . *What are you talking about?*

"All I know is people keep saying to me, 'We'd like to get you over here, but the Trump name is toxic.'"

He gave a small jolt at "toxic." He asked who I'd been speaking with. I didn't want to rat anybody out. At the same time, I knew the kinds of reactions I'd been getting from people I knew and liked, who had said they wanted to hire me. Donald nodded without offering any specific suggestions. Then, just as I was leaving, he said to me: "By the way, don't ever say that the Trump name is toxic. Never say that."

"*I* didn't say it," I assured him. "*People* are saying it. That's what they're saying to *me.*"

In fact, it wasn't only in the work world that others considered the Trump name toxic, whether Donald wanted to hear about it or not. I'd had much the same experience trying to help families in need at charitable events. Over the years, I had helped raise money for groups working to improve the lives of people with developmental disabilities. That was something I could do, and I was happy to do it. I began to enjoy the charitable efforts more than my work. But even that had gotten tough because of Donald.

The trouble accelerated in 2015 when he publicly mocked Serge Kovaleski, a *New York Times* reporter who had a disability called arthrogryposis. My uncle's cruel gesture and comments got a deluge of media coverage, all of it negative, and generated understandable outrage among families, advocates, and decent people everywhere. Donald dismissed the incident and moved on. Our community could not. It cut deeply and personally for me as I tried to move on.

At the same time, I was organizing another golf-outing fundraiser for the disabled community. My cousin Eric had helped me get the golf course donated. He'd even helped secure discounts on the food and other items. But with all the uproar over Donald's cruel comments, we had to cancel the event. And when we tried again the next year, we were hit with a petition and online threats that all added up to: *How dare you use a Trump location to host this fundraiser.* Even though the golf course was donated and the extras were deeply discounted, any association with my name, which was also William's name, could not be tolerated.

Once the local social media heated up, angrily tying my name to the cause, one of our biggest supporters got death threats. One active parent in our community stood up for us when no one else would. Terry Torok, the father of a special-needs child, knew how important fundraising was to our community. He understood our family's true intention. He helped squelch the fire at the time. But it would burn again. To this day, people remain fearful about contributing to this important charity, to support this critical cause, to help caregivers, even to assist with this book. Once they see the T-name they fade quickly. Lawsuits and death threats? No thanks.

I reluctantly decided to back away. I wanted to be a help, not a burden. Suffice it to say we haven't been asked to host a golf outing at a Trump golf course ever since.

Now that Donald and Melania were spending most of their time in Florida, I didn't get to see him as often as I used to. They still had the triplex at Trump Tower. The Trump Organization offices were still in the building on Fifth Avenue. But unless he had a speech, a rally, a fundraiser, or a court case—that last one becoming more frequent—Donald was almost certainly at Mar-a-Lago. Even when he traveled, he still liked sleeping in his own bed at night.

He, Melania, and Barron did come up to Bedminster for the summer when Palm Beach was too hot for anyone, even someone with a beautiful swimming pool, a blasting air conditioner, and what passes for Atlantic breezes down there in July and August. Still, most of the time, we were 1,250 miles apart.

The last few times I saw him were—where else?—on the golf course.

He seemed more resigned than relaxed, and maybe just a bit older. There was one obvious difference since he'd left the White House. His security detail was far more relaxed. He still had Secret Service agents at his side whenever he went out somewhere, but no more commandos in military gear or snipers on the rooftops. Even so, you couldn't call the presence totally casual.

The last time I saw him was at Bedminster. We were both in carts. He was coming up the ninth fairway. I was going up the first fairway. They're parallel. I stopped and waited for him. That's when a stern-looking gentleman walked over to me. I'm not sure if he was Secret Service, but if he wasn't, he should probably apply. He'd fit right in.

"What's going on?" he said to me in that special tone where a question isn't quite a question. It's more like a challenge.

"That's my uncle," I answered.

"Okay, stay here."

As the man walked off, I waved to Neville, Donald's caddie. He saw me. I watched him say something to Donald, who turned his cart and rode over to us. He looked tanned and relaxed.

"Hey, pal," he said, his old, familiar greeting. "Looks like you lost weight."

I laughed. "I can assure you I didn't lose any weight."

"Well, you still got the greatest hair."

"Thanks," I said.

And that was kinda it.

That might have sounded like a mundane exchange, and I guess it was.

But it was the kind of thing that happens in normal families. Just normal banter. Given all we'd been through, that was oddly reassuring to me.

Robert wasn't the only member of that generation who seemed to be approaching the end. By late 2023, Maryanne was under hospice care as she battled cancer. With the exception of Donald, who seemed like he might go on forever, the generation ahead of me was really moving on.

Maryanne's time as a judge hadn't ended well. She'd left the Third Circuit under a cloud in February 2019, a cloud that had blown in from the business dealings of the family. Four months earlier, *The New York Times* had published an investigation detailing the Trump family's alleged "dubious tax schemes" throughout the 1990s aimed at transferring Fred Trump Sr.'s fortune to his children. One of the most egregious examples was a "sham corporation," their words, called All County Building Supply & Maintenance, a purchasing agent supposedly set up by the Trump family in 1992 that served as a vehicle to "siphon millions of dollars" from Trump-owned apartment buildings by padding invoices; the extra money then flowed directly to the owners—Maryanne, her siblings, and a cousin—essentially as untaxed gifts.

The New York State Department of Taxation and Finance launched an investigation. The Court of Appeals for the Second Circuit began a judicial-misconduct probe in February 2019, and ten days later, Maryanne announced her retirement from the bench, effectively ending the misconduct investigation.

I felt bad for her. She'd had a sterling career as a lawyer and a judge. She'd never been involved in the family business. She let her high-profile brother pursue his dreams in business and politics without ever trying to horn in on his spotlight. And yet it was an ancient piece of family business that had felled her in the end.

How much she even knew about it, I can't say. But for a woman who cared very much about projecting an image of integrity, I know the whole experience had hurt her a whole lot.

She and I discussed the news and how she was reacting to it. Her stories got more and bitter, revealing the true depth of her anger. She always had an angry undertone—always. And now it had grown even more intense. She never spoke about my father, her late older brother. And I had learned over and over that even when I tried to keep sore subjects out of our conversations, she found her way to bitterness, no matter what I avoided or said.

She could certainly be prickly. She could be harsh. Many times I'd been on the receiving end of Maryanne's cruelty. But I never stopped going to see her, taking her to lunch or stopping by her dark Fifth Avenue apartment. During the Great COVID Toilet Paper Shortage, I even brought her food and toilet paper.

Certainly, there were not many people Donald looked up to more than his older sister, Maryanne. And now she was gone.

The police were called to her apartment on November 13, 2023, where they found her. She was eighty-six years old.

Knowing Donald the way I do, almost nothing he does at this point could possibly surprise me, other than giving a press conference to shout, "I'm a yuuuuuge loser." Anything else . . . I'll probably have to shrug and say "of course."

That's how it was for me when he announced he was running a third time for president.

Once he'd refused to accept the results of the 2020 election and had revved up his four-year Stop the Steal campaign, he almost *had* to run in 2024. How else could he prove the last election was stolen? How else could he show everyone he wasn't the loser that the Democrats and the media were saying he was? It's a classic double-or-nothing bet. If he wins in November, he'll be able to say, "I told you so." If he loses—well, he'll say this latest election was stolen too, though it'll be a whole lot harder to convince most people he was that big a victim *twice*.

Why not go for broke?

He knew he had the Republican nomination in the bag. He still dominates his party as few politicians ever have. He has a genuine path back to the White House. Not a guaranteed path. Nothing is guaranteed in today's fast-moving politics. But I don't know anyone—Trump lover or Trump hater—myself included—who will confidently count him out this time.

He's proven he can win, and he could easily do it again, especially considering his competition.

As for the avalanche of criminal charges that would have sunk any other politician, they clearly haven't sunk Donald Trump. Even thirty-four guilty convictions in New York will not deter his ambitions.

The debate now is a much narrower one: whether all these prosecutions are helping or hurting him.

What these cases have done, it seems to me, is only intensify everyone's feelings.

The people who love him see him as more of a martyr now. The people who loathe him see him as even more of a fiend. And once again, hardly anyone is left in the middle. Except for me. I always seem to be caught in the middle. But where's the rational place for reasonable dialogue?

Whether Donald wins or loses in 2024, I will still be a Trump, and I know more than ever what a double-edged sword that can be. And if he loses, mark my words: He won't be a loser; he will run again in 2028.

America isn't close to finished with the Trumps, and neither, it seems, am I.

EPILOGUE

PAGE-TURNER

I t's time to turn the page.

Write a new chapter. Break the cycle. Pick whichever analogy you find most comforting. It's time—long past time—to move beyond the past.

It may be "the end of the world as we know it," as the R.E.M. song goes, but I am ready for the line . . . "and I feel fine." One Trump may not be able to redefine the brand that's been breaking news for so long, but I won't be changing my name, and I will no longer be the quiet private citizen. We have some things to be proud of in this family and so much left to do.

A new generation is coming along. A promising generation. My children's generation. Whether Maryanne was or wasn't cruel, what Donald did or should have done, the fact that Grandpa looked down on Freddie's high-flying dreams—those were the dramas that defined earlier decades. They don't need to define our future.

Enough, already. Let it rest.

My generation and the ones that follow, we didn't launch these hostilities. My children and their cousins, they weren't even born yet. I appreciate whatever connections I have with my cousins. I am sure that keeping a balance of family and privacy is extremely challenging for Eric, Donnie, and Ivanka. They also know what it's like to be responsible parents and how that becomes what you work to protect most.

As a parent, we get to choose what we carry and what we bury.

Over the past couple of years, I have made some changes in my life, many of them propelled by my role as a father. I have begun to face an issue I'd been avoiding, a challenge in my own life that had helped to wreck my father's future, a challenge he had explicitly warned me about.

Alcohol.

I think my father was right: We really may have "a bad gene" in this family.

I came to the conclusion that, like my father, I was drinking too much and I wasn't always able to control it. In the fall of 2023, I decided I'd had enough. It wasn't easy stopping. I thought about it for a long time. Lisa and my children had been encouraging me, sometimes quite forcefully. And I am proud to say I am sober.

For all he went through, I believe my father would be proud of me. I make no vows about forever. I say what others have said who've preceded me down this road to recovery. I say, "One day at a time."

After almost four decades in the commercial real-estate world, I began winding down my career. I'd worked for terrific companies. Been part of some fascinating deals. Spent an awful lot of time and energy to build a nice lifestyle and support my family. All that was great. I am proud that my career reached such levels. At the same time, I was starting to reappraise what was most important to me.

Did I really want to spend the next ten years making commercial real-estate deals? My focus, my passion, seemed to be shifting somewhere else, toward things that felt more gratifying and more important to me. As Grandpa told those people at the Horatio Alger gala: "You must like what you do." That, ultimately, is the road to successful living. Wouldn't we have all been better off if Grandpa had applied that rule *without exception*?

I have always been a proponent of small business, family-owned and -operated. I believe in the entrepreneurial spirit that our economy is built on. Anything that erodes the opportunity of the underdog is not good for any of us. As noted in the annual Edelman Trust Barometer, the trust we have in those businesses still runs high, while trust in government and media slumps to an all-time low. As the report affirms, the political divide of the world and our country further erodes trust in each other. From our Congress to our campuses, we have to get back to reasonable and real conversations or the anger will surely heat up beyond control. And we can't let families get ripped apart.

Caregiving and mental health are worth fighting for. I loved bringing people to the White House to advocate for kids and caregivers and families like ours. Giving needed support, I knew that's where my heart was. There is not a loud enough voice in America advocating for those who deserve to be equally alive, to experience the basic quality of life they have every right to.

That's the path I choose to follow, the cause that calls me into the future. I choose to continue on this path and devote the rest of my life to it. It is worth fighting for families. It is worth fighting for inclusion, and that most definitely includes people with intellectual and developmental disabilities.

As a parent, you get a good sense of how your children are going to do in life. Andrea and Cristopher are smart and kind and have good values. Growing up with William gave them a sense of compassion and taught them what genuine inclusion means. They also have a sense of fighting *for* family, not *against* it. They will be fine. As for William: On my deathbed, I will still be wondering if I have done enough. Did I do everything I possibly could have done for him?

That's what families do, right? In ways large and small, for better and for worse, we remain tied to each other through it all. I am reminded of it every time I close my car door and walk up to the house. I always let out a little whistle to let everyone know I'm home. I don't even think about it. It just comes out.

And the notes? The very same ones my grandfather whistled. After all those decades, that little tune is deeply embedded in my brain.

Wherever life takes us, I will always be a Trump.

AFTERWORD

OUR WILLIAM

So, how's our younger son doing? As Lisa likes to say, "our hunk-a-chunk of love is full of love, finding the best in every day."

The whirlwind continues. The hurdles are high. That's life.

The never-changing news for William is that he is deeply loved. His life has its steady challenges, but most days he has a smile on his face. He remains on his seizure meds, which have gone from three times a day—breakfast, snack, and dinner—to twice a day. One game changer: He can often get by now with an ambulatory EEG, permitting him to come home with the wires attached and return to the hospital after forty-eight hours for the data to be analyzed.

That may not sound like much of a difference. It is huge.

All through his school years, William remained busy with activities and therapies . . . of every imaginable sort. Aquatic. Music. Occupational. Physical. Feeding. Speech. Vision. I'm sure I'm forgetting a few. All things he needs, and he has been guided by dedicated professionals who have known him for years and have watched him grow and thrive. As parents, Lisa and I have always done our best to be there every moment to cheer all our children on—from the soccer sidelines to the black-diamond ski slopes in Vermont. It always took some juggling. Sometimes, Lisa might drop off Cristopher for the start of a game, and I'd get there for the second half, while Lisa went home and got dinner started. But we made it work, as busy parents do, managing the different schedules, the different schools, lives that sometimes intersected and sometimes ran on separate tracks. And our younger son was on a track all his own.

For William, we cheered for what might seem like tiny moments. Going underwater and holding his breath for a few seconds was a huge deal for us at aquatic therapy. Harmoniously matching a single musical note, even for seconds, as we shouted, "Yes, yes, that's a C!" The day he used assistive technology to find the right page in an e-book on his computer—wow, that was a giant celebration for all of us.

One day, Lisa was asked to speak with the children in William's class. They had a lot of questions. "What does William like to eat? . . . What does he like to watch on television?" One student asked, "Will William ever be able to walk?" The school therapist blurted out a "No," a *no* that Lisa wouldn't stand for.

"How many of you have seen William standing with his walker in the hallway?" she asked. Hands shot up. "How many have watched him take steps?"

"I have, I have."

"Then you've seen that William can walk," she said. "It's just different from the way that you do. When you see someone who walks differently than you do, you can be sure they're trying very hard to do the best they can."

Lesson learned.

When it came to caregivers, we really struck gold. The amazing Patti Bourne was William's primary person for more than ten years, from ages two to twelve. Patti was a major part of William's childhood. Without her, Lisa and I never could have balanced our three children the way we did. She set the bar high. She helped us find other caregivers, who came to love our growing boy and have stuck with us ever since then, starting a lifelong chain. As much as we advocated for William, so did they. They've been with him through his seizures, his illnesses, his injuries, and his therapies. They've shared his outings and his music, and become our new family. They know his wants and needs and how to make him feel happy and cared for, safe and sound. With William at the center, they've all come to admire each other and work as a team.

Now that William is well into his twenties, he is no longer a "special-needs kid." He has grown into a handsome young man, who lives in a group home with four other developmentally challenged adults a short drive from our house. That independence is an important part of growing up. Still, we constantly ask ourselves: What's the best living situation for William? How can we be sure he is getting the care, attention, and socialization that's best? What can we do so he's living a fulfilled life? What will happen when Lisa and I are gone? We won't live forever. His brother and sister love him dearly, but what is fair to expect from them?

It turns out William and I share a deep love for music.

He has a collection of stuffed animals and musical cards that play classic rock songs, his own big fuzzy album collection. From Bob Marley's "One Love" to Peter Gabriel's "Road to Joy," neither one of us ever tires of our music therapy.

William spends many of his waking hours in a wheelchair he can't move by himself. He stretches and stands with assistance, and it's crucial that he does. Like all of us, he needs daily exercise to keep his arms and legs strong. He needs his muscle memory, and staying in motion helps with that. But it takes a small team, all synced together, to pull it off. He loves taking rides on his adaptive bicycle and hanging out in his lounge chair. He loves swimming. He'd be in a pool every day if he could. We've figured out how to rig a special life vest with noodles so he can navigate on his own, with one of us in the water beside him. He loves that weightless buoyancy and knowing he can go wherever he wants to. The way my father and I loved to fly, William loves to swim. We often "fly him through the pool." The water makes him feel like he can do anything.

Did I mention something that William inherited from our family? No, not my adamant opinions. It's his heart-melting blue eyes. Those eyes are vitally important. They are a big part of how we communicate. Whether it's a cry for help or him saying, "I'm okay, Dad" or the whole world of possibilities in between, I can read my son's eyes, and he can read ours. I wished that I'd been able to explain that to Donald, when he said William didn't recognize me.

William's tells are subtle, but they are there. Though I often greet him with, "Hey, bud-bud, how was your day?," there is no, "It was okay, Dad," and off to the fridge. I still ask the question, but I've learned to pause and, in that moment, listen differently. I look for the signs from a nonverbal boy—his face, his posture, his expressions, his eyes.

I've learned to "speak" that language too.

William operates through gestures, expressions, and assistive technology. Though he doesn't have the motor skills for an iPad, tech is more and more a part of his daily independence. Voice-output and eye-gaze devices. Switch access that can turn on a blender or play a game, a book, or a song. All this tech is arriving rapidly.

Almost nothing for William comes without effort and assistance. He had to *learn* how to bite and chew. For William, all food still needs to be blended or finely chopped and balanced on a spoon, a spoon he cannot hold himself. The taste-and-swallow process is dependent on caregivers. We take the victories as they come. When William could eat a peanut butter and jelly sandwich, we were ecstatic. When he could sit and enjoy a chopped-and-prepared Thanksgiving meal specifically for him, our whole family was thrilled.

We're always asking, "Did William get enough to eat? . . . Did he get to the toilet? . . . Is his jacket warm enough?"

This goes on forever.

He can't tell us when something is broken, whether it's his bone or his heart. We are the chief investigators of all things William, and it's made us incredibly intuitive. Lisa calls this intuition her blessing and her curse. It means she sometimes feels like she's interrogating the very people who are responsible for his care 24/7. Trust is precious, and it is slowly earned. Trust can also be lost in an instant. Instead of focusing on his disabilities, we try to focus on what William can *do*, constantly encouraging and nurturing his abilities and loving him with all our might.

As much as we have gotten to know William, he has gotten to know us. His brother, Cristopher, is all over him with wrestling moves that make him laugh out loud and tossing balls that William tries his best to return. The two of them lie on William's bed together, watching sports on TV, while William glances over to check his brother's reaction to an amazing dunk or a touchdown. Andrea treats both her brothers the same, more observant, less physical, letting the boys be boys and do their thing. The love we keep getting from William is unbreakable. This unbreakable family love is worth fighting for.

There are endless things to be concerned about.

As the parent of a child with intellectual and developmental issues, you become acutely aware of all the physical challenges out there—the stairways, paths, parking places, and the doorways that might or might not be wide enough. But the ideas of inclusion and access are much broader than that. Looking back, the grade-school years were easier than the middle-school years, which were easier than the high-school years, which were easier than young adulthood. The stigmas of middle school and high school could be brutal. And many of the therapeutic and educational programs provided during the school years come to an end at age twenty-two.

You're pretty much on your own after that.

The lack of living options for adults with developmental disabilities is terrifying. The waitlists at group-care homes are daunting. And group living isn't for everyone, whatever the "community living" advocates may claim. Resources are scarce. Funding is limited. Finding qualified staff has never been harder. And nonverbal, nonambulatory people like William with complex medical needs can often end up in places they don't belong, just because that's what may be available. We question this all the time for William.

The caregiver challenge is especially concerning. The work is tough. The pay is demeaning. Too many people in the field have found easier ways to make a living. Many of these caregivers give their all, then go home to take care of their own families. We need to find new ways to recruit these angels, just like we need to find ways for adults with disabilities to live.

To me, that sounds like a challenge, just the kind of thing I'd like to take on.

As the grandson of a great New York builder, I do have to ask: Why isn't it possible to build homes and schools and public facilities that can accommodate *everyone*? Why can't we design new styles of living that match people's individual needs?

Don't tell me it's not possible. It's time to try.

Now, that would be using the Trump name to do good.

A note to my son, William . . . Remember what your great-grandfather said: "Find what you like, and learn everything about it."

My addition: Then go ahead and include everyone.

ACKNOWLEDGMENTS

Thank you to William's amazing angels over time: Patti, Emma, Jessica, Clare, Javier, Guerrier, Anna, Yhon, Miriam, Melvin, Jake, Jarrett, Charles, the Friendship Circle, and Enzo the Barber.

Deep appreciation to special ed lawyers like Jen Laviano who fight like crazy for the rights of neurodiversity and equal education.

Thank you to the medical professionals that have supported William throughout his life, including nurses Muriel and Evelyn, Yale New Haven Health, Dr. Orrin Devinsky and his NYU team, Next Generation Pediatrics, Dr. Josh Herbert, Dr. Michael Burruano, Dr. Jeremy Dixon, and William Potter. PTs, OTs, SLP, and every note of music therapy, Ailene, Andrea, Billy, Denise, Joe, Kate, Paul, and Voytek, LOF Adaptive Skiers, and conductors Edina, Kati, and Klara.

Abilis: From the Birth to Three program to adulthood, thank you for your dedication to William, our family, and the families of our community. We are grateful to important places like The Center for Discovery and North Street School.

A special thank-you to Terry Torok, for your friendship, trust, tenacity, and belief that made this book and the work ahead possible. Thank you to his family, Alicia, Justice, and Elijah.

Thank you to our and Lisa's family, parents, sisters, niece, and nephews for their unconditional love and support. To my oldest friend, Michael Siegel, who has seen it all and is my political junkie comrade. To Bruce Orr, just a good guy. To my Norwalk golf buddies. To John Hamilton for your commitment and patience. Thank you to Pam and Bill and their angel, Olivia.

Natasha Simons, you are dedicated and kind; you made our decision to go with Gallery the right one. Thank you to Jonathan Karp, Jennifer Bergstrom, Aimée Bell, Sally Marvin, Caroline Pallotta, Jill Siegel, Kell Wilson, Lisa Litwack, Christine Masters, Mia Robertson, Brigid Black, Karen Pearlman, Chris Lynch, Elisa Shokoff, Tom Spain, and the entire team at Gallery Books and Simon & Schuster for believing in this book; you know who you are, and the world should too.

Thank you to Ellis Henican for the flow of thoughts, words, and a list of superlatives that belong to you. Thank you to Beatrice Hogan for her expert research edits and attention to detail. I'm grateful for the incredible fact-finding of Roberta Teer and sound guidance of Steve H.

Thank you to the online, ongoing resource support of John Phane, Sam Sokol, Rowan Smith, and team.

Thank you to the good people behind the Edelman Trust Barometer, measuring the importance of what matters most, and to the Chopra Foundation's Never Alone Alliance at NeverAlone.love.

I am grateful for the dedicated representation of the Creative Intelligence Agency: www.therealcia.com.

Thank you to the extended network of friends and family who are ALL IN, fighting for the community of Intellectual and Developmental Disabilities.

And finally, thank you to the rebels with a cause and the underdogs to be found at: www.allin.family.

MORE TO THE STORY

For more of the story, media, and resources to support mental health and communities of intellectual and developmental disabilities, go to www.allin.family or scan the QR code below.